Fraud Examination

Prevention, Detection, and Investigation

Second Edition

Steven M. Bragg

 AccountingTools®

For more information about AccountingTools® products, visit our Web site at www.accountingtools.com.

ISBN-13: 978-1-64221-027-9

Printed in the United States of America

Table of Contents

Preface

Every organization can be impacted by fraud, with the potential to lose its assets and reputation as the result of improper actions by its own employees and outsiders. While the accounting department is best known for being a locus of fraud activities, fraud can actually be found anywhere in a business, from the mail room to the executive suite. Given the breadth and severity of fraud, an organization needs a reference for how to prevent, detect, and deal with fraud. *Fraud Examination* is that book, since it covers every possible fraud topic – the types of schemes that can be used against a business, specific prevention activities to undertake, and how to investigate fraud.

The book is divided into three sections. In Chapters 2 and 3, we cover the many types of fraud and theft schemes, with particular attention to financial statement fraud. In Chapters 4 through 6, we cover the methods used to prevent fraud from occurring, including the use of fraud-specific controls, and describe the indicators of fraud. Finally, in Chapters 7 through 11, we address the investigation process when fraud is suspected, including interviewing techniques, writing the final report, and the legal aspects of fraud.

You can find the answers to many questions about fraud examination activities in the following chapters, including:

- What are the triggers that can cause someone to engage in fraud?
- How does money laundering work?
- How can the reported sales of a business be falsely inflated?
- What types of corporate policies can be used to combat fraud?
- What types of controls can be used to mitigate the risk of payroll fraud?
- What accounting anomalies can indicate the presence of fraud?
- How does the chain of custody impact the ways in which documents are handled?
- How is an interview conducted with an unfriendly interviewee?
- What information is included in a fraud report?
- How does civil litigation vary from criminal litigation?

Fraud Examination is designed for professionals and students, who can use it as a reference tool for preventing, detecting, and investigating fraud.

Centennial, Colorado
May 2019

About the Author

Steven Bragg, CPA, has been the chief financial officer or controller of four companies, as well as a consulting manager at Ernst & Young. He received a master's degree in finance from Bentley College, an MBA from Babson College, and a Bachelor's degree in Economics from the University of Maine. He has been a two-time president of the Colorado Mountain Club, and is an avid alpine skier, mountain biker, and certified master diver. Mr. Bragg resides in Centennial, Colorado. He has written the following books and courses:

7 Habits of Effective CEOs
7 Habits of Effective CFOs
7 Habits of Effective Controllers
Accountant Ethics [for multiple states]
Accountants' Guidebook
Accounting Changes and Error Corrections
Accounting Controls Guidebook
Accounting for Breweries
Accounting for Casinos and Gaming
Accounting for Derivatives and Hedges
Accounting for Earnings per Share
Accounting for Income Taxes
Accounting for Intangible Assets
Accounting for Inventory
Accounting for Investments
Accounting for Leases
Accounting for Managers
Accounting for Mining
Accounting for Retirement Benefits
Accounting for Stock-Based Compensation
Accounting for Vineyards and Wineries
Accounting Information Systems
Accounting Procedures Guidebook
Activity-Based Costing
Activity-Based Management
Agricultural Accounting
Auditor Independence
Behavioral Ethics
Bookkeeping Guidebook
Budgeting
Business Combinations and Consolidations
Business Insurance Fundamentals
Business Ratios
Business Valuation
Capital Budgeting

CFO Guidebook
Change Management
Closing the Books
Coaching and Mentoring
Conflict Management
Constraint Management
Construction Accounting
Corporate Bankruptcy
Corporate Cash Management
Corporate Finance
Cost Accounting (college textbook)
Cost Accounting Fundamentals
Cost Management Guidebook
CPA Firm Mergers and Acquisitions
Credit & Collection Guidebook
Crowdfunding
Developing and Managing Teams
Effective Collections
Effective Employee Training
Employee Onboarding
Enterprise Risk Management
Entertainment Industry Accounting
Ethical Frameworks in Accounting
Ethical Responsibilities
Excel Charts and Visualizations
Excel Data Analysis Tools
Excel Data Management
Excel Formulas and Functions
Fair Value Accounting
Financial Analysis
Financial Forecasting and Modeling
Fixed Asset Accounting
Foreign Currency Accounting
Franchise Accounting
Fraud Examination

(continued)

On-Line Resources by Steven Bragg

Steven maintains the accountingtools.com web site, which contains continuing professional education courses, the Accounting Best Practices podcast, and thousands of articles on accounting subjects.

Fraud Examination is also available as a continuing professional education (CPE) course. You can purchase the course (and many other courses) and take an on-line exam at:

www.accountingtools.com/cpe

Chapter 1
Introduction to Fraud

Introduction

Fraud is pervasive in many parts of the world, and exists even in those areas where people are generally considered to maintain high ethical standards. The amount of losses that businesses suffer from fraud is not minor, with many estimates exceeding 5% of sales. Given the prevalence of fraud and its inordinate cost, anyone involved in managing a business should be deeply concerned with how fraud can be detected and prevented. When fraud can be curtailed, a business may experience profits that its competitors cannot match, thereby giving it a long-term financial advantage.

In order to detect and prevent fraud, it is first necessary to understand what it is, why people engage in fraud, the types of fraud, and the indicators of fraud risk. These topics are covered in the following sections.

What is Fraud?

Fraud is a false representation of the facts, resulting in the object of the fraud receiving an injury by acting upon the misrepresented facts. Fraud is proven in court by showing that the actions of an individual involved the following elements:

- A false statement of a material fact;
- Knowledge that the statement was untrue;
- Intent by the individual to deceive the victim;
- Reliance by the victim on the statement; and
- Injury sustained by the victim as a result of the preceding actions.

The key element in the preceding definition is *intent*. A company could make false representations in its financial statements simply because the accounting staff made a mistake in compiling certain financial information. This is not fraud (though it may be incompetence), since there was no intent to misstate the financial statements. Conversely, if a controller intentionally reduces the bad debt reserve in order to increase profits and thereby triggers a bonus for the management team, this *is* fraud, because a false statement was intentionally made.

For the purposes of this book, we are adding to the definition of fraud any type of theft from a business. Doing so expands the number of crimes enormously. For example, the theft of funds before they are recorded (skimming) and the theft of assets from a business (larceny) can now be considered fraud. These additional crimes do not fall within the classic definition of fraud. However, the detection and prevention of these activities involve actions that are quite similar to those used for "classic" fraudulent activities. By including additional types of crime, we are providing the reader with a broader knowledge of activities to guard against.

Confidence

One of the key elements of fraud, as noted in the last section, is the reliance by victims on the statements made by the perpetrator. In essence, the victims have confidence that the perpetrator is honest. Confidence may be obtained in many ways. For example, a well-dressed person is more likely to gain the confidence of others than someone who is dressed in a shabby manner. Or, someone with excellent interpersonal skills is more likely to gain the confidence of listeners. Another possibility is someone who establishes a cover story of having the same background or beliefs as others, and so insinuates himself into their social circles.

The most successful frauds are perpetrated when the victims have an extremely high level of confidence in the perpetrators. In these situations, the victims are more than willing to hand over astonishing amounts of assets. They also express disbelief when informed that a fraud has been carried out, since their level of confidence was so high that the possibility of fraud never even occurred to them.

The Effects of Fraud

The size of frauds appears to be increasing. This is because perpetrators no longer have to remove physical assets from the premises of the target. Instead, with the broad use of electronic systems to manage records, a person could transfer massive amounts of funds from the accounts of a victim without ever leaving his home.

The size and frequency of financial statement fraud is also on the rise. Publicly-held entities are always under pressure from the investment community to increase their reported income, so management teams are more likely to engage in financial shenanigans to do so. These issues, when uncovered, have resulted in massive declines in the trading prices of company shares, which have severely impacted investors.

When fraud is perpetrated on an organization, this has a direct impact on profits – that is, a $1,000 fraud loss reduces before-tax income by the same amount. When a business has a relatively small gross margin, it may require a substantial amount of additional revenues to make up the lost profit.

EXAMPLE

The sales manager of Kelvin Corporation is discovered to have submitted duplicate expense reports, resulting in a fraud loss of $50,000. The company earns a relatively low 20% gross margin on the sale of its thermometers. For the company to make up this loss, it will need to generate an additional $250,000 of sales (calculated as $50,000 loss ÷ 20% gross margin).

Further, most companies operate in highly competitive markets, so generating the additional sales needed to overcome a fraud loss will likely require a price cut in order to increase sales, which in turn reduces gross profits and therefore requires even more sales to earn back the lost profits.

EXAMPLE

To continue with the preceding example, the president of Kelvin Corporation decides to make an all-out effort to generate the required additional $250,000 of sales to recoup the fraud loss. However, the company is locked in a price war with a competitor, so the extra sales will require a price drop that brings Kelvin's gross margin down to 10%. At this margin, Kelvin will need to sell an additional $500,000 of thermometers to recoup the loss (calculated as $50,000 ÷ 10% gross margin).

Consequently, it is far less expensive to prevent fraud than to recoup losses after fraud has already occurred.

Fraud Triggers

Under what conditions does someone commit fraud? There are three interlocking conditions, known as the *fraud triangle*, under which fraud is most likely to flourish. These conditions are:

- *Perceived pressure*. A person may be liable for significant liabilities, such as the cost of supporting sick relatives, college loans, car loans, and so forth. Or, they may have an expensive habit that requires ongoing funding. When the individual sees no way out of the situation, they may resort to fraud. However, there may only be a *perceived* level of pressure, such as earning comparatively less than one's friends. This latter situation can trigger expectations for a better lifestyle, perhaps involving a sports car, foreign travel, or a larger house. When a person does not see a clear path to meeting these expectations by honest means, he or she may resort to dishonest alternatives.
- *Opportunity*. When the preceding pressures are present, a person must also see an opportunity to commit fraud. For example, a maintenance worker may realize that there are no controls over checking out and returning tools; this is an opportunity for theft.
- *Rationalization*. An additional issue that is needed for fraud to continue over a period of time is the ability of the perpetrator to rationalize the situation as being acceptable. For example, a person stealing from a company's petty cash box might rationalize it as merely borrowing, with the intent of paying back the funds at a later date. As another example, a management team adjusts reported earnings for a few months during mid-year, in the expectation that sales will rise towards the end of the year, allowing them to eliminate the adjustments by year-end.

The issues noted here tend to interact. For example, if a person is under an intense amount of financial pressure and there is a serious opportunity for fraud, then the level of rationalization needed to justify committing fraud will be quite low. Conversely, if there is little pressure and only a modest opportunity to do so, then it will take a much higher level of rationalization to justify the fraud. Consequently, a good approach to proactively dealing with fraud is to work on all of these areas – reducing the financial pressure on employees and minimizing the number and size of opportunities for fraud.

We cover the pressure, opportunity, and rationalization issues in more detail in the following sub-sections.

Perceived Pressure

The most obvious type of pressure that may impact a person is financial pressure. While one might associate real financial pressure with someone living in a car or under a bridge, anyone can have a perceived amount of financial pressure even when they already earn a substantial amount of money. Consider the following situations:

- A person is living well beyond his means. For example, a production worker loves sports cars and is determined to have one, even though his hourly wage does not begin to qualify him for a car loan. Or, a corporate executive wants a private jet, so he will misrepresent his company's profits in order to sell shares at a higher price and then buy the jet.
- A person has incurred a large amount of debt. His current wage might have been sufficient under all normal circumstances, but the additional amount of debt payments renders his situation much less tenable. The same situation arises when a person's wages are being garnished.
- A person is suddenly confronted with a large expenditure. For example, a person's spouse is uninsured, and she must now undergo expensive radiation therapy to treat cancer.
- A person wants to be perceived as being successful. This calls for the acquisition of a large home, a cabin in the country, a fishing boat, and other toys. This person is more concerned with the image being conveyed than having a low level of integrity.

Financial pressure can extend to the management team when they are trying to protect the viability of the company. For example, an entity's financial results have been gradually declining, and it is in danger of breaching its loan covenants, which will trigger a loan call by the bank. To avoid this situation, the management team adjusts the financial statements to keep the entity's reported results just higher than the thresholds stated in the loan covenants.

A type of behavior that can cause financial problems is any type of vice. For example, a person may be unable to stop gambling, and racks up enormous gambling debts. Or, an individual is addicted to hard drugs, and is always in need of cash to fund the habit. As another example, a person has a mistress and needs to support her lifestyle.

A different type of pressure is the desire to get even with an employer. For example, a person might have been denied a promotion, and so elects to commit fraud in order to make the employer "pay" for this decision. A person might feel the same way if he perceives his compensation to be unusually low, or if his contributions to the business have not been acknowledged.

Yet another type of pressure comes from the employer. This pressure usually comes in the form of a performance standard that must be met. For example, the senior management team imposes a very difficult commission plan on the sales staff; to meet their targets, the sales staff needs to sell more to customers than they really need. Similarly, if a very high profit goal has been set, the accounting staff feels that it needs to use subterfuge, such as keeping the books open into the following month in order to record additional sales.

Opportunity

A key factor contributing to fraud is the presence of a perceived opportunity to steal assets. These opportunities can come in many shapes and sizes. The opportunity for fraud is certainly enhanced when the environment within an organization is permissive, as would be the case in the following situations:

- *Absence of controls*. A key control might be missing that would otherwise prevent a theft from occurring, or at least detect it after the fact. This situation is more likely to arise when new systems are installed or existing ones are modified without paying attention to the underlying controls. In addition, a business that is not audited is less likely to have an independent review of its system of controls, and so may have no idea that it is lacking a key control. When any of the following types of controls are missing, it represents an opportunity for fraud to occur:
  - The presence of authorizations for transactions, so that a manager must issue an approval before a transaction can be completed, or employees are only authorized to engage in transactions up to a certain dollar limit.
  - Segregation of duties, so that it would require more than one person to commit fraud.
  - Independent reviews of a person's work, perhaps involving job rotations or supervisory reviews, so that a person could not keep up a fraud for a long period of time.
  - Controls over physical access to assets, so that someone would need to break into a controlled area in order to steal assets.
  - Proper supporting documentation for records, to identify the nature of a transaction and any related authorizations.
- *Accountability*. The level of accountability for all tasks should be quite clear within a business. When this is not the case, controls are significantly weaker, since no one is required to engage in preventive or detective activities.
- *Internal audit*. When there is an active internal audit department that is visibly examining transactions, this presents a significant deterrent. When there is no such group within a business, employees are more likely to engage in fraud, since there is no one in an oversight role.

- *Transitions*. Whenever there are layoffs, spin-offs, mergers, and plant closures, there is an increased risk that the control environment will break down, frequently because the key employees with a deep knowledge of controls are no longer working for the company.
- *Management example*. There may be a general environment of permissiveness within an organization. For example, if the management team is known to "play loose" with their expense reports, employees are more likely to follow their example. Or, if management is known to be creating fictitious customers in order to increase the reported sales level, employees will be more tempted to cheat the company and its investors in other ways. In this environment, the effectiveness of even a strong set of controls is weakened, since employees are more likely to work together to defeat the control system.
- *Management communication*. Ideally, management should be communicating constantly with employees regarding acceptable behavior, using training, a code of conduct, and other tools. If these communications are not present, employees do not have a clear indication of what is right and wrong, and so will be more inclined to step over the line and commit fraud.
- *Work environment*. In a negative work environment, employees have a vastly lower association with the business, and so are more likely to engage in fraudulent activities. Situations that can contribute to a negative work environment are:
  - A persistently high level of negative feedback from management
  - A strongly hierarchical management structure, where consideration is rarely given to suggestions from people lower in the organization
  - A widespread sense of job inequity, such as advancement being given to a small group of favored employees
  - Extremely difficult performance targets that are rarely attained
  - Minimal acknowledgement of good employee performance
  - Unusually low compensation and benefit packages
- *Vetting practices*. The human resources department must spend the time to research the backgrounds of all job candidates prior to hiring them. Otherwise, people with criminal backgrounds, questionable performances at prior employers, or falsified resumes will be hired, which leads to a higher incidence of fraud.

Rationalization

Someone committing fraud almost always needs to have some way to rationalize this conduct. There are many possible rationalizations, such as:

- I am taking the money from a corrupt organization
- I am using the money to help others
- The organization should have paid me this money
- This is only borrowing for a short time, and I will pay it back

- We will correct the books once we get through this rough patch and sales increase
- I have already paid enough income taxes
- If I pay more income taxes, the government will waste it anyways

With these kinds of rationalizations, a person can lie to himself that there is a good reason for engaging in fraud.

Fraud Addiction

As we have just noted, a person is likely to be under a certain amount of pressure when committing fraud. What if that pressure goes away because the person collects enough money through the fraud scheme? At this point one might think that the person would stop. Instead, the reverse occurs. Frauds tend to become larger over time, because the act of committing fraud can be addictive. A person might succeed with one fraud, and then chooses to expand the amount stolen or engage in a series of other frauds. The eventual result is the collection of a great deal more money.

When a fraud investigator finds a fraud situation, it makes sense to assume that the individual responsible for it has not been engaged in just the fraud that was found. That might be a small percentage of the total. Instead, the investigator should not only assume that the same fraud has been perpetrated multiple times, but also that the same person has spread his activities into other areas. The end result may be that the discovery of a small initial fraud balloons into something much larger.

Collusion

Many ways to combat fraud assume that people act alone. Thus, if a control is being developed to prevent fraud from occurring, it may involve having two people work on a task together, on the assumption that a person acting alone will not commit fraud in the presence of someone else. But what if this assumption is wrong, and people *do* collude to commit fraud? This is a worst-case scenario, since groups of people intent on committing fraud can sidestep many preventive measures.

Why do people collude to engage in fraud? It frequently involves how the power of persuasion impacts their relationships. For example:

- *Monetary inducement*. One employee is able to convince others that they will receive a benefit as the result of a fraudulent activity. For example, the managers of a subsidiary know they will earn a bonus from the parent company if they report a certain minimum profit. In this case, the entire management team might actively collude to ensure that the profit figure is reached.
- *Personal linkage*. A person may take advantage of a personal relationship with others to convince them to go along with a scheme. In this case, a pre-existing close relationship between the parties forms the basis for the collusion.
- *Possible punishment*. A person in a more powerful position convinces a more junior person that he will be punished in some way if he does not participate

in a scheme. For example, the junior person could be denied a pay raise or a promotion.

- *Superior knowledge*. One person may be able to convince others that he has a superior level of knowledge, and so should be followed. In this case, the others submit to the supposedly superior knowledge of the ringleader, and follow his lead.

In short, there are a number of ways in which groups can coalesce to perpetrate fraudulent activities. These groups can become particularly large when the initial founder of a group is able to convince the original members of the group to proselytize among other people, thereby further increasing the size of the group.

Types of People More Likely to Engage in Fraud

There is no "classic" personality type that is more likely to engage in fraud. Instead, literally anyone can switch from being a completely reliable employee to someone who commits fraud on a regular basis. If the fraud triangle conditions noted earlier are present, then they can tip anyone over into being a fraud perpetrator. Further, someone can be a completely reliable employee for years and then suddenly commit fraud, if they are impacted by the fraud triangle. Given the problem with identifying potentially fraudulent employees, a business needs to enact strong preventive measures that impact *all* employees.

Types of Fraud

There are a number of types of fraud that a business can experience. At the highest level, they can be broken down into two general categories, which are fraud committed *on behalf of* the organization and fraud committed *against* the organization. In the first case, employees alter the reported financial results of the business in order to make it look better than is really the case. This could be done in order to bolster the stock price, earn bonuses, or avoid a loan default. The benefit to the perpetrator may be indirect. In the latter case, employees are directly stealing from the organization, so they experience a direct benefit. Within these two classifications are a number of fraud types, which we describe in the following sub-sections.

Financial Statement Fraud

In financial statement fraud, the management team alters the financial statements in order to reveal more sales, better profits, a more robust financial position, and/or better cash flows than is really the case. The victims of this fraud are investors and creditors. Investors are relying on the financial statements to judge the prices at which to buy or sell a company's shares, and so could make incorrect investment decisions. Creditors are relying on the statements to determine whether to loan funds or extend credit to the company, and could potentially lose these funds if the company turns out to be a poor credit risk.

Embezzlement

When embezzlement occurs, employees either directly take assets from the company for their own use, or assist in diverting assets from the company. For example, a warehouse person could walk out with finished goods inventory, a maintenance staffer could steal tools, and a sales clerk could steal cash from the cash register. When a person assists in diverting assets, this involves taking bribes or kickbacks from outsiders who are engaged in fraudulent activities. For example:

- *Supplier kickback.* A purchasing department employee accepts a 5% kickback from a supplier in exchange for approving its bid in a competitive bidding situation. The supplier bids at a higher price than would normally be accepted, so the company is losing funds as a result of the situation.
- *Supplier bribery.* A supplier bribes the receiving manager to overlook low-quality raw materials being delivered to the company. The company suffers from a higher failure rate in its production processes as a result of using the low-quality materials.

The level of embezzlement depends on the position occupied by the perpetrator, with more senior positions having a greater ability to embezzle. It is also possible that a person with a less-senior position can also embezzle a significant amount if they take advantage of a control weakness.

Supplier Fraud

There are a number of ways in which a supplier can commit fraud against a company. Consider the following possibilities:

- *Bid rigging.* In a competitive bidding situation, several suppliers could collude to not bid excessively low prices, thereby keeping the company from reaping the gains normally experienced in this situation.
- *Overbilling.* A supplier could agree to one price, and then bill a higher price. This may not be obvious when the billing is obfuscated with many smaller or add-on charges. This is a particular concern in cost-plus billing arrangements where suppliers can bill the costs they have incurred; they may overload these billings with unrelated expenses.
- *Lower quality goods.* A supplier could ship lower-quality goods. This is especially hard to detect when the lower-quality items are mixed in with higher-quality goods or are integrated into completed components.
- *Short ship goods.* A supplier may slightly under-ship the number of goods ordered, and bill for the full amount. This is most common when the number of units ordered is extremely large, and it is difficult for the receiving department to affirm the exact amount received.

These issues can occur when there is not a sufficient level of oversight of the purchasing process or the receiving department. The level of fraud can be more pronounced when a supplier is bribing an employee to overlook the overbillings and other issues.

This type of fraud can be subtle and unusually hard to detect when suppliers only engage in it at a very low level.

Customer Fraud

Customer fraud occurs when a customer refuses to pay the company or pays too little with no justification, or demands more goods or services in exchange for the amount paid. This situation most commonly arises when a customer has a significant amount of power over a company, typically because it represents a large part of the company's revenues.

A variation on the concept is for a person to impersonate a customer. For example, a bank could be persuaded to issue a bank check to a person who has misrepresented himself as being a wealthy client.

Investment Scams

In essence, an investment scam seeks to extract funds from an investor in exchange for illusory profits. There are a number of investment scam types, including the following:

- *Advance fee fraud.* Under this arrangement, a person is required to make an advance payment in order to obtain access to a loan or investment opportunity. For example, a perpetrator could promise a needy business owner that a loan will be forthcoming once a fee is paid, after which the person vanishes with the fee.
- *Financial assistance fraud.* In this scam, bulk e-mails are sent that request financial assistance in shifting a large amount of cash out of another country, usually in exchange for a portion of the proceeds.
- *Identity theft.* Perpetrators of this scam steal information about a person and use it to buy goods in the person's name, obtain tax refunds, and so forth. The personal information may be obtained from (for example) on-line phishing e-mails, by examining a person's trash, and stealing credit card information from retailers.
- *Ponzi schemes.* This is a type of fraud under which cash from subsequent investors is used to pay premiums or interest to prior investors. These schemes continue to grow until the pool of new investors dries up, at which point the scheme collapses. A Ponzi scheme advertises unusually large returns in order to attract investors; the type of investor that responds to this type of advertising is more likely to be greedy for unusually high returns, and so is willing to ignore the patent falsity of the advertising. A key element of a Ponzi scheme is the level of confidence that the perpetrator can generate among investors. To do so, the perpetrator must be willing to pay funds back to investors on demand, which convinces them that the scheme is actually a legitimate business.

- *Telemarketing fraud.* In this arrangement, victims are convinced by callers to hand over their credit card or other personal information in association with a prize, free gift, or unusually low-priced offer.

In the following Fraud and Theft Schemes chapter, we will delve into the various types of fraud in considerably more depth, with a focus on situations that impact businesses, rather than individuals.

Common Fraud Risk Indicators

There are a number of factors that make it more likely that fraud will occur or is occurring in a business. These fraud risk factors include:

Nature of Items

- *Size and value.* If items that can be stolen are of high value in proportion to their size (such as diamonds), it is less risky to remove them from the premises. This is a particularly critical item if it is easy for employees to do so.
- *Ease of resale.* If there is a ready market for the resale of stolen goods (such as for most types of consumer electronics), this presents an increased temptation to engage in fraud.
- *Cash.* If there is a large amount of bills and coins on hand, or cash in bank accounts, there is a very high risk of fraud. At a local level, a large balance in a petty cash box presents a considerable temptation.

Nature of Control Environment

- *Separation of duties.* The risk of fraud declines dramatically if multiple employees are involved in different phases of a transaction, since fraud requires the collusion of at least two people. Thus, poorly-defined job descriptions and approval processes present a clear opportunity for fraud.
- *Safeguards.* When assets are physically protected, they are much less likely to be stolen. This can involve fencing around the inventory storage area, a locked bin for maintenance supplies and tools, security guard stations, an employee badge system, and similar solutions. A lack of these safeguards encourages thieves.
- *Documentation.* When there is no physical or electronic record of a transaction, employees can be reasonably assured of not being caught, and so are more inclined to engage in fraud. This is also the case if there *is* documentation, but the records can be easily modified.
- *Time off.* When a business requires its employees to take the full amount of allocated time off, this keeps them from continuing to hide ongoing cases of fraud, and so is a natural deterrent. Thus, *not* having a time off policy is a fraud risk factor.

- *Related party transactions*. When there are numerous transactions with related parties, it is more likely that purchases and sales will be made at amounts that differ considerably from the market rate.
- *Complexity*. When the nature of a company's business involves very complex transactions, and especially ones involving estimates, it is easier for employees to manipulate the results of these transactions to report better results than is really the case.
- *Dominance*. When a single individual is in a position to dominate the decisions of the management team, and especially when the board of directors is weak, this individual is more likely to engage in unsuitable behavior.
- *Turnover*. When there is a high level of turnover among the management team and among employees in general, the institutional memory regarding how transactions are processed is weakened, resulting in less attention to controls.
- *Auditing*. When there is no internal audit function, it is unlikely that incorrect or inappropriate transactions will be spotted or corrected.

Pressures

- *Level of dissatisfaction*. If the work force is unhappy with the company, they will be more inclined to engage in fraud. Examples of such situations are when a layoff is imminent, benefits have been reduced, bonuses have been eliminated, promotions have been voided, and so forth.
- *Expectations*. When there is pressure from outside investors to report certain financial results, or by management to meet certain performance targets (perhaps to earn bonuses), or to meet balance sheet goals to qualify for debt financing, there is a high risk of financial reporting fraud.
- *Guarantees*. When the owners or members of management have guaranteed company debt, there will be strong pressure to report certain financial results in order to avoid triggering the guarantees.

Responsibility for Fraud Prevention

One of the main reasons why fraud exists is that no one believes it is their primary responsibility to prevent or detect fraud. For example, here are the areas of responsibility of the people who might be tasked with combatting fraud:

- *Corporate security*. This group is responsible for protecting company assets and personnel, and may be involved in the prosecution of anyone found to have committed fraud. Nonetheless, its activities are only peripheral to the general topic of combatting fraud.
- *Human resources*. This group has a broad range of activities which can include some aspects of fraud prevention, such as examining job candidates for honesty, conducting background checks, and managing employee assistance programs. The bulk of its activities are elsewhere, in the recruiting, compensation planning, and benefits administration functions.

- *Internal auditors.* The internal audit staff spends most of its time testing whether the existing control systems function properly, with a secondary task of spotting areas in which operational improvements can be made. They are not normally tasked with fraud-related activities.
- *Outside auditors.* The outside auditors are primarily tasked with verifying the fairness of presentation of the financial statements. Their audit tests are conducted at a relatively high level of materiality, so it is likely that they will not detect fraudulent activities.

In short, there are numerous positions within a business that either are or should be involved in fraud prevention and detection to some extent, but there is no overriding authority that is clearly responsible for it. Given this fragmented approach to dealing with fraud, it is no surprise that fraud is such a common event in organizations.

The Fraud Examiner

Once a fraud situation has been found, how is it investigated? This is the job of the fraud examiner. In general, a fraud examiner investigates fraud cases, examining documents and interviewing those having any related information. A fraud examiner is deeply familiar with the different types of fraud that can be committed, understands how control systems operate and can be circumvented, and assists with bringing perpetrators to justice. More specifically, a fraud examiner engages in the following activities:

- Reconstructs how fraud cases were accomplished
- Calculates the amount of assets stolen
- Reconstructs accounting records
- Collects documents pertaining to a case
- Interviews witnesses
- Coordinates activities with law enforcement agencies
- Constructs a report that contains the trail of documents collected, interviews conducted, and surveillance completed in relation to the case
- Creates supporting evidence for court cases
- Provides testimony in court as an expert witness
- Evaluates business operations to detect control weaknesses
- Advises management regarding fraud prevention techniques

Fraud examiners may be employed within a large business, but more commonly operate from separate practices, sometimes as sole practitioners, but more frequently as part of larger accounting and consulting firms.

We will refer to the role of the fraud examiner throughout the remainder of this book.

Summary

The key point in this chapter was that certain conditions will make fraud much more likely. When there is a high level of perceived pressure, a clear opportunity, and the ability to rationalize the conduct of a fraud, then there is a good chance that a person will engage in fraud. When several of these issues are taken away, the incidence of fraud declines considerably. In the Fraud Prevention chapter, we will discuss how to reduce the effects of these three issues. But before we engage in fraud prevention, it is useful to first consider the massive range of activities that can result in fraud (if only to frighten the reader into wanting to prevent fraud). In the next chapter, we cover the dozens of fraud and theft scams to which a business can be subjected.

Chapter 2
Fraud and Theft Schemes

Introduction

Later in this book, we will describe the many controls that a business can install to protect itself from fraud, as well as the detection systems that can be used to spot it. One might ask whether it is worthwhile to spend the time on these prevention and detection activities. Our intent in this chapter is to make a convincing argument in favor of prevention and detection systems by outlining the vast number of fraud and theft schemes that can be deployed against a business. Even the briefest perusal of this chapter should convince the most optimistic manager that these issues are a real and present danger to any organization.

> **Related Podcast Episodes:** Episodes 215, 216, 217, 239, 245, 247, and 260 of the Accounting Best Practices Podcast discuss a variety of fraud schemes. They are available at: **accountingtools.com/podcasts** or **iTunes**

Cash Theft

There are a number of ways in which an individual can steal cash from a business. Since cash is essentially untraceable once stolen, someone intent on stealing assets will be particularly focused on this type of asset.

Here are several ways in which cash theft can be committed:

- *Intercept at cash register*. An employee could pocket cash at the cash register, and never ring up the sale on the register. This approach can be detected after the fact by comparing actual inventory levels to the amount of sale transactions. If the inventory level is lower than indicated by the cash register transactions, someone may be removing cash.
- *Intercept in mail room*. Though rare, it is possible that a customer will send cash through the mail in payment of an invoice. If so, a mail room clerk can pocket the mailed cash and destroy the letter with which it came. Since there is no in-house evidence that the cash ever arrived, a reasonable claim can be made that the payment was lost in the mail.
- *Conduct off-hours sales*. An employee can continue to conduct sales during off-hours. All of these additional sales are not recorded, with the employee retaining all funds collected.
- *Substitute check for cash*. When an unusual payment is received in the form of a check, employees know that the receipt is an anomaly. For example, a refund may be received. An employee holds onto this check until there is an

opportunity to steal the same amount of cash. The employee then enters the check as having been received. By doing so, the total amount of receipts remains normal, so the theft is less detectable.

- *Scrap payments*. Many manufacturing businesses produce a fair amount of metal scrap as part of their ongoing operations. This scrap is then sold to a scrap dealer, who may pay cash on the spot. Anyone handling these cash receipts could take the cash, without recording the transaction at all. Since scrap is typically not tracked, this type of theft can easily go undetected, especially if the theft only occurs infrequently.

- *Create refund at cash register*. An employee rings up a supposed customer return of merchandise for a refund, and then pockets the amount of the refund. The flaw in this approach is that the refund creates a debit to increase inventory, even though no inventory was returned. When the next physical inventory count occurs, the amount counted will be lower than the amount indicated by the inventory records.

- *Void a sale at cash register*. A sale may occasionally be voided at the cash register, in which case the customer is paid back the amount of the original sale. The normal controls for this transaction mandate that a copy of the customer's receipt be attached to the void slip, which is evidence of the original sale and the void. Someone can circumvent this process by retaining a customer receipt instead of giving it to a customer, and later processing a void sale transaction and retaining the cash. The customer receipt and void slip are processed as normal. The flaw in this approach is the same as for the preceding cash refund fraud – the system assumes that the related inventory has been returned, when this is not actually the case.

- *Intercept at cashier*. The cashier can remove cash and simply not record the associated transaction in the accounting records. This issue can be detected after the fact by recording the amount of cash prior to delivering it to the cashier, and then comparing the initial record to the cashier's record of cash received.

- *Intercept in deposit pouch*. The person delivering cash deposits to the bank can remove cash from the pouch on the way to the bank. This issue can be mitigated by handing off the cash to an armored truck for delivery. It can also be detected after-the-fact by comparing the deposit slip from the bank to the cashier's record of cash received.

- *Petty cash removal*. One of the easier ways to abscond with cash is to take cash out of the petty cash box when it is unguarded. Another option is to steal the entire box, thereby ensuring that all cash and coins are removed.

- *Pay envelope removal*. A person could remove cash from pay envelopes before they are delivered to employees. This issue can be detected by having employees count the cash in their pay envelopes and sign for receipt of the envelopes.

The first five types of cash fraud are known as *skimming*, where someone takes cash before it can be entered into the accounting system. This usually occurs on the front end of the sales process. For example, a sales clerk could pocket a customer's cash payment without entering it into a cash register. Or, a cover charge for entrance to a club could be pocketed in the same manner. Skimming can be difficult to spot without direct observation. Since sales are being reduced but any related expenses are still being incurred, this should result in a decline in the gross margins of the business. If there are different sales-generating parts of a business, one detection technique would be to examine the trend of gross margins in each business segment to see if they are below expectations.

The remaining types of cash fraud are known as *larceny*, where cash is removed from the premises after it has been recorded in the accounting system. Because this type of theft requires modification of the existing records, it is easier to detect, and is therefore less commonly encountered. Larceny works best when the amount stolen per event is quite small; in this case, the issue is usually considered a miscount problem and is written off with no further investigation.

The activities noted here only relate to the theft of cash, which means bills and coins. In addition, a person could use the company's account access codes to illegally wire company funds to an outside bank account. The amount stolen via a wire transfer can be enormous, potentially eliminating a company's cash reserves with a single transfer. Given the extreme risk of corporate failure, wire transfers need an exceptional level of control, including a call-back confirmation from the bank to verify that wire transfers over a certain amount should be initiated.

Disbursement-Related Theft

There are multiple situations in which employees can gain from incorrect payments being made by their employer. In the following sub-sections, we describe a number of these schemes.

False Expense Reports

There are many ways in which an employee can file an expense report that contains false expenses. When reimbursed for these false claims, an employee is stealing funds. Here are multiple examples of the ways in which an expense report can be falsified:

General Issues

- *Multiple reimbursements.* An employee makes multiple copies of a receipt and continues to submit these extra receipts in successive expense reports, thereby being reimbursed several times for the same expenditure. A cleverer alternative is to submit several different types of support for the same expense in successive expense reports. For example, an employee could submit the itemized detail for a hotel room on one expense report, and the credit card receipt for the room on the next report. A variation is to charge an item to the company credit card, and then claim reimbursement for it on his expense report, using the transaction receipt.

- *Personal expenditures*. An employee includes various personal expenditures in an expense report. For example, a personal meal is characterized as a business lunch.
- *Adjusted receipts*. An employee deliberately alters a receipt to increase the amount to be reimbursed. If the alteration is visible, the person is more likely to submit a photocopy instead, on which the adjustment is less likely to be noticed.
- *Fake receipts*. An employee creates entirely fake documentation for a reimbursement claim, including an official-looking form, a fake company logo, and multiple line items that appear quite detailed and authentic.

Specific Situations

- *Educational reimbursement*. An employee submits a claim for expense reimbursement, using a receipt that shows he paid a college to enroll in a course. Once reimbursed, the employee cancels the class and is paid back by the college.
- *Meals reimbursement*. An employee is on an extended out-of-town consulting trip, and is reimbursed for all grocery store receipts, since he likes to cook his own meals. When at the grocery store, he collects additional receipts from other people who have just gone through the checkout line, and submits these additional receipts for reimbursement.
- *Hotel reimbursement*. An employee buys meals at the hotel restaurant and has them charged to his room. He then submits a reimbursement request for the total hotel bill, while separately submitting a request for meal reimbursement.
- *Cab reimbursement*. An employee takes a cab ride, pays the driver in cash, and asks for a blank receipt, which he then fills out with a higher amount and submits for reimbursement.
- *Mileage reimbursement*. An employee overstates the amount of miles actually traveled on company business, in order to receive extra reimbursement.

In short, the amount of expense report padding is limited only by the inventiveness of employees.

Mis-use of Company Credit Card

An employee may be entrusted with a company credit card, and then uses it to make personal purchases. This scam works especially well when the employee is in a position to approve his own purchases. A variation on the concept is to use the corporate travel card to pay for personal airfare, hotels, and so forth.

Billings from Fake Suppliers

An employee can create a shell company and enter it into his employer's accounting system as a valid supplier. This may be a state-registered company with a mailing address, and usually its own bank account – thereby giving it an air of authenticity.

The employee then creates dummy invoices and submits them to the company for approval. If the employee knows what the minimum cutoff level is within the company for invoice approvals, he can set the invoices at amounts just under this threshold, thereby escaping detection.

This type of fraud is quite difficult to detect if the amounts billed are kept low. If a person becomes bolder and submits larger invoices, then it will also be necessary for the person to override the invoice approval process, personally approve the invoices, or collude with an approved signer. This increased level of control over larger invoices makes it more difficult for anyone to sustain a large-dollar fraud with fake supplier billings. Nonetheless, the sheer volume of funds that can be stolen via fake suppliers continues to make this a popular fraud.

Self-Insurance Fraud

A business may self-insure its medical insurance. This usually involves directly paying for smaller claims, with catastrophic coverage by an outside insurer for larger claims. In this situation, doctors are supposed to submit claims directly to the company for reimbursement. An employee in the claims department can take advantage of this arrangement by creating several fake doctors, and forwarding fake claims from them to the company's claims department. The individual can then approve the claims for payment. The payables department then issues payments to the mailing addresses of the fake doctors, which the employee collects.

Unauthorized Shipments

A common form of fraud is for someone in the company to take a phone call from an outside party that is offering an uncommonly good deal on copier toner, or some other office supplies. Any agreement by the employee is considered a verbal purchase order, which is used as the basis for a delivery of substandard goods to the company's receiving dock a short time later. The seller then bills the company, referencing the name of the person who gave verbal approval.

Redirected Payments

An outsider could contact the company and request that all future payments made to a particular supplier be made to a new bank account or mailing address. Once these payments are made, the individual absconds with the funds, leaving the company still having an obligation to pay its suppliers. This type of fraud is becoming increasingly difficult to spot, since requests to redirect payments can be included in quite convincing-looking e-mails or letters.

Check Theft

An employee can steal blank check stock and use it to create checks payable to her. This is especially easy if the company keeps a signature stamp or signature plate in the same storage area as the check stock, so that breaking into just one cabinet gives the perpetrator all of the tools needed to engage in this kind of theft. A variation is the concealed check scam, where a payables clerk creates a check made payable to herself or an associated entity, and slips it into a stack of checks to be signed by an authorized check signer. If the check signer has a reputation for signing anything without question, there is a good chance that the payables clerk will soon have a valid payment that can be cashed with impunity.

A variation on this concept is to intercept outgoing checks intended for suppliers, and modify them sufficiently to be able to deposit them into the individual's own account. The modification of an existing check can include forging the name of the payee and/or the amount paid. Doing so provides the person with a valid check that already has an authorized signature on it. Here are several variations on the concept:

- Intentionally pay a supplier twice, and then demand that one of the checks be returned. The returned check is then intercepted and cashed.
- Intentionally pay the wrong supplier, and then demand that the check be returned. The returned check is then intercepted and cashed.

Check theft is especially pernicious when the person engaging in the fraud is an authorized check signer, such as an in-charge bookkeeper or controller. This person has ready access to the check stock, and no one will question the checks being issued. The situation is especially bad if the person sets up fake suppliers (as noted in a preceding sub-section), so that she can submit fake invoices, and is then authorized to issue the checks to pay for her own invoices.

ACH Debits

An outside party that knows a company's bank account information can set up an ACH debit, which extracts money from the account through an ACH transaction. This approach is most likely to succeed if the amount is relatively small, thereby passing under any threshold that the company may have imposed that requires the bank to first contact the company to verify that such a debit is authorized. If someone were to use an ACH debit to extract a small sum from a bank account on a monthly basis, this could add up to quite a substantial amount over time.

Compensation Fraud

There are multiple ways in which employees can falsely obtain payment for compensation that they have not earned. For example, any hourly wage earner can submit a timesheet with overtime hours stated that he or she did not actually work. If there is not a control in place for formally approving these hours, the overtime may be paid with no review at all. Or, if an employee claims just a minor amount of overtime on an ongoing basis, this could pass beneath the attention of a supervisor, who allows the payment to be made.

There are several ways for a payroll clerk to engage in compensation fraud. Consider the following possibilities:

- *Alter hours*. No matter how many hours were approved by supervisors, a payroll clerk can still enter a different number of hours into the payroll system.

The recipient could then kick back some of the difference to the clerk, as compensation.

- *Alter rate.* The payroll clerk can alter the pay rate paid to one or more employees. The recipients kick back some of the difference to the clerk, as compensation.
- *Alter commission.* The compensation of a salesperson can be enhanced by artificially increasing the amount of sales credited to the person, so that a larger commission is paid. Alternatively, a payroll clerk can inflate the commission rate paid to a sales person.
- *Use ghost employees.* When an employee leaves the company, a payroll clerk continues to pay the person for a few additional pay periods, and changes the direct deposit information to route money into his or her bank account. At a more egregious level, these ghost employees can be maintained in the system for long periods of time.

Executive Loans

Corporate executives may authorize that loans be made by the company to themselves. These loans have unusually favorable terms, and may even be forgiven at a later date. In effect, these are cash handouts to the benefiting executives. Loans to members of management should be approved in advance by the board of directors. However, executives can use their authority within the organization to override this requirement, so that the board never knows that loans have been granted or forgiven. Given the participation of senior managers in this scam, it can be difficult to develop any type of valid control for it, since the managers can override the controls.

Workers' Compensation Fraud

An employee can fake having incurred an injury while on the job, and files a workers' compensation claim. He then receives compensation while recuperating from the "injury". Though the cost of these claims is initially borne by the insurer, the insurance premium charged to the employer will rise, so that the fake claim will eventually become an expense of the employer.

An especially pernicious version of workers' compensation fraud is when the employee is in cahoots with a doctor, who files fake medical treatment claims and then splits the proceeds with the employee.

Check Kiting

Check kiting is the deliberate issuance of a check for which there is not sufficient cash to pay the stated amount. The mechanics of this fraud scheme are as follows:

1. Write a check for which there is not sufficient cash in the payer's account.
2. Create a checking account at a different bank.
3. Deposit the fraudulent check in the checking account that was just opened.
4. Withdraw the funds from the new checking account.

The entity harmed by check kiting is the bank that has allowed funds to be withdrawn from the new checking account without first waiting for funds to arrive from the paying bank.

Banks combat this problem by not allowing funds to be withdrawn from an account until a certain number of days have passed, by which time the lack of funds in the payer's account will have been discovered. Also, there are a number of kiting indicators to look for, including the following:

- A large number of check deposits each day
- Many checks are drawn on the same bank
- A large proportion of cash in an account that has not yet cleared the paying bank
- Deposits are being made through multiple bank branches, in order to make the volume of deposits less obvious to the bank staff

Check kiting is extremely intentional. Someone engaged in kiting has a detailed knowledge of how long it takes for checks to clear the bank, and will take advantage of the timing delay to withdraw cash (even partial amounts) just before the bank discovers that there is a problem. A sophisticated check kiting scheme can result in multi-million dollar losses.

Kiting is particularly effective when an individual engages in a reasonable amount of normal check writing and depositing activities in an account over a period of time, so that the related account appears perfectly normal, and so is subject to fewer bank-imposed restrictions than might be the case for a newly-opened account.

A kiting scheme may involve multiple banks, where an individual is constantly shifting check payments among numerous accounts, just keeping ahead of the funds clearing mechanism. This can be a particular problem when a kiting scheme is finally shut down, for one of the banks in the group may be stuck with the bulk of the losses, depending on which checks were written from which accounts, and the timing of the payments.

Banks have software that reviews customer transactions to see if anyone has a high volume of checking transactions within a short period of time. If so, these customers are flagged for further examination by the bank's internal audit staff.

Solicitations Disguised as Invoices

A lower dollar amount of fraud involves the receipt of solicitations that are designed to look like invoices. If the document looks particularly official and the amount is not that large, the recipient is more likely to submit the document to the payables department for payment, on the assumption that the item is a valid invoice.

It is illegal for anyone to create a solicitation that is disguised as an invoice, unless there is a large-font statement on the document that it is actually a solicitation. This statement must be in bold font capital letters, and in a color that contrasts prominently with the document background. Consequently, anyone approving or processing these documents for payment should peruse them for a solicitation notice.

Lapping

Lapping occurs when an employee steals cash by diverting a payment from one customer, and then hides the theft by diverting cash from another customer to offset the receivable from the first customer. This type of fraud can be conducted in perpetuity, since newer payments are continually being used to pay for older debts, so that no receivable involved in the fraud ever appears to be that old.

Lapping is most easily engaged in when just one employee is involved in all cash handling and recordation tasks. This situation most commonly arises in a smaller business, where a bookkeeper may be responsible for all accounting tasks.

Lapping typically requires that the person engaged in the fraud be involved every day, and so does not take any vacation time. Thus, having a person refuse to take the vacation time that they have earned can be considered a possible indicator of the existence of lapping.

Lapping can be detected by conducted a periodic review of the cash receipts records, to trace payments to outstanding receivables. If there is ongoing evidence that cash receipts are routinely being applied against the wrong customer accounts, then either the cashier is astonishingly incompetent or there is an active lapping scheme in progress.

Inventory Theft

There are numerous ways in which employees can steal inventory from the premises. These losses appear as shrinkage in the ending inventory balance, so that the losses are included in the cost of goods sold. Several ways in which to steal inventory are:

- *From the receiving area.* The receiving staff can remove items from incoming shipping containers. This can take the form of declaring certain receipts as having been damaged in transit, documenting that these items were returned, and then keeping the goods. The returned goods gambit is especially effective, for the stolen goods never enter the company's inventory tracking systems.
- *From the warehouse.* Inventory may be retained for some time in the warehouse, which therefore gives employees the longest time to figure out how to steal the goods. However, this is also a controlled environment, with fencing and inventory tracking procedures. Nonetheless, someone can still walk out of the warehouse with inventory during odd hours, or check out inventory as though it is being delivered to production and removing the goods as soon as they leave the warehouse.
- *From the production floor.* The production area is a much less controlled environment than the warehouse, so it is easier to remove inventory from this area. Theft is especially common when complete inventory kits are positioned in the production area at the start of each job; this is a ready source of all possible inventory items. In addition, fittings and fasteners are commonly stored in bulk next to the production area for easy access, which makes them easy to steal.

- *From the rework area.* When goods are tested on the production floor and found to be out of specification, they are sent to the rework area for further evaluation. An easy theft is for the people working in this area to declare these items incapable of recovery and then take the goods, rather than scrapping them.
- *From the shipping area.* Completed goods that are ready for shipment can be easier to steal from the shipping area than the warehouse, since the level of control is lower here. A variation is for the theft to occur while the goods are in transit to the customer; this requires the connivance of the driver, who can remove selected items from the shipment.

It is not that common for employees to cover up their inventory thefts by also adjusting the inventory balances. Instead, these thefts simply appear as shrinkage, with ongoing inventory counts noting that the amounts on hand are regularly lower than what the book balances indicate should be on hand.

A fancier form of inventory theft that is not so easy to locate is when an employee requisitions inventory for a specific project, and then takes the inventory. The items were never actually needed for the project. Since the goods were charged to the internal project, there is no inventory shortfall in the warehouse records. A bolder perpetrator might even create an entirely fake project in order to charge inventory and other assets to it.

One should not assume that only finished goods will be stolen. Raw materials and components may also be removed from the premises, and then sold on an auction site. In short, any type of inventory can be converted into cash by the more enterprising perpetrators.

Product Replacement Fraud

Employees can steal significant amounts of inventory if they create fake credit memos to customers that have allegedly returned defective goods. The supposedly returned items are designated in the warehouse records as having been scrapped, and are then stolen from the warehouse. The employees liquidate the stolen inventory and pocket the proceeds. This fraud will only work when there is collusion between the warehouse staff (which steals the inventory) and selected accounting staff (who process the credit memos).

This fraud will create a spike in the inventory returns level, and should trigger an investigation by the product design team, which will want to know why so many products are being returned. Given these risks, the perpetrators will have the best chance of success if they keep the theft level fairly low, so that the extra credit memos only register as a slight uptick in the historical product returns rate.

Fixed Asset Theft and Misuse

Despite their name, fixed assets are not always fixed in nature, and so can be removed from the premises of a business. There are multiple ways to do so, usually involving simple theft. In addition, fixed assets may be misused, which is another form of fraud that damages an organization. Several ways in which fixed assets can be misused or stolen are as follows:

- *Theft of idle assets.* If fixed assets are not used on a regular basis, there is a tendency for them to be shunted off to one side and ignored. When assets are idle, there is much less chance that anyone will notice their absence. At this point, someone can remove quite substantial assets from the premises, and the absence may never be noticed.
- *Interception of disposal funds.* When a fixed asset is declared to be no longer necessary, the purchasing department is usually tasked with finding a buyer, and then sells the asset. If there is not a strong system of controls in place, it is quite possible that a buyer declares an asset to have instead been scrapped, and pockets the proceeds from the buyer.
- *Improper asset use.* A person may elect to employ a company-owned asset for personal use. This is incorrect behavior, since the result is an asset that has a shorter useful life or a lower residual value as a result of the excess use. For example, when a salesperson continues driving his company-owned car for personal use, it reduces the resale value of the car. This is, in effect, a theft from the business.

Bust-Out Scams

A common practice for the credit department of a business is to grant small amounts of credit to newer customers, and then gradually build up the amount of credit allowed when there is a history by customers of paying on time. Someone can take advantage of this pattern by setting up a business, placing small orders, and paying the resulting bills within normal terms. At this point, the credit manager is more likely to allow credit for a much larger order. The perpetrator then accepts delivery, shuts down his business, and moves away – without paying the bill. The goods are then liquidated for cash. This is called a *bust-out scam*.

The process can also work in reverse. The perpetrator sets up a company and begins offering goods at excellent prices, but only when payment is made in advance. Once customers become comfortable with the arrangement, the company offers exceptional pricing for a short period of time in order to attract even larger orders, takes the prepayment money, and walks away from the business.

Advance-Fee Loan Schemes

A business may have difficulty obtaining a loan through normal sources, perhaps due to a poor record of previous loan repayments, or poor fundamentals in its financial statements that are scaring away traditional lenders. If so, the owners may examine alternatives that are essentially fraud schemes. These schemes usually involve the offer of a guaranteed loan if the company first pays a fee. The perpetrator promises to represent the business with a recognized lender, saying that he has the connections needed to secure a loan. Once the fee is paid, the person either vanishes or puts off the firm with various excuses.

A variation on the concept is to require a fee to obtain an introduction to a lender. In this case, the fee agreement may be structured so that there is no actual fraud – the business is simply paying for a referral. If the lender to which the business is being referred then demands an exorbitant fee, the referring person can claim to only being responsible for the initial introduction.

In an advance-fee scheme, the fee is frequently stated as a percentage of the gross amount of the loan that the organization is trying to obtain. For example, a 5% fee might be charged in order to secure a $100,000 loan, so the person is paid a $5,000 fee. When the business is only paying for an introduction, the payment is more likely to be a fixed sum, such as $10,000.

A reasonable degree of caution will keep a business from falling into this type of scheme. A key preventive point is to consider why a promoter can obtain a loan on the company's behalf when it is impossible to do so directly. Also, be sure to obtain the name of the lender that will be extending a loan, and verify with that lender the representations made by the promoter. In addition, ask for contact information for other entities that have used the promoter in the past, and contact them to see if they actually obtained the promised loan amounts. Finally, conduct a background investigation on the promoter to see if there have been any issues with him in the past, or if there are indicators of fraud in his prior business dealings.

Kickbacks

In a kickback scheme, a supplier pays a buyer a bribe in exchange for selecting the supplier to sell goods and services to the buyer's company. This results in inflated prices and/or substandard quality levels for the company. A variation on the concept is for the supplier to hire a relative of the purchasing agent, typically at an inflated level of compensation; by doing so, there is no traceable payment being made to the supplier. Other variations are for the kickback recipient to take out a loan and have the loan payments paid by the supplier, or for the supplier to issue the person a credit card, with all payments on the card being made by the supplier.

This type of fraud can be found by comparing the prices paid to suppliers to the market price, to see if there is price inflation. This task is usually taken on by the internal audit department, which will probably only invest the investigation effort for larger purchasing contracts. Consequently, if the two conniving parties are careful, they can probably get away with smaller kickback schemes for a long time, and go undetected.

A less common variation on the kickback scheme is for a customer to pay the collections staff of a company in exchange for allowing their payments to extend longer than usual without designating the receivables as overdue (which might trigger an interest charge). There is a significant opportunity for fraud in this area when the amounts outstanding are quite large, and especially when there is a continuing series of invoices to be paid. This issue can be prevented to some extent by routinely shifting customer assignments among the collections staff, so that no one can take advantage of such a deal for long. The arrangement may also be detected by tracking the days outstanding for larger invoices.

Bid Rigging

A variation on the preceding kickback scheme is when an employee (usually a buyer in the purchasing department) assists a supplier in winning a competitive bid. Under a competitive bidding arrangement, a number of suppliers are asked to provide bids. A buyer can assist a preferred supplier by altering the terms of the bid solicitation to favor that supplier's goods and services, by informing the supplier of the terms of other bids already received, and by influencing the subsequent selection process to favor the indicated supplier. Another variation is to set up such a narrow time window within which to submit bids that most bidders are unable to submit bids on time, and so are rejected.

A bid rigging situation is not easily pinpointed, since the methods used may be so subtle that there is no clear indicator on an individual bid basis that anything is wrong. The situation is more obvious when a number of bids are aggregated, at which point it will become clear that a particular supplier is winning a disproportionate number of contracts.

Bribery

The reverse of accepting kickbacks is offering bribes. In this case, a business is offering to pay a third party for influence in obtaining a contract with a customer, or some other arrangement that benefits the business. The bribery of foreign officials is illegal under the Foreign Corrupt Practices Act (see the Legal Aspects of Fraud chapter). Bribery payments are usually spotted by examining the contracts associated with these payments that allegedly authorize the payments in exchange for valuable services. If there is no contract at all, this is a good sign that a business is engaging in bribery.

Bribery can be extremely tempting when a business is trying to obtain licenses, permits, and other types of assistance when opening new locations or entering new territories. This is especially the case when local officials make it clear that a payment is expected, or else roadblocks will slow down an organization's expansion plans. When a business has many alternatives for growth, senior management can choose to focus elsewhere, and not pursue growth in areas where corruption is endemic. However, when those other revenue sources have already been tapped and an entity is now looking for short-term gains in order to avoid being tagged as a slow-growth business, senior management may put increased pressure on local managers to increase sales, which then presents them with the awkward issue of having to pay bribes in order to achieve their assigned numbers.

Bribery is combatted by instituting a program of training, policies, and controls that reinforce the message that the company does not engage in bribery under any circumstances. This program must be reinforced regularly with existing staff, as well as with new staff, until there is a high level of integrity throughout the organization. This can be difficult in new locations where the entire staff may have just been hired, so it is imperative for management to initiate immediate integrity training programs as soon as a new company location opens for business.

Conflicts of Interest

Conflict of interest fraud occurs when an employee has divided loyalties in a business arrangement. That is, he benefits from both sides of a deal. For example, an individual could be part-owner of a supplier that provides cleaning services to the person's employer. In these situations, the person has a monetary interest in continuing to direct business toward the third party in which he has an interest.

There is no conflict of interest when the employer knows about the arrangement. Once the situation is known, business dealings take into account the existence of the relationship, so it can no longer be said that the individual in question is taking advantage of his employer.

Examples of other situations that can be construed as conflicts of interest are:

- Directing business to a supplier that is owned by friends or family
- Selling goods or services at below-market rates to a customer that is owned by the employee, or his friends or family

Insider Trading

Insider trading occurs when employees have knowledge of information that is not yet available to the public, and use this information to buy or sell company securities at advantageous prices. For example, the CFO of a business knows that reported sales levels will decline in the next quarterly financial statements, so he sells his shares in the company in advance of the information release. The CFO avoids a loss in the market value of his shares by timing the sale of the shares.

Insider trading does not harm the company, but most definitely harms its investors, since they may be buying securities from or selling securities to people who have better knowledge of what those securities are really worth.

There are significant insider trading legal penalties, which are classified as felonies. If that is not a sufficient deterrent, all insiders who hold company stock can be regularly advised of the penalties associated with insider trading.

Stock Option Backdating

Stock options give their holder the right to purchase the common stock of a corporation at a specific price. This right is available over a date range, such as for the next five years. Once a stock option is used to buy shares, these shares are typically sold right away, in order to pay any related income taxes. Consequently, a person who has been awarded stock options will only use them if the current market price is higher than the exercise price built into the options. The exercise price is usually the market price of the shares on the date when the options were awarded. For example, a person is awarded 1,000 stock options that allow him to buy the shares of the employer for

$10.00 per share. After three years have passed, the price of the shares has increased to $12.00. The investor exercises the options to buy 1,000 shares from his employer for $10,000. He immediately sells the shares on the open market for $12,000, pocketing a profit of $2,000.

An issue with stock options that management can illegally take advantage of is to backdate the options. The date at which the option price is set is shifted backward to that date on which the market price of the stock was the lowest. By doing so, those awarded stock options can now buy the shares at a lower exercise price, so that they reap larger profits when they sell the shares. To use a variation on the preceding example, management backdates the stock options by three weeks, to a day on which the company's stock price was $9.00 per share. The person awarded the options later buys the shares at $9.00 and sells them for $12,000, resulting in a profit of $3,000. Because of the backdating, the individual earned a 50% larger profit than would otherwise have been the case.

This type of fraud is difficult to spot, since it is not immediately apparent in a company's financial statements. Instead, one must examine the date of the board of directors minutes to see when the options were authorized, and then trace this date back to when the options documentation was completed. A disparity between the dates indicates that backdating has occurred.

Information Theft

Fraud can also involve the loss of intangible assets. An employee could steal the trade secrets of a company and market them to the highest bidder, or use the information to bargain for a job with a competitor. This information can take many forms, such as:

- Business strategies
- Customer lists
- Employee compensation lists
- Food recipes
- Manufacturing configurations
- Product designs
- Software code

There are many ways to steal trade secrets, such as storing information on a thumb drive, taking pictures of documents with a phone, and e-mail transfers of files.

Time Theft

The preceding types of fraud can cause a direct decline in the cash flows of a business, and so tend to attract the most attention from an anti-fraud campaign. A more widespread but less noticeable type of fraud is the theft of time. This occurs when employees take time out during the normal working day to engage in personal activities. In effect, they are still being paid *by* the company, but are not providing value *to* the company. Several examples of time theft are:

- Arriving at work late and leaving early
- Both taking and making personal phone calls
- Conducting a private business on the premises
- Deliberately slowing down the normal work rate
- Trolling the Internet during work hours

Since no money is being stolen, time theft is not a criminal offence. Nonetheless, it can result in significant losses for a business.

Money Laundering Schemes

Money laundering is the process of obscuring the origins of illegally-obtained cash, so that it appears to be legitimate. By using money laundering, one can avoid the risk of having cash appropriated by the government.

The basic concept behind money laundering schemes is to shift illegally-obtained cash into a different entity, usually in another country, and then convert it into legal assets. The process works best when the cash is shifted through a series of other entities in multiple countries, thereby making it more difficult to ascertain the origins of the cash.

Once the cash has been shifted through the bank accounts of a sufficient number of enterprises, it is invested in an entity that is entirely legitimate, such as a restaurant, office building, farm, or manufacturing facility.

The best money laundering schemes involve shifting funds through numerous people, thereby making it more difficult for anyone to associate funds obtained by one party as being the funds now held by someone else. The risk to the money launderer is that one of these parties will abscond with the cash, so hefty fees or commissions are allowed as money shifts through the various entities that are laundering money.

The basic steps in a money laundering scheme are as follows:

1. *Placement in a financial institution*. Cash is deposited in bank accounts. This can be difficult, since banks are required to notify the government of large cash deposits. Accordingly, deposits are made in small and irregularly-sized amounts, using a variety of accounts at different banks. Also, bank officials may be bribed to not report these cash deposits.
2. *Cash movement*. Once deposited, the cash is transferred in differing amounts to many other accounts in banks in several other countries, with the intent of making the transfers as difficult to follow as possible. Examples of the ways in which this cash movement is conducted are:

    - *Underground banking*. There are undocumented "underground banking" systems in some countries that do not report their transactions to the government. Money is shifted into and out of these banking systems.
    - *Shell companies*. Shell companies are created that offer fake goods and services in exchange for cash. Once received, this cash is the

property of the shell company, which is likely to be under the control of the original cash owner or an associate.

- *Legitimate businesses*. Cash is injected into a legitimate business by having that business bill for additional revenues and paying it with laundered cash.
- *Asset purchases*. The form of the cash is changed into some type of asset, such as real estate, jewelry, paintings, and so forth.
- *Currency conversion*. Cash is exchanged into a different currency, possibly going through several conversions, in order to hide its origins.

3. *Cash conversion*. Once the origins of the cash have been sufficiently obscured, it is used to purchase assets, varying from commodities to real estate. This represents the "cleaned" version of the cash - it cannot be traced, and it appears to be legitimate. At this point, the cash can be used by the actual owner.

Money laundering operations can be quite complex, requiring the services of lawyers, bankers, and accountants to continually dream up new laundering schemes and keep track of the flow of money.

Money laundering can result in unusual transactions that serve as red flags. For example:

- Owning expensive assets without an obvious source of wealth to pay for them
- Paying for expensive assets in cash
- Paying for ongoing expenses in cash
- Using a corporation to buy assets that are obviously for personal use
- Using an unusual number of cashier's checks or money orders

Financial Statement Fraud Schemes

The last type of fraud that we describe in this chapter is financial statement fraud. This involves the deliberate alteration of the reported results, financial position, or cash flows of a business in order to mislead the readers of the financial statements. In the following sub-sections, we describe a multitude of ways to falsify financial statements.

Sales Inflation

The managers of a business might try to falsely increase sales. Their intent could be to cover a shortfall in projected sales for a short period of time, or perhaps to artificially bolster sales over a longer period. Here are several options they might attempt to use:

- *Accelerate recognition on mixed sale arrangements*. When a company sells a mix of goods and services, it overstates the price of the goods (which can be recognized at once), while underpricing the price of the services (which are recognized over a longer period of time).

- *Bill and hold transactions*. Under these arrangements, the seller recognized revenue while retaining the goods that should have been shipped to the customer, allegedly because the customer wants the seller to store the goods on the customer's behalf. The seller may forge documents, stating that the customer has authorized this arrangement.

- *Billing of cost overruns*. Under several types of construction reimbursement contracts, the buyer compensates the seller for cost overruns – but only after the customer approves a formal change order. If the seller were to record these cost overruns as revenue prior to a change order, it would constitute falsification of revenues.

- *Combine a business unit sale with guaranteed future product sales*. A company may choose to sell off one of its business units. In order to falsely generate more sales in future periods, the transaction is structured to sell the unit at an artificially low price, while requiring the buyer to purchase goods from the parent company for a certain period of time and at an inflated price. The net effect of the deal is that the parent company converts a one-time gain on the sale of its subsidiary into operating revenue that it can recognize in the future.

- *Consignment sales*. A business sends goods to a third party, which has agreed to sell the goods to the ultimate buyer on behalf of the company. Under a consignment arrangement, there is no sale until delivery is made to the ultimate buyer. When the business records a sale at the point when it delivers goods to the consignee, this is a fraudulent acceleration of the related sale.

- *Create revenue journal entries*. Management can simply create a journal entry that credits sales and debits accounts receivable, thereby instantly generating sales even when there is no underlying transaction at all. This is called a *topside entry*, for it is made to the general ledger, not to any supporting subledgers. Topside entries are a favorite tool for falsely adjusting revenue, because they do not require collusion with other departments; management simply makes its own entries.

- *Delay recordation of discounts*. When discounts are granted to customers on sales transactions, the amount eventually collected from the customers will be reduced, which means that the initial sales figure should be reduced by the amount of these discounts. Delaying the recordation of sales discounts into a later period will result in a temporary boost in the sales figure.

- *Delay recordation of returns*. When goods are returned by customers, this is recorded as a reduction of sales. When management wants to keep sales as high as possible in the current period, they delay the recordation of sales returns until a later period.

- *Grossing up revenue*. An entity that acts as an agent for another party should only recognize as revenue the commission it earns on a sale, not the entire amount of the sale. An organization can use various pretexts under the accounting rules to claim that it can actually recognize all of these types of sales.

For example, an airline ticket broker may claim the entire amount of a sold ticket as revenue, when it should really be just the amount of the commission earned on the deal.

- *Keep the period open.* The end of the reporting period is allowed to stay open into the following day (or in egregious cases, for several days), so that shipments occurring on the next day are recorded as sales in the previous reporting period.
- *Manipulate the percentage of completion.* When there are lengthy projects associated with revenues (such as the construction of a building), revenue is recognized based on the estimated percentage of completion. Thus, a 50% completion rate means that 50% of the contract revenue can be recognized. Sales can be inflated simply by increasing the assumed percentage of completion.
- *Misclassify sales.* A one-time gain on an asset sale is mis-classified as being part of revenues. Another variation is to classify investment income as sales.
- *Pipeline stuffing.* A business could encourage its customers, retailers, and distributors to accept additional products in order to achieve a short-term boost in sales. This may be accomplished by offering to take back unused goods, offering long-term payment terms, or large discounts from the normal list price. The intent behind doing so is to create a burst of sales that will be misconstrued by the readers of the entity's financial statements as an increase in long-term sales.
- *Recognize sales on incomplete orders.* There may be customer orders in process that have not been completed as of the end of the reporting period, so managers authorize these orders to be recognized as complete.
- *Related-party sales.* A company sells assets to an entity that is controlled by the corporate parent or a common investor, resulting in a gain. However, since the ownership of both entities is the same, it is really an intercompany transaction that should have been backed out of the financial statements.
- *Round-tripping.* An organization sells certain assets to another party, promising to buy them back at a later date. Doing so creates revenue, though there is no economic justification for the continual shifting of assets back and forth. The more elaborate forms of this arrangement may even involve three parties, so that the nature of the activity is more obscure and difficult to detect.
- *Ship excess inventory.* A company ships extra goods to customers and bills them for the excess. The intent behind doing so is to book additional sales. Some customers may accept the extra merchandise, though most can be expected to return the goods after the end of the reporting period. The result for the company is a spike in sales, followed by a sharp decline when the sales returns are booked.
- *Ship goods early.* A customer may only want to have goods delivered as of a certain date, perhaps because it is operating a just-in-time system, and there is no room for the on-site storage of early deliveries. The company may ship early in order to record the sale within the reporting period.

- *Ship to company-owned warehouse.* A business can ostensibly ship goods and recognize the revenue associated with those goods, while actually just sending the goods to a warehouse that is owned by the company. The warehouse is essentially a way-point for goods that allows a business to recognize sales early, holding the goods for a short time and then forwarding them to the ultimate customer.
- *Side agreements.* A company can enter into undocumented side agreements with its customers that grant the customers special rights, such as the right to send back goods for an inordinately long time. Because these agreements are not documented, there is no proof that sales are being recorded sooner than should really be the case.

If the intent is to artificially increase sales for a long period of time, the fraud involves the creation of entirely new customer orders. This can include fake customer purchase orders, with a fake set of supporting documents to show how the orders were handled within the company and fulfilled.

Expenses Falsification

The preceding list of falsifications related to sales was enormous. The list of possibilities for adjusting expenses is quite a bit smaller, but can still have a significant impact on reported profit levels. The key expense falsifications are:

- *Capitalize expenses.* A business can recognize expenses as assets, thereby deferring expense recognition until a later period. These expenses are usually parked in one or more fixed asset accounts, but can be stored in a number of imaginatively-named asset accounts. Certain types of expenses are more likely to be incorrectly capitalized, such as advertising and other marketing costs, where the argument is that marketing expenditures are a cost of attracting new customers. Under this logic, the costs are then charged to expense over the period of time that the company expects to have the customers.
- *Slow the amortization rate.* When expenditures have been capitalized, management can further slow the rate of their conversion to expenses by slowing down the rate of amortization. Amortization is the process of charging assets off to expense. For example, marketing costs are capitalized into a customer acquisition asset, and management then decides that the amortization rate will be 10 years. Doing so spreads the expense recognition over quite a long period of time, and keeps profit levels unusually high in the interim. Management can alter all types of asset amortization periods, including depreciation rates for fixed assets, in order to defer expense recognition.
- *Do not record invoices.* Management holds supplier invoices until the following reporting period, and then allows the accounts payable staff to record them in the accounting system. Doing so shifts the expense out of the current period and into the next one. This approach is typically only used for a few larger invoices.

- *Do not accrue expenses.* Management may skip the accrual of various expenses, such as accrued wages, bonuses, commissions, and so forth. By doing so, the related expense recognition is shifted into the following period.
- *Avoid loss reserves.* A prudent business will record loss reserves for warranty claims, lawsuit payouts, and so forth. A management team that is intent on minimizing reported expense levels will avoid creating any of these reserves. Instead, they only recognize expenses as they actually occur, which could be at a later date.
- *Reduce loss reserves.* When there are existing loss reserves, management reverses some or all of the amounts in them, thereby reporting a negative expense in the income statement. A more conniving management team will establish one or more generic loss reserve accounts, and shift expenses into and out of them in order to manage the earnings level from period to period.

Marketable Securities Falsification

A business is supposed to record its marketable securities at their market values as of the ending date of each reporting period. The market value is derived from the reported prices at which shares sell. This might initially appear to be an area in which little fraud is possible, since the calculation is based on publicly-available information. However, the securities of many public companies are not traded on formal exchanges. Instead, they are listed on the over-the-counter market, where trading is much thinner. In these cases, a company could bid up the price of a stock just before month-end with just a few small purchases, and then value all of its holdings in that stock at the month-end value. The falsification is only apparent when looking at the trend line of prices for the stock on a daily basis.

Prepaid Expenses Falsification

The prepaid expenses account is supposed to contain expenditures that have been paid for in one accounting period, but for which the underlying asset will not be entirely consumed until a future period. An example of a prepaid expense is insurance, which is frequently paid in advance for multiple future periods; an entity initially records this expenditure as a prepaid expense, and then charges it to expense over the usage period.

When a company wants to make its financial results look better, it overloads the prepaid expenses account by adding expenses that should have been charged to expense at once. Instead, these expenses are recognized in a future period. The alteration of this account is typically used to make smaller adjustments to the financial statements on a short-term basis, where the intent is to clean up the account shortly thereafter.

Receivables Falsification

There are multiple ways to falsify an organization's accounts receivable. In the following points, we outline several of the more common ones. They are:

- *Date alteration.* When a business engages in suspect sales activities, the related accounts receivables will eventually age to the point where they are clearly overdue for payment, and should be written off (thereby causing a loss). To prevent a write-off, the accounting staff alters the dates on the invoices or credits the invoices to eliminate them, and replaces them with debit memos or invoices that have a more current date.
- *Minimize reserves.* A relatively common financial statement adjustment is to maintain an excessively low allowance for doubtful accounts. When this happens, the allowance does not accurately reflect the amount of bad debt that is contained within accounts receivable. The result is that bad debts are more likely to be charged to expense in a later period, when specific invoices are written off. This means that the current period profit is overstated by the understatement of this allowance.
- *Delay bad debt recognition.* A variation on the last concept is to delay recognizing bad debts until a later period. When a bad debt is recognized, it is written off by offsetting it against the allowance for doubtful accounts. By delaying this recognition, the allowance looks bigger than it really is, making it appear that no additional charge to bad debts expense is needed.
- *Offload questionable receivables.* When it appears that some receivables will not be collected, the company sells them to another entity, usually at full value. The buying entity could be controlled by a related party, so that the sale is a sham.
- *Shift to notes receivable.* A company can convince some of its customers to sign paperwork that converts trade receivables into notes receivable. By doing so, the company can remove these items from its accounts receivable line item, thereby producing a misleading comparison of sales to receivables, indicating that receivables are more current than is really the case.

Loss Reserves Falsification

A business could record a large loss reserve, taking a massive charge against earnings in one period. The argument favoring the use of this reserve is that the business is about to discontinue some of its operations, engage in a restructuring, complete an environmental cleanup, and so forth, and wants to recognize all related losses at once. As expenditures are incurred in later periods, they are charged against the reserve, for which the expense was already recognized.

This is fine, except when the amount of the loss is overstated. When there is too much of a loss, the reserve turns into a bank that can be reversed whenever needed to offset operating expenses, resulting in incorrectly high profits. For example, a business recognizes a $1,000,000 charge against earnings that relates to the forthcoming shuttering of its widget production facility. However, management knows that the actual amount of these losses will be much closer to $300,000, leaving a reserve of $700,000 that is available for other uses. A few periods later, the company records an inordinately high legal expense, so the controller is instructed to debit the reserve by $60,000 and credit the legal expense in the same amount, resulting in a reduction in the reported legal expense.

The use of excessive loss reserves is particularly common in the following circumstances:

- *New team.* A new management team has been hired to replace a poorly-performing team, and sets up a loss reserve right away, under the guise of needing to write off any number of things to clean up the mess. Actually, the loss is then used to manage earnings for the next few accounting periods in order to show gradual improvement in reported results.
- *Excess earnings.* Earnings are already quite good, but management foresees that earnings could begin to decline, so it writes off a large amount into a loss reserve under a pretext. The reserve is then used to bolster subsequent earnings.
- *Losses add-on.* A company is already suffering massive losses and a large decline in its stock price. Management presumes that adding on more losses at this point will make little difference, so it adds on a loss reserve, which can be used to manage earnings in the future.

The use of loss reserves can be detected by keeping track of the loss reserve balance on the balance sheet. As it gradually declines over time, inquire as to how the reserve was used.

Inventory Falsification

When the ending valuation of inventory is adjusted, this has a direct impact on the reported amount of income. The reason is that the cost of goods sold is calculated using the following formula:

Beginning inventory + Purchases – Ending inventory = Cost of goods sold

Thus, if the amount of ending inventory is artificially increased, this reduces the cost of goods sold, which increases profits. Given this effect, it should be no surprise that multiple scams have been originated to modify ending inventory, including the following:

- *Claim consigned inventory.* When a business holds consigned inventory on behalf of a consignor, it does not own the inventory. One can easily count these items and include them in ending inventory in order to inflate inventory levels.
- *Delay purchase recordation.* When purchases are recorded, they form the middle part of the cost of goods sold calculation that was just described. Thus,

if someone wants to report a lower cost of goods sold, the entry of a supplier's invoice is just delayed until the following reporting period. Of course, this will then increase the cost of goods sold in the next reporting period.

- *Delay shrinkage charges.* The inventory may shrink for any number of reasons, including theft, damage, and inventory items exceeding their usage dates. These items should be promptly subtracted from inventory, which reduces profits. If the management team simply refuses to authorize the shrinkage charges, then inventory will be overstated.

- *Double counting.* Two separate count teams could be routed to the same inventory area at different times, resulting in each team innocently counting the same inventory. Doing so doubles the ending inventory count for the targeted items.

- *Inflate overhead.* Factory overhead is allocated to ending inventory, and can form a substantial part of the total inventory balance at month-end. This amount can be manipulated by altering the accounts that are included in factory overhead, or by altering the allocation methodology.

- *Mis-calculate inventory extensions.* The computer program used to multiply ending unit counts by costs per unit can be programmed to yield inflated figures. Or, if an electronic spreadsheet is used, a selection of manual overrides can be made to achieve the same result.

- *Move inventory.* Management can arrange to have inventory counted at one location on one day, and then moved to another location and counted again the next day. This scam requires that counts be staggered across several days.

- *Overstate the percentage of completion of work-in-process.* When goods have not yet been completed by the end of a reporting period, a cost is assigned to them based on their percentage of completion. When this percentage is artificially raised, so too is the inventory valuation.

- *Recognize fictitious inventory.* Someone could record entirely fake inventory, along with supporting purchase and storage documents. This approach works best when there are no scheduled inventory counts in the near future, so that there is no risk of someone spotting these items.

- *Repackage scrap inventory.* Inventory items designated as scrap or rework can be packaged into finished goods boxes at month-end and counted as normal finished goods.

- *Use incorrect costs.* When an inventory count is conducted at the end of a reporting period, the units on hand are supposed to be multiplied by the relevant unit cost, depending on the cost flow assumptions being used by the business (such as the first in, first out method). One could replace a selection of these costs with an adjusted amount, thereby altering the amount of ending inventory.

Inventory-related fraud tends to be used to manufacture artificial results for just a short period of time, since modifications to ending inventory balances are self-correcting. This is because the modified ending inventory balance for one period becomes the beginning inventory balance for the *next* period. Therefore, if someone does not continually alter the ending inventory balance in each consecutive month, the false reporting will be automatically flushed out of the system.

Fixed Asset Falsification

There are several ways to shift expenses into a later period by altering the fixed assets accounts, thereby increasing profits in the current period. These adjustments are as follows:

- *Allocate purchase costs to land.* The land asset is not depreciated. The ramification from a fraud perspective is that, when a grouping of land and buildings is acquired as part of a single deal, as much of the purchase price as possible should be allocated to the land portion of the deal. The result is that a large part of the purchase is never depreciated.

- *Capitalize compensation costs.* Management could capitalize an excessive amount of labor costs into the costs of fixed assets. This is especially common for constructed assets, where there is a better justification for doing so.

- *Create fake assets.* A business could report fixed assets that have no basis in reality. The assets may simply be added to the books, perhaps with an offset to an equity account. Doing so appears to increase the amount of assets that can be used as collateral for loans, while also increasing equity, which makes the organization appear more financially stable.

- *Create intangible assets.* Management could capitalize a variety of operating expenses as fixed assets, thereby deferring recognition of the related expense. For example, software development costs could be capitalized into the cost of software, as well as research & development costs and start-up costs. The accounting standards limit the circumstances under which operating costs can be capitalized, so this approach requires some aggressive stretching of the rules.

- *Increase useful lives.* The assumed useful lives of fixed assets can be increased, thereby spreading depreciation expense over a longer period of time. Useful lives may be extended for just the largest fixed assets, thereby making this alteration more difficult to spot while still maximizing the amount of depreciation expense that is deferred into future periods.

- *Increase salvage values.* Salvage values are assigned to fixed assets that do not currently have one, and existing salvage values are increased. By doing so, the amount of depreciation that will be charged against fixed assets is reduced. This approach is less easy to detect when only a few assets are assigned salvage values.

- *Increase interest capitalization.* The accounting staff liberally interprets the rules for assigning interest costs to long-term fixed asset projects, so that more interest costs are assigned to these projects, rather than being charged to expense as incurred.

- *Lower capitalization threshold.* The cutoff point at which expenditures are recorded as fixed assets is dropped, so that more expenses are converted into fixed assets. This spreads the recognition of expenses over several years.
- *Avoid asset write-offs.* When an asset is impaired, the amount of the impairment is supposed to be charged to expense at once. This is a particular issue with the goodwill derived from acquisitions; many organizations find that their goodwill balances must be written down. Management could mandate that all impairments are to be ignored. This also involves misleading the auditors, who will make inquiries about whether any asset impairments exist.

Liability Falsification

When a business does not record liabilities, the associated expenses are not recorded, thereby leading to increased profits. The following scams are used to achieve a lower level of liabilities:

- *Reduced accruals.* When an asset is consumed, there should be a related expense in the same period. When there is no associated supplier invoice for a period of time, the accounting staff is supposed to record an expense accrual. When this does not happen, the expense is shifted into a later period, when the invoice eventually arrives. This can be a particular problem with property taxes, since the bill is only sent once a year. Other types of accruals that may be ignored or understated are:
    - Insurance payable
    - Interest payable
    - Payroll taxes payable
    - Pension payments payable
    - Rent payable
    - Utilities payable
    - Vacations payable
    - Wages payable
- *Recognize self-insurance as incurred.* When a business self-insures, the accounting staff could incorrectly defer expense recognition by waiting until claims are actually received, which could be months or even years later.
- *Delayed recordation.* When a large supplier invoice arrives near month-end, it is withheld from the accounting system, and only recorded in the following month after the current month has closed. This effectively shifts the expense into the next reporting period.
- *Inflate purchase returns.* The amount of returns to suppliers can be inflated, which creates credits that offset the amounts owed to suppliers. This scam is especially pernicious, because it can originate in the shipping department rather than the accounting department. Someone in shipping forges product return documentation and sends it to accounting, so that the accounting staff thinks the returns are valid.

- *Inflate purchase discounts*. A company may claim to qualify for purchase discounts, such as volume discounts that are calculated following the end of each year. These discounts can be accrued even in the absence of actual credits being issued by suppliers.

- *Avoid setting up a warranty reserve*. A business might have a number of ongoing warranty claims from customers, in which case it should set up a warranty reserve when sales are initially generated, so that the related warranty expense is recognized at once. When there is no warranty reserve, the related warranty expense is only recognized when an actual customer claim is received, which could be months later.

- *Record deposits as revenue*. When a customer pays a deposit on an order, this amount is supposed to be recorded as a liability until such time as the related product or service has been shipped or completed, respectively. At that time, the deposit liability is eliminated and a sale is recorded. The accounting department could instead record these deposits as revenue right away, thereby understating liabilities. A more aggressive form of this fraud is when a deposit is supposed to be returned to a customer at a later date, as occurs when a renter makes a deposit that is to be paid back when the lease term expires. A company could record this type of deposit as revenue; doing so manufactures revenue that does not actually exist.

- *Use aggressive pension assumptions*. In a defined benefit pension plan, employees are guaranteed certain benefits. This type of plan calls for constant, ongoing accounting adjustments by the employer over the life of the plan, based on estimates of how much will be earned on invested pension funds and various assumptions regarding benefit usage levels and the death rates of participants. A business can use aggressive assumptions when calculating its pension obligation, such as assuming that an unusually high return will be generated on invested funds.

- *Waffle on contingent liabilities*. A contingent liability is supposed to be recorded when it is probable that the loss will occur, and it is reasonably possible to estimate the amount of the loss. A company can waffle on recording these liabilities by either ignoring them or by understating the probable amount of the liability. If it is reasonably possible that a contingent liability will occur, the liability should be disclosed in the accompanying footnotes to the financial statements. Again, management could choose to ignore these liabilities, not reporting them in the disclosures at all.

Debt Falsification

There are several ways in which to alter the amount of debt liability that a business is recording in its financial statements. Consider the following types of fraud:

- *Misrepresentation of debt*. A relatively common occurrence is for the owner of a closely-held business to contribute funds to the organization, and to characterize it as equity. By doing so, the business appears to be more stable, with a lower ratio of debt to equity. However, the owner's real intent is that the contribution is a loan, for which there is an expectation of repayment, along with interest. This situation may not become apparent until a later date, when the owner alters the underlying documents to shift the equity payment into a debt payment.

- *Not recording loans.* The owners of a business may take out loans that are collateralized by company assets, and retain the proceeds from the loans. These arrangements are not stated in the financial statements of the company, even though they are liabilities of the company.
- *Claiming forgiveness of debt.* Management can claim that a debt was forgiven by a lender, either in whole or in part. Not only does this eliminate a potentially major liability, it also creates a gain on the forgiveness of debt, which bolsters profits. This situation can appear to be correct in substance, especially when the debt is unsecured and the company refuses to pay the lender; in effect, the loan will not be paid, so the question is whether the loan is in default or has been forgiven.

Discontinued Operations Stuffing

The accounting standards mandate that the results of those operations scheduled to be discontinued should be shifted below the income from operations line, where it is typically ignored by investors. An easy ploy is for the management team to declare that a business unit is scheduled to be shut down and then tag it as a discontinued operation. Better yet, they stuff all possible expenses into this business unit, thereby increasing the reported profit level from continuing operations. The end result is a total profit figure for the entire business that has not changed, but with a much higher operating profit number.

Cash Flow Reclassifications

The statement of cash flows reveals the cash inflows and outflows of an organization, grouped into sub-categories for cash flows from operations, investing activities, and financing activities. The types of cash flows that are supposed to be associated with these classifications appear in the following three tables.

Operating Activity Cash Inflows and Outflows

Cash Inflows	Cash Outflows
Cash receipts from the sale of goods and services	Cash payments to employees
Cash receipts from the collection of receivables	Cash payments to suppliers
Cash receipts from lawsuit settlements	Cash payment of fines
Cash receipts from settlement of insurance claims	Cash payments to settle lawsuits
Cash receipts from supplier refunds	Cash payments of taxes
Cash receipts from licensees	Cash refunds to customers
	Cash payments to settle asset retirement obligations
	Cash payment of interest to creditors
	Cash payment of contributions

Investing Activity Cash Inflows and Outflows

Cash Inflows	Cash Outflows
Cash receipts from the sale of equity investments	Cash payments made to acquire equity investments
Cash receipts from the collection of principal on a loan	Cash payments made to acquire debt securities
Cash receipts from the sale of fixed assets	Cash payments made to acquire fixed assets

Financing Activity Cash Inflows and Outflows

Cash Inflows	Cash Outflows
Cash receipts from the sale of company shares	Cash payments to pay dividends
Cash receipts from the issuance of debt instruments	Cash payments to buy back company shares
Cash receipts from a mortgage	Cash payments for debt issuance costs
Cash receipts from derivative instruments	Cash payments to pay down principal on debt

There is a temptation for the management team to bolster the cash flows from operations classification, since this makes the operational activities of the firm appear to be quite robust. To this end, the general goals are:

- To reclassify cash inflows relating to investing and financing activities into the operating activities section; and
- To reclassify cash outflows relating to operating activities into the investing and financing activities section.

Here are several ways in which these goals are accomplished:

- *Buy and sell capacity*. A business can enter into an arrangement where it buys the capacity of its competitors, while also selling competitors its own capacity. The practice was prevalent in the telephone industry at one time. Under this scheme, cash flows received from competitors are classified as cash flows from operating activities, while payments to competitors are classified as cash flows from investing activities.
- *Capitalize operating expenses*. When management incorrectly capitalizes operating expenses, this not only means that the expenditures are now classified as assets on the balance sheet, but also that the cash outflow is now classified as an investing activity, rather than an operating activity.
- *Delay supplier payments*. When payments to suppliers are delayed, this reduces the amount of cash outflows for operating activities. This is not necessarily fraud – a company may simply be abusing its supplier relationships.
- *Make purchases with debt*. A company can acquire goods and services in exchange for a longer-term loan, rather than the usual credit terms that require payment in a month or so. By doing so, the cash outflow (when it occurs) is considered to be the repayment of a loan, which is classified as a financing activity, rather than an operating activity.
- *Retain receivables when selling a subsidiary*. A company could sell a subsidiary while retaining the related receivables, which it then collects. By doing so, the company can recognize the cash inflows related to the receivables as being an operating activity, rather than an investing activity (which would be the classification for the rest of the sale transaction).
- *Sell inventory and buy it back*. When a company enters into an arrangement to sell off its inventory and then buy it back shortly thereafter, this is essentially a loan that uses inventory as collateral. However, because inventory was "sold," the transaction can be mis-characterized as the sale of goods, which then appears as a cash inflow in the operating activity section of the statement of cash flows. The reverse side of the transaction, where the inventory is "bought" back, is then classified as a financing activity.

- *Sell receivables.* A company can validly choose to sell its accounts receivable in order to obtain more immediate use of the related cash. This transaction accelerates the amount of cash inflows reported in the operating activity section. There is nothing illegal about this practice, but it can be misleading, since it accelerates the reported receipt of cash flows into the current period, leaving fewer cash inflows to report in later periods.

Acquisition Falsification

When an organization acquires another business, there are several opportunities to fudge the transaction in the accounting records in order to meet the needs of the acquiring entity. Consider the following:

- *Adjust market values.* An acquirer is supposed to record the assets and liabilities of the acquiree at their market values on the acquisition date. The managers of the acquirer can exert pressure to alter the accounting for this transaction, so that the highest "market value" is assigned to those assets that have the longest depreciable lives, thereby incorrectly extending the period over which expenses will be recognized.
- *Delay sales.* The acquirer in an acquisition arrangement may ask the acquiree to slow down or even halt its recognition of sales in the months leading up to the acquisition date. By doing so, the sales are then recognized after the acquisition date, which allows the acquirer to record a significant boost in its sales.
- *Designation of acquirer.* The designation of the acquirer can be altered, so that the actual acquiree is designated as the acquirer. By doing so, the assets of the "acquiree" can now be marked up to their market values. This approach works from a fraud perspective when there is a clear difference in the potential asset markups between the two entities.

The Most Difficult Financial Statement Fraud Areas to Detect

Some types of fraud are not hard binary solutions, where a business has clearly committed fraud or it has not. Others are more a matter of opinion, and so are difficult to prove. In this sub-section, we note some of the most difficult cases of financial statement fraud to detect.

One of the hardest areas is in the treatment of contingent liabilities. As the name implies, these liabilities may or may not occur. Further, they may never have occurred in the past, so there is no historical record from which a pattern can be extrapolated forward. Instead, the examiner must use his knowledge of the business and the industry within which it operates, as well as its contracts and legal proceedings, to decide whether there are any contingent liabilities.

Another difficult area is revenue recognition when the amount to be recognized is based on an estimate of the percentage of project completion. Only a person intimately familiar with the conduct of a project may be able to determine the best percentage of completion to use. Realistically, there is room to waffle these percentages by several percent up or down, without being able to prove that the amount used is incorrect. The examiner can review these percentages of completion over time, to see if the percentage used tends to be at the high end of the possible range in order to inflate sales, or if the rate seems to be varying in order to manage earnings.

Yet another difficult area is unrecorded liabilities. Because these items have never been recorded, there is no evidence within the business that a liability exists. Sometimes, a reference to these liabilities is made in the board minutes or in letters or billings from attorneys, so be sure to examine this documentation for clues. In many cases, fraud in these areas will only be found well after the fact, when the liabilities come due for payment.

Financial Statement Disclosure Fraud

The accounting standards require that certain additional disclosures be made in addition to the financial statements themselves. These disclosures cover a broad range of topics, and are intended to provide supplemental information that gives the reader a more complete view of the financial performance and condition of a business. Further, a publicly-held company is also required to include in its financial statement reporting the MD&A (management's discussion and analysis) section. The MD&A section describes an organization's opportunities, challenges, risks, trends, future plans, and key performance indicators, as well as changes in revenues, the cost of goods sold, other expenses, assets, and liabilities. These requirements are based on three objectives related to financial reporting, which are:

- To give a narrative explanation of the financial statements from the perspective of management
- To enhance the numerical disclosures in the financial statements, as well as to provide a context within which to review this information
- To discuss the quality and possible variability of an entity's earnings and cash flows

The managers of a business can commit fraud by including incorrect or misleading information in these disclosures, or by not including essential information at all. Here are several examples:

- A company fails to describe the extent to which its sales were boosted by recent acquisitions, leaving investors to assume that the increase was caused by increases in its existing product lines.
- A company does not describe any contingent liabilities, so investors are unaware of the possibility of additional expenditures in the future.
- A company does not reveal the existence of long-term purchase obligations, which may create a substantial burden for several years into the future.
- A company targets its sales at lower-income customers, and earns material amounts from them in the form of interest on late payments. The company does not describe the source of this income, leaving investors to assume that the interest income comes from its investments.

- A company sells assets to a related party and buys them back at a later date. The company does not describe the ownership of the other entity, nor does it note the full extent of the arrangement. This is a clear case of disclosure fraud, since the activities that should be disclosed were likely used to pump up the reported sales level.
- A business discloses that there is a contingent gain, when in fact the gain is highly unlikely to occur, and misleads investors into thinking that the company will soon experience a notable windfall.
- A business fails to disclose that it is investing its excess cash in highly risky investments, in hopes of obtaining major returns.

Disclosure fraud can occur when the relevant disclosure is indeed present, but the description has been so thoroughly muddled that it is impossible for any but the most discerning reader to understand what is being said.

A variation on the disclosure fraud concept is when a business issues non-GAAP financial information. GAAP (generally accepted accounting principles) mandates that financial information be presented in a certain way that includes all expenses. When a business issues non-GAAP disclosures, it is usually subtracting certain one-time expenses that it does not consider to be relevant, inevitably resulting in a higher profit figure than would have been the case under GAAP reporting.

Another type of disclosure fraud occurs when management thoroughly misrepresents the nature of the business and its products in general informational issuances to the public. These issuances can include press releases, brochures for general distribution, speeches, and its website. This type of fraud is most frequently targeted at prospective investors, to convince them to invest funds in what is effectively a worthless business.

It can be difficult to prove this type of fraud, since it must be intentional. In cases where there is no disclosure at all, and especially when the accounting department is not used to producing detailed disclosures, the error may not be intentional.

Fraud Schemes More Common in Closely-Held Businesses

Fraud schemes can be perpetrated in any type of business. However, the situation is made more difficult in family-run businesses, since a small number of people have absolute control over the business, and so can readily breach any controls. Here are several examples of what can be accomplished when family members want to extract illicit gains from a business:

- *Sales skimming.* Members of the family route customer payments directly to their own bank accounts before any sales transactions can be recorded by the company. This means that the company appears to be earning quite a low profit (if any), while the family is earning profits that are not recognized for tax purposes. An even more egregious case arises when the family then wants to take the company public, and so stops engaging in skimming, which falsely shows an increase in sales just before the initial public offering, thereby resulting in a higher valuation.

- *Personal expenses*. Family members tend to treat a business like their own personal piggy bank, and so will routinely have the company pay their personal expenses. This tends to result in an especially bloated travel and entertainment expense.
- *Personal assets*. Family members can direct the company to buy assets that are intended for the personal use of the family, such as cars, mountain cottages, and sailboats.
- *Liability assumptions*. The family takes out loans and secures them with company assets. Or, the company is directed to pay down the loans. The loaned funds are intended for the personal use of family members.

Summary

It should be particularly telling that a listing of the types of fraud and theft to which a business can be subjected is the longest chapter in this book. There are many ways in which assets can be stripped from a business, or outsiders abused through the compilation of incorrect financial statement information. Employees in all parts of a business can engage in theft and fraud, making it critical to comprehensively guard against losses.

The number of ways in which the financial statements can be falsified is a particular concern, since the falsifications can extend into every corner of the financial statements. Further, financials are the lynchpin of the relationship between a business and its investors, lenders, and creditors. If financial statement fraud were to become a rampant problem, it would seriously undermine the ability of the debt and equity markets to function. The nature of financial statement fraud and how it can be detected is the focus of the next chapter.

Chapter 3
Financial Statement Fraud

Introduction

Financial statement fraud involves the intentional alteration of the financial results and financial position of a business, as well as the subsequent concealment of this information. It requires a higher level of authorization to alter the financial statements, so one or more members of the management team is likely to be aware of the manipulation. There are several reasons why management would engage in this practice, including personal gain, meeting investor expectations, and to keep an organization current with its loan requirements.

When a management team is clever enough in how it alters financial statements, it is not immediately evident that there is anything wrong. Luckily, financial statements can contain a number of indicators of potentially fraudulent reporting. These indicators typically involve relationships between the numbers stated on different line items in the financial statements. When these indicators are supplemented by a number of red flag conditions, a person has a reasonable chance of figuring out when financial statements are being manipulated.

In this chapter, we cover the reasons why people alter financial statements, the nature of the financial statements, and the many analyses that can be conducted to gain some hint of the existence of fraud in this area.

Reasons for Financial Statement Fraud

There are always new cases being publicized in which companies falsify their financial statements. Why would anyone do this? There are many reasons that can strongly motivate people to falsely adjust financial statements. Consider the following:

- *Bonuses*. A management team is presented with an aggressive bonus package under which they receive massive payouts, but only if they attain stretch goals for financial performance. This is a strong incentive for the management team to connive to adjust the stated financial results in order to trigger their bonus payments. The situation is even more likely to result in fraud if the bulk of management compensation is skewed toward bonuses.
- *Covenants*. There may be covenants associated with a loan that allow the lender to call the loan if the business no longer displays certain performance or liquidity metrics. If the loan is called, the business may fail. This situation also presents a powerful motivation to adjust the financials to ensure that the covenant thresholds are surpassed.
- *Investor expectations*. A publicly-held business is under constant pressure from investors to continually report better results. This is especially the case

if there are threats from investors to take over the board of directors and then oust the management team. In essence, the management team is tempted to manage the stock price, rather than just running the business and letting the stock price fall where it may. This situation also routinely results in financial statement fraud.

- *Loan guarantees*. In a closely-owned business, some members of management may have personally guaranteed the company's debt. If so, these individuals could see their personal savings and assets wiped out if the business fails. This prospect gives them a major incentive to report adequate financial results for the business.
- *Ownership impact*. Many managers have large stock holdings in their businesses. If the share price were to fall, these people would suffer substantial losses in their investment portfolios. Consequently, they prop up reported earnings to keep the stock price high.
- *Stock options*. The management team may have a substantial number of stock options, and will benefit from exercising the options at a high stock price. Therefore, they have an incentive to enhance the results of the business during the dates when they can exercise their stock options.
- *Tax concerns*. In a business where earnings flow through to a small group of owners, there is a reverse incentive to report the *smallest* possible amount of taxable income, so that tax payments are minimized. This can result in efforts to minimize or defer reported revenues, while maximizing or accelerating the recognition of expenses.
- *Temporary shortfalls*. A business may suffer what appears to be a temporary shortfall in revenues or profits, so management covers the shortfall by adjusting the books. Then, when the shortfall turns out not to be temporary, the shifting of revenues and other adjustments leaves a gaping hole in the financial statements in later periods, which must then be covered up with further financial trickery. In essence, a small adjustment gradually builds into a major accounting fraud.

A key factor that underlies several of the preceding points is that there is a significant value associated with presenting sales and earnings that continue to increase at a smooth pace. When there are no unexpected spikes or dips in these growth rates, investors assume that a business has a lower risk of failure, and so will bid its stock price higher. This means that managers are motivated to present a steady and predictable rate of increase, which may diverge quite a bit from what is actually happening.

Financial statement fraud is most likely to occur in situations where there are few controls over the actions of the management team. For example, if the board of directors is entirely comprised of buddies of the chief executive officer, it is quite unlikely that board members will exercise a vigorous watch over the business. This situation also arises when there is no outside audit, thereby eliminating yet another third party that would otherwise be able to detect improprieties. Yet another situation that can give rise to financial statement fraud is when a business routinely engages in highly complex business transactions; in this environment, it is relatively easy for a canny management team to engage in financial chicanery that no one will be likely to spot.

Instigators

Other types of fraud can be caused by people throughout an organization, but financial statement fraud is centered on the senior management team. As noted in the preceding section, this type of fraud is triggered by the existence of large potential bonuses, loan covenants, and investor relations – all factors in which the management team has a deep interest. The person most likely to initiate financial statement fraud is the chief executive officer, who has an obvious level of influence over the rest of the management team. It is also entirely possible that *all* of the "chief" officers – CEO, COO, and CFO – will be deeply involved in the misstatement of financial results.

How Financial Statement Fraud Begins

Financial statement fraud tends to build over time. It usually begins with a management team that routinely makes small adjustments to the financial statements in order to cover small shortfalls in predicted results. The rationalization is that these shortfalls and the offsetting adjustments are minuscule, and only require somewhat aggressive accounting to "correct".

The management team continues to do this as the business grows, and then makes a larger adjustment in period when there is a significant shortfall. What they do not realize is that sales and profits have topped out or will now grow at a significantly reduced rate, which is common for any business as it enters a more mature phase of its growth. The managers make the mistake of continuing to manage the numbers with larger and larger falsifications, while actual results fall further and further behind. After some time has passed, the management team sees no way out of the situation, and so acts as a group to falsify vast portions of the reported results. At this point, management is spending more time servicing the fraud than the company, so actual operational results are more likely to decline as the fraud increases in size.

The Financial Statements

A person who wants to learn about the manipulation of financial statements must first understand how they are used and what they contain. The financial statements include three documents, which are the balance sheet, income statement, and statement of cash flows, as well as a set of accompanying footnotes. These documents describe the financial results, position, and cash flows of an organization. We describe each one in the following sub-sections.

The Balance Sheet

A balance sheet (also known as a statement of financial position) presents information about an entity's assets, liabilities, and shareholders' equity, where the compiled result must match this formula, which is called the *accounting equation*:

$$\text{Total assets} = \text{Total liabilities} + \text{Equity}$$

This equation drives the name of the document, where the total of all assets must *balance* the total amount of liabilities and equity. This balancing concept is necessary, since the ownership of an asset can only occur if an organization either pays for it with an obligation (such as a loan) or with the funds invested by shareholders or the ongoing profits of the business (which is equity).

In essence, a balance sheet describes what a business owns, what it owes, and what residual amount net of the first two items is left over for its shareholders. It is used to assess an entity's liquidity and ability to pay its debts.

The balance sheet reports the aggregate effect of transactions as of a specific date. For example, if a balance sheet has been produced as part of a package of financial statements for the month of April, the information contained within the balance sheet is as of April 30, which is the last day of the month. Thus, it essentially represents a snapshot of the financial condition of a business as of a moment in time.

The basic format of a balance sheet is noted in the following exhibit. It contains a header, which describes the name of the entity whose financial information is being reported on, the name of the report, and the date as of which the report was constructed. In the following line items, we have noted how each one adds up into the various subtotals and totals in the document.

Sample Balance Sheet Format

Lowry Locomotion
Balance Sheet
As of December 31, 20X1

ASSETS	
Current assets	
Cash	A
Investments	B
Accounts receivable	C
Inventory	D
Prepaid expenses	E
Total current assets	A + B + C + D + E = F
Non-current assets	
Fixed assets	G
Goodwill	H
Other assets	I
Total non-current assets	G + H + I = J
Total assets	F + J
LIABILITIES AND EQUITY	
Current liabilities	
Accounts payable	K
Other payables	L
Accrued liabilities	M
Unearned revenues	N
Total current liabilities	K + L + M + N = O
Noncurrent liabilities	
Long-term debt	P
Bonds payable	Q
Total noncurrent liabilities	P + Q = R
Total liabilities	O + R = S
Shareholders' equity	
Common stock	T
Preferred stock	U
Additional paid-in capital	V
Retained earnings	W
Treasury stock	X
Total shareholders' equity	T + U + V + W + X = Y
Total liabilities and shareholders' equity	S + Y

To see how these calculations are used in a balance sheet, the following example replaces the line item computations with numbers taken from the general ledger of a business.

Sample Balance Sheet with Numeric Presentation

Lowry Locomotion
Balance Sheet
As of December 31, 20X1

ASSETS	
Current assets	
Cash	$45,000
Investments	80,000
Accounts receivable	425,000
Inventory	415,000
Prepaid expenses	15,000
Total current assets	$980,000
Non-current assets	
Fixed assets	800,000
Goodwill	200,000
Other assets	20,000
Total non-current assets	$1,020,000
Total assets	$2,000,000
LIABILITIES AND EQUITY	
Current liabilities	
Accounts payable	$215,000
Other payables	30,000
Accrued liabilities	28,000
Unearned revenues	12,000
Total current liabilities	$285,000
Noncurrent liabilities	
Long-term debt	200,000
Bonds payable	350,000
Total noncurrent liabilities	550,000
Total liabilities	$835,000
Shareholders' equity	
Common stock	10,000
Preferred stock	50,000
Additional paid-in capital	320,000
Retained earnings	825,000
Treasury stock	-40,000
Total shareholders' equity	$1,165,000
Total liabilities and shareholders' equity	$2,000,000

The line items appearing in the preceding balance sheet example are stated in a particular order, which is derived from a concept called the *order of liquidity*. This refers to the presentation of assets in the balance sheet in the order of the amount of time it would usually take to convert them into cash. Thus, cash is always presented first, followed by investments, then accounts receivable, then inventory, and then fixed assets. Goodwill is listed last. The approximate amount of time required to convert each type of asset into cash is noted below:

1. *Cash*. No conversion is needed.
2. *Investments*. A few days may be required to convert to cash in most cases.
3. *Accounts receivable*. Will convert to cash in accordance with the company's normal credit terms.
4. *Inventory*. Could require multiple months to convert to cash, depending on turnover levels and the proportion of inventory items for which there is not a ready resale market.
5. *Fixed assets*. Conversion to cash depends entirely on the presence of an active after-market for these items.
6. *Goodwill*. This can only be converted to cash upon the sale of the business for an adequate price.

In short, the order of liquidity concept results in a logical sort sequence for the assets listed in the balance sheet. The same concept applies to the liabilities section of the balance sheet, where those obligations most likely to be paid off first are listed first.

The Income Statement

The income statement contains the results of an organization's operations for a specific period of time, showing revenues and expenses and the resulting profit or loss. The typical period covered by an income statement is for a month, quarter, or year, though it could cover just a few days.

An income statement is used to measure the ability of an organization to achieve sales, and its efficiency in servicing customers. If a business does well in both respects, then it earns a profit. A profit is the amount by which sales exceed expenses. Instead, if expenses exceed sales, then the entity generates a loss. The cumulative amount of this profit or loss, net of any dividends paid to investors, appears in the retained earnings line item in the balance sheet.

The basic format of an income statement is noted in the following exhibit. It contains a header, which describes the name of the entity whose financial information is being reported on, the name of the report, and the date range for which information is being presented. In the following line items, we have noted how each one adds up into the various subtotals and totals in the document. The flow of information in the statement is to begin at the top with sales, subtract out expenses directly related to sales, then subtract all other expenses to arrive at before-tax income, and then subtract income taxes to arrive at the net income figure.

Sample Income Statement Format

Laid Back Corporation
Income Statement
For the month ended December 31, 20X1

Net sales	A
Cost of goods sold	B
Gross margin	$A - B = C$
Operating expenses	
Advertising	D
Depreciation	E
Rent	F
Payroll taxes	G
Salaries and wages	H
Supplies	I
Travel and entertainment	J
Total operating expenses	$D + E + F + G + H + I + J = K$
Other income	L
Total income before taxes	$C - K + L = M$
Income taxes	N
Net income	$\underline{M - N}$

To see how these calculations are used in an income statement, the following example replaces the line item computations with numbers taken from the general ledger of a business.

Sample Income Statement with Numeric Presentation

Laid Back Corporation
Income Statement
For the month ended December 31, 20X1

Net sales	$1,000,000
Cost of goods sold	480,000
Gross margin	$520,000
Operating expenses	
Advertising	10,000
Depreciation	8,000
Rent	32,000
Payroll taxes	25,000
Salaries and wages	359,000
Supplies	5,000
Travel and entertainment	11,000
Total operating expenses	$450,000
Other income	10,000
Total income before taxes	$80,000
Income taxes	30,000
Net income	$50,000

In short, the balance sheet provides a point-in-time picture of a business, while the income statement provides a report card on its results in between these point-in-time snapshots.

The Statement of Cash Flows

The statement of cash flows is used to identify the different types of cash payments made by a business to third parties (cash outflows), as well as payments made to a business by third parties (cash inflows). Though less frequently used than the balance sheet and income statement, this additional report provides valuable information about the cash status of a business.

This statement is needed, because the information in the income statement does not exactly correspond to cash flows. Instead, an accrual-basis income statement may record revenues and expenses for which cash flows have not yet occurred. In addition, there is no information in the income statement regarding the cash required to support investments in receivables, fixed assets, inventory, and other assets, nor is there any information about cash flows related to the sale of stock, obtaining or paying back loans, and similar matters.

The basic format of a statement of cash flows is noted in the following exhibit. It contains a header, which describes the name of the entity whose financial information is being reported on, the name of the report, and the date range for which information is being presented. In the following line items, we have noted how each one adds up into the various subtotals and totals in the document. The flow of information in the statement is to begin with a derivation of cash flows generated by the operations of a business, followed by the cash flows associated with investing activities and financing activities, which results in a net change in cash for the period. Cash flows are separated into the operating, investing, and financing activities classifications in order to give the reader more information about how cash is generated and used.

Sample Statement of Cash Flows Format

Newton Enterprises
Statement of Cash Flows
For the year ended 12/31/20X1

Cash flows from operating activities		
Net income		A
Adjustments for:		
Depreciation and amortization	B	
Provision for losses on accounts receivable	C	
Gain/loss on sale of assets	D	
		B + C + D = E
Increase/decrease in accounts receivables	F	
Increase/decrease in inventories	G	
Increase/decrease in trade payables	H	
		F + G + H = I
Cash generated from/used in operations		A + E + I = J
Cash flows from investing activities		
Purchase of fixed assets	K	
Proceeds from sale of equipment	L	
Net cash generated from/used in investing activities		K + L = M
Cash flows from financing activities		
Proceeds from issuance of common stock	N	
Proceeds from issuance of long-term debt	O	
Dividends paid	P	
Net cash generated from/used in financing activities		N + O + P = Q
Net increase/decrease in cash and cash equivalents		J + M + Q = R
Cash and cash equivalents at beginning of period		S
Cash and cash equivalents at end of period		R + S

To see how these calculations are used in a statement of cash flows, the following example replaces the line item computations with numbers taken from the general ledger of a business.

Sample Statement of Cash Flows with Numeric Presentation

Newton Enterprises
Statement of Cash Flows
For the year ended 12/31/20X1

Cash flows from operating activities		
Net income		$100,000
Adjustments for:		
Depreciation and amortization	12,000	
Provision for losses on accounts receivable	18,000	
Gain on sale of assets	-10,000	
		20,000
Increase in accounts receivables	-80,000	
Decrease in inventories	30,000	
Decrease in trade payables	-16,000	
		-66,000
Cash generated from operations		54,000
Cash flows from investing activities		
Purchase of fixed assets	-80,000	
Proceeds from sale of equipment	24,000	
Net cash used in investing activities		-56,000
Cash flows from financing activities		
Proceeds from issuance of common stock	120,000	
Proceeds from issuance of long-term debt	57,000	
Dividends paid	-32,000	
Cash generated from financing activities		145,000
Net increase in cash and cash equivalents		143,000
Cash and cash equivalents at beginning of period		230,000
Cash and cash equivalents at end of period		$373,000

Some elements of the statement of cash flows are derived from the other financial statements. The net income figure comes from the income statement, along with several of the net income adjustment items. The cash balances at the bottom of the report are taken from the balance sheet, while the increases and decreases in the various assets and liabilities are derived by calculating the differences between the line items in the most recent balance sheet and the same line items in the balance sheet pertaining to the end of the immediately preceding reporting period. For example, the change in accounts receivable noted in the statement of cash flows is derived by calculating the difference in the accounts receivable line items in the last two balance sheets.

Interactions between the Financial Statements

When a business transaction is recorded in the accounting records, it may impact several of the financial statements at the same time. In this section, we describe a number of these interactions. The intent is to point out how someone reading the financial statements can see how information flows through and is represented in the balance sheet, income statement, and statement of cash flows. Key interactions are as follows:

- *Sales on credit*. When sales are made on credit, the amount appears as both a sale in the income statement and an increase in accounts receivable in the balance sheet. If goods are sold, then this also reduces the inventory line item in the balance sheet by an amount that appears in the cost of goods sold in the income statement.
- *Cash receipts*. When cash is received from a customer in payment of an invoice, this reduces the accounts receivable balance and increases the amount of cash, both of which are located in the balance sheet. This also appears within the operating activities section of the statement of cash flows, since it impacts cash.
- *Buy inventory on credit*. When merchandise and raw materials are acquired from suppliers on credit, the amount appears as both an increase in the inventory and accounts payable line items, which are located on opposite sides of the balance sheet.
- *Receive expenses invoice*. When an invoice is received from a supplier for goods or services that are consumed at once, the amount appears as an expense in the income statement and an increase in the accounts payable liability in the balance sheet.
- *Pay suppliers*. When an invoice is paid, this reduces both the cash and accounts payable line items, which are located on opposite sides of the balance sheet. This also appears within the operating activities section of the statement of cash flows, since it impacts cash.
- *Sell shares*. When cash is received from investors when they buy shares from a business, this increases both the cash balance and the amount of shareholders' equity; these line items are located on opposite sides of the balance sheet. This also appears within the financing activities section of the statement of cash flows, since it impacts cash.
- *Acquire debt*. When cash is received from a lender under the terms of a loan, this increases both the cash and debt liability line items, which are located on opposite sides of the balance sheet. This also appears within the financing activities section of the statement of cash flows, since it impacts cash.

Horizontal Analysis

An excellent way to examine financial statements for evidence of fraud is to use horizontal analysis. Horizontal analysis is the comparison of historical financial information over a series of reporting periods, or of the ratios derived from this information. The analysis is most commonly a simple grouping of information that is sorted by period, but the numbers in each succeeding period can also be expressed as a percentage of the amount in the baseline year, with the baseline amount being listed as 100%.

When conducting a horizontal analysis, it is useful to do so for all of the financial statements at the same time, to see the complete impact of operational results on the company's financial condition over the review period. For example, as noted in the next two illustrations, the income statement analysis shows a company having an excellent second year, but the related balance sheet analysis shows that it is having trouble funding growth, given the decline in cash, increase in accounts payable, and increase in debt.

Horizontal analysis of the income statement is usually in a two-year format such as the one shown in the next exhibit, with a variance also reported that states the difference between the two years for each line item. An alternative format is to simply add as many years as will fit on the page, without showing a variance, in order to see general changes by account over multiple years.

Income Statement Horizontal Analysis

	20X1	20X2	Variance
Sales	$1,000,000	$1,500,000	$500,000
Cost of goods sold	400,000	600,000	-200,000
Gross margin	600,000	900,000	300,000
Salaries and wages	250,000	375,000	-125,000
Office rent	50,000	80,000	-30,000
Supplies	10,000	20,000	-10,000
Utilities	20,000	30,000	-10,000
Other expenses	90,000	110,000	-20,000
Total expenses	420,000	615,000	-195,000
Net profit	$180,000	$285,000	$105,000

Horizontal analysis of the balance sheet is also usually in a two-year format, such as the one shown next, with a variance stating the difference between the two years for each line item. An alternative format is to add as many years as will fit on the page, without showing a variance, in order to see general changes by line item over multiple years.

Balance Sheet Horizontal Analysis

	20X1	20X2	Variance
Cash	$100,000	$80,000	-$20,000
Accounts receivable	350,000	525,000	175,000
Inventory	150,000	275,000	125,000
Total current assets	600,000	880,000	280,000
Fixed assets	400,000	800,000	400,000
Total assets	$1,000,000	$1,680,000	$680,000
Accounts payable	$180,000	$300,000	$120,000
Accrued liabilities	70,000	120,000	50,000
Total current liabilities	250,000	420,000	170,000
Notes payable	300,000	525,000	225,000
Total liabilities	550,000	945,000	395,000
Common stock	200,000	200,000	0
Retained earnings	250,000	535,000	285,000
Total equity	450,000	735,000	285,000
Total liabilities and equity	$1,000,000	$1,680,000	$680,000

Vertical Analysis

The preceding horizontal analysis tool is an excellent one for detecting spikes and drops in numbers as compared to the general trend line. However, total sales and related expenses may vary so much from month to month that it is difficult to discern any trends. In this situation, we use vertical analysis, which is the proportional analysis of a financial statement, where each line item on a financial statement is listed as a percentage of another item. Typically, this means that every line item on an income statement is stated as a percentage of gross sales, while every line item on a balance sheet is stated as a percentage of total assets.

The most common use of vertical analysis is within a financial statement for a single time period, to see the relative proportions of account balances. Vertical analysis is also useful for timeline analysis, to see relative changes in accounts over time, such as on a comparative basis over a five-year period. For example, if the cost of goods sold has a history of being 40% of sales in each of the past four years, then a new percentage of 48% would be a cause for alarm. An example of vertical analysis for an income statement is shown in the far right column of the following condensed income statement.

Income Statement Vertical Analysis

	$ Totals	Percent
Sales	$1,000,000	100%
Cost of goods sold	400,000	40%
Gross margin	600,000	60%
Salaries and wages	250,000	25%
Office rent	50,000	5%
Supplies	10,000	1%
Utilities	20,000	2%
Other expenses	90,000	9%
Total expenses	420,000	42%
Net profit	$180,000	18%

The information provided by this income statement format is primarily useful for spotting spikes in expenses.

The central issue when creating a vertical analysis of a balance sheet is what to use as the denominator in the percentage calculation. The usual denominator is the asset total, but the total of all liabilities can also be used when calculating all liability line item percentages, and the total of all equity accounts when calculating all equity line item percentages. An example of vertical analysis for a balance sheet is shown in the far right column of the following condensed balance sheet.

Balance Sheet Vertical Analysis

	20X1	Percent
Cash	$100,000	10%
Accounts receivable	350,000	35%
Inventory	150,000	15%
Total current assets	600,000	60%
Fixed assets	400,000	40%
Total assets	$1,000,000	100%
Accounts payable	$180,000	18%
Accrued liabilities	70,000	7%
Total current liabilities	250,000	25%
Notes payable	300,000	30%
Total liabilities	550,000	55%
Capital stock	200,000	20%
Retained earnings	250,000	25%
Total equity	450,000	45%
Total liabilities and equity	$1,000,000	100%

The information provided by this balance sheet format is useful for noting changes in a company's investment in working capital and fixed assets over time, which may indicate that these items are being artificially altered as part of a fraud scheme to either create better income statement results or to make the financial condition of the business appear to be more robust than is actually the case.

Interrelationships Analysis

When certain types of financial statement fraud are present, the outcome is usually a skewing of the relationships between different numbers in the financial statements. In this section, we address several of the relationships that can point toward the potential existence of financial statement fraud.

Revenue Interrelationships

When a business records a sale, there is usually an offsetting increase in accounts receivable. If not, the only legitimate excuses are that the credit terms were so short that payment was received within the same month, or that the payment was made in cash. In either of these cases, there should be an increase in cash inflows on the statement of cash flows that shows the cash receipts.

When management books a fake sale, the offset is to the accounts receivable account, which will increase. The item to then watch for is the total amount of trade receivables to continually increase in size, since the receivables will never be collected. This should result in a continually increasing days sales outstanding (DSO) measurement: To calculate DSO, divide 365 days into the amount of annual credit sales to arrive at credit sales per day, and then divide this figure into the average accounts receivable for the measurement period. Thus, the formula is:

$$\frac{\text{Average accounts receivable}}{\text{Annual sales} \div 365 \text{ days}}$$

EXAMPLE

An analyst examining the financial statements of Oberlin Acoustics, maker of the famous Rhino brand of electric guitars, wants to derive the days sales outstanding for the company for the April reporting period. In April, the beginning and ending accounts receivable balances were $420,000 and $540,000, respectively. The total credit sales for the 12 months ended April 30 were $4,000,000. The analyst derives the following DSO calculation from this information:

$$\frac{(\$420,000 \text{ Beginning receivables} + \$540,000 \text{ Ending receivables}) \div 2}{\$4,000,000 \text{ Credit sales} \div 365 \text{ Days}}$$

$$=$$

$$\frac{\$480,000 \text{ Average accounts receivable}}{\$10,959 \text{ Credit sales per day}}$$

$$= 43.8 \text{ Days}$$

A slight variation on the concept of detecting fake sales is when a company is selling long-term contracts, but recognizes all of the revenue at the beginning of the arrangement. In this case, the offset to the revenue is the unbilled receivables account, rather than the accounts receivable account, since the bulk of the recognized revenue has not yet been billed to the customer, and may not be for several more years. The impact on DSO is the same, as long as the receivables figure in the calculation includes unbilled receivables.

In addition to an increase in accounts receivable, an increase in sales should also trigger an increase in the cost of goods sold. Sales minus the cost of goods sold equals the gross margin, which is then divided by sales to arrive at the gross margin percentage. For an established company, the gross margin percentage should only fluctuate slightly over time, since it has an established set of products. If the management team fraudulently increases sales, it must be careful to report a similar cost of goods sold that will result in the historical gross margin percentage. If not, the margin could fluctuate dramatically, which could attract an auditor.

When a company buys the inventory needed to build the goods required to generate sales, this also results in an increase in the amount of accounts payable. The increase should be a proportional one that reflects the purchases presumably needed to generate the sales. This means that the days payables outstanding (DPO) should remain approximately the same over time. To calculate days payables outstanding, summarize all purchases from suppliers during the measurement period, and divide by the average amount of accounts payable during that period. The formula is:

$$\frac{\text{Total supplier purchases}}{(\text{Beginning accounts payable} + \text{Ending accounts payable}) \div 2}$$

This formula reveals the total accounts payable turnover. Then divide the resulting turnover figure into 365 days to arrive at the number of accounts payable days.

EXAMPLE

An analyst wants to determine a company's accounts payable days for the past year. In the beginning of this period, the accounts payable balance was $800,000, and the ending balance was $884,000. Purchases for the last 12 months were $7,500,000. Based on this information, the accounts payable turnover calculation is:

$$\frac{\$7,500,000 \text{ Purchases}}{(\$800,000 \text{ Beginning payables} + \$884,000 \text{ Ending payables}) \div 2}$$

$$=$$

$$\frac{\$7,500,000 \text{ Purchases}}{\$842,000 \text{ Average accounts payable}}$$

$$= 8.9 \text{ Accounts payable turnover}$$

Thus, the company's accounts payable is turning over at a rate of 8.9 times per year. To calculate the turnover in days, divide the 8.9 turns into 365 days, which yields:

$$365 \text{ Days} \div 8.9 \text{ Turns} = 41 \text{ Days}$$

Another interrelationship to consider is the amount of cash collected in relation to reported revenue levels. When sales have been falsified, the related fake accounts receivable will not be collected, since they do not exist. This means that cash collections as a percentage of sales will decline. An interesting side effect of this relationship is that one can estimate the amount of actual sales based on the amount of cash received. Simply assume that the historical percentage of cash collections to sales is still correct, and then apply that percentage to the actual amount of cash received.

EXAMPLE

A fraud examiner has been called in to review the financial statements of Quirky Corporation. There is a suspicion that sales have been falsified. She does a historical analysis of sales and cash receipts, and assembles the following information:

(000s)	20X1	20X2	20X3
Sales	$14,625	$16,804	$23,092
Cash receipts	13,482	13,701	13,883
Sales : Cash receipts	1.08x	1.23x	1.66x

Based on this information, she presumes that the fraud probably commenced sometime part-way through 20X2. Based on the initial 1.08x sales to cash receipts ratio for 20X1, she estimates that actual sales were $14,797,000 in 20X2 and $14,994,000 in 20X3. This means that approximately $2,007,000 of sales were falsified in 20X2 and $8,098,000 in 20X3.

Revenue Acceleration Interrelationships

A business may have longer-term contracts with its customers, under which revenue is gradually recognized over the term of these contracts based on how rapidly the company is fulfilling the terms of the arrangement. The recognition of these revenues could be falsely accelerated, so that most of the revenue is recognized up front, thereby improving short-term results at the expense of longer-term results.

If a business reports the amount of its backlog of customer orders, the effect of the accelerated revenue will be a decline in the backlog. However, it is possible that a company could also fake the amount of its reported backlog in order to mask the amount of potential revenue that it will earn in the future.

Cost of Goods Sold Interrelationships

When management wants to manipulate the reported amount of profitability, it usually does so by increasing the ending inventory balance. This is because the cost of goods sold is calculated using the following formula:

Beginning inventory + Purchases − Ending inventory = Cost of goods sold

So, if someone wants to artificially increase profits, they need to decrease the cost of goods sold. If they can artificially increase the ending inventory balance, the result will be a decrease in the cost of goods sold. The concept is described in the following example.

EXAMPLE

A manager at Henderson Industrial wants to increase the reported amount of before-tax income, so that he can earn a $50,000 bonus. Initially, the cost of goods sold calculation for the final month of the year is:

$2,000,000 Beginning inventory + $800,000 Purchases - $1,800,000 Ending inventory

= $1,000,000 Cost of goods sold

The manager needs to increase the before-tax profit by $70,000. To do this, he falsely increases a few inventory balances to arrive at an ending inventory balance of $1,870,000. The revised cost of goods sold calculation is now:

$2,000,000 Beginning inventory + $800,000 Purchases - $1,870,000 Ending inventory

= $930,000 Cost of goods sold

The alteration results in a $70,000 drop in the cost of goods sold, which in turn increases before-tax income by $70,000.

If management cannot return the ending inventory figure to its actual level, the inventory balance will eventually exceed the historical inventory balance by a substantial amount. This inflation will be most evident in the inventory turnover calculation, which compares the inventory balance to sales. To calculate inventory turnover, divide the ending inventory figure into the annualized cost of sales. If the ending inventory figure is not a representative number, then use an average figure instead. The formula is:

$$\frac{\text{Annual cost of goods sold}}{\text{Inventory}}$$

The result of this calculation can be divided into 365 days to arrive at days of inventory on hand. Thus, a turnover rate of 4.0 becomes 91 days of inventory.

EXAMPLE

An analyst is reviewing the inventory situation of the Hegemony Toy Company. The business incurred $8,150,000 of cost of goods sold in the past year, and has ending inventory of $1,630,000. Total inventory turnover is calculated as:

$$\frac{\$8{,}150{,}000 \text{ Cost of goods sold}}{\$1{,}630{,}000 \text{ Inventory}}$$

$$= 5 \text{ Turns per year}$$

The five turns figure is then divided into 365 days to arrive at 73 days of inventory on hand.

When the inventory turnover figure displays a trend of continually declining turns per year, there is a good chance that the inventory balance has been artificially inflated to hide fake profits.

Capitalization Interrelationships

A company could commit fraud by capitalizing more of its expenses as fixed assets or inventory. This can be done by lowering the capitalization threshold for fixed assets, so that minor items such as desks and chairs are capitalized. A higher level of inventory capitalization can be achieved by shifting non-factory expenses (such as administrative costs) into the overhead cost pool, from which the costs are then allocated to inventory.

When capitalization occurs, the items that were formerly expenses now appear as assets, so there should be a significant decline in expenses. If the person conducting the capitalization is not careful, the capitalized expenses will only come from one or two accounts, so these expenses will likely experience drastic declines in the income statement, while the fixed asset and inventory accounts will increase.

Another capitalization interrelationship is that the funding for new assets must come from somewhere, so either the cash balance must decline or a liability account must decrease. If neither occurs, then either the asset does not exist or a liability has not been recognized.

Ratio Analysis

A good way to detect the possible presence of fraud is by conducting a thorough ratio analysis of the financial statements, and then applying all three of the following analyses to the ratios:

- Compare the ratios over time to see there are any disparities on the trend line of ratio results. Any upward or downward change could be grounds for further investigation.
- Examine the ratios to see if they make sense. For example, if a business is reporting a rapid increase in sales, the increase should mean that it needs

additional financing to support the growth, so one would reasonably expect to see a change in the debt/equity ratio that reflects the addition of more debt.
- Compare the ratios to industry averages. Most organizations within an industry have roughly the same financial structure and profitability levels, so their ratios should be about the same.

There are many ratios that can be used to examine a company's financial statements. The exact ones used will vary depending on the circumstances, but a core group of ratios will be found in most fraud analyses. We suggest starting with the ratios noted in the following table.

Suggested Financial Analysis Ratios

Ratio Name	Ratio Description	Ratio Calculation
Liquidity Ratios		
Cash coverage ratio	Shows the amount of cash available to pay interest	$\dfrac{\text{Earnings Before Interest and Taxes} + \text{Non-Cash Expenses}}{\text{Interest Expense}}$
Current ratio	Measures the amount of liquidity available to pay for current liabilities	$\dfrac{\text{Current assets}}{\text{Current liabilities}}$
Quick ratio	The same as the current ratio, but does not include inventory	$\dfrac{\text{Cash} + \text{Marketable securities} + \text{Receivables}}{\text{Current liabilities}}$
Activity Ratios		
Accounts payable turnover	Measures the speed with which a company pays its suppliers	$\dfrac{\text{Total supplier purchases}}{\text{Average payables}}$
Accounts receivable turnover	Measures a company's ability to collect accounts receivable	$\dfrac{\text{Net Annual Credit Sales}}{\text{Average receivables}}$
Fixed asset turnover	Measures a company's ability to generate sales from a certain base of fixed assets	$\dfrac{\text{Net annual sales}}{\text{Gross fixed asset} - \text{Accumulated depreciation}}$
Inventory turnover	Measures the amount of inventory needed to support a given level of sales	$\dfrac{\text{Annual cost of goods sold}}{\text{Inventory}}$
Sales to working capital ratio	Shows the amount of working capital required to support a given amount of sales	$\dfrac{\text{Annualized net sales}}{\text{Accounts receivable} + \text{Inventory} - \text{Accounts payable}}$
Working capital turnover ratio	Measures a company's ability to generate sales from a certain base of working capital.	$\dfrac{\text{Net sales}}{\text{Average working capital}}$
Leverage Ratios		
Debt to equity ratio	Shows the extent to which management is willing to fund operations with debt, rather than equity	$\dfrac{\text{Long-term debt} + \text{Short-term debt} + \text{Leases}}{\text{Equity}}$
Debt service coverage ratio	Reveals the ability of a company to pay its debt obligations	$\dfrac{\text{Net Annual Operating Income}}{\text{Total of Annual Loan Payments}}$
Profitability Ratios		
Gross profit ratio	Shows revenues minus the cost of goods sold, as a proportion of sales	$\dfrac{\text{Sales} - (\text{Direct materials} + \text{Direct Labor} + \text{Overhead})}{\text{Sales}}$
Net profit ratio	Calculates the amount of profit after taxes and all expenses have been deducted from net sales	$(\text{Net profit} \div \text{Net sales}) \times 100$
Return on equity	Shows company profit as a percentage of equity	$\dfrac{\text{Net income}}{\text{Equity}}$
Return on net assets	Shows company profits as a percentage of fixed assets and working capital	$\dfrac{\text{Net profit}}{\text{Fixed assets} + \text{Net working capital}}$

Financial to Non-financial Relationships

Some organizations are unusually good at falsifying financial statements so that they appear to be correct. The management team understands the interrelationships between the various financial statement line items, and is careful to construct a façade that passes a cursory examination. In these cases, it can make sense to compare the reported financial results to the non-financial metrics of the business. For example:

- The number of salespeople should roughly keep pace with the sales level, on the assumption that the sales per salesperson stays constant over time.

- The amount of sales per retail store should remain relatively constant over time, so the number of stores should increase as sales increase.
- The amount of assets on a per-store basis should be about the same over time, unless the entity started building stores of a different size.
- The sales per employee should be roughly consistent over time (unless the business model changes), so employee levels should track sales.
- The sales per sales region should be fairly consistent over time. When sales suddenly increase and no new sales regions have been added, it is possible that fake sales have been recorded.
- The amount of reported inventory will require a certain amount of storage space, so see if the reported amount of warehouse space is sufficient to house the inventory.
- Sales should not be higher than the proven production capacity of the business.

It is possible that a management team will report non-financial data that matches its falsified financial statements. However, non-financial information can be independently verified in some cases (such as by counting the number of retail stores). Further, the adjustment of non-financial information may require the management team to bring additional people into their scheme, which increases the probability that word of the scheme will leak out.

Time-Based Analysis

A great many transactions related to the falsification of financial statements occur during the last few days of each reporting period. The reason is that management wants to run preliminary financial results for the period to see how far off the results may be, and then creates transactions to adjust the books at the last minute. This presents an opportunity for the auditor, whose research can be confined to this short period of time.

One way to spot false transactions is to look for journal entries that are not part of the standard list of entries to be completed as part of the closing process. Or, look for sales to customers that only occur on the last few days of each month.

In both of these cases, pay particular attention to transactions that appear to be inordinately large. As a fraud progresses, the size of the financial statement adjustments will likely become greater, so there may be a trend of unusual transactions that increase in size over time.

Other Red Flags

Besides the analyses already listed, there are other indicators that a company may be falsifying its financial statements. The examiner should be aware of the following red flags:

- *Excessively smooth results.* There are always economic factors that will cause sales and expenses to fluctuate over time, resulting in a jagged trend line. When there are no spikes or dips in the reported results, this can indicate that earnings are being managed. This is a particular concern when the growth rate follows a consistent pattern over a long period of time, such as always growing by 3% per year.
- *Change in top customers.* It is easier for managers to falsify just a small number of sales transactions. For these transactions to have any noticeable effect on financial results, sales will be created for just a few customers. This means that the mix of top customers will likely change, with several fake customers included in the top 10, or real customers for which additional fake sales have been added. The examiner can profitably focus on just these few customers to locate fake sales.
- *Changes in sales mix.* The mix of the different products and services that a business sells tends to be relatively stable from year to year. When sales are falsified, the person doing so is probably not taking this mix into account, and so will concentrate sales on just a few items. The result will be a sudden change in the sales mix.
- *Claims of a breakthrough.* When a business claims to have made a major breakthrough that will cause its value to increase exponentially, this may mean that the management team is simply pumping up the stock price before it sells more shares. Breakthrough claims should only be believed once they have been verified by one or more reputable third parties.
- *Contract win rate.* If a business earns its sales by engaging in competitive bidding, it probably has a win rate (percentage of wins to total bids submitted) that is fairly consistent. When there is a sudden and continued increase in the win rate, it can indicate that fake contracts are being added by management.
- *Decline in sales commission percentage.* When sales are falsified, it is unlikely that management will be willing to pay the sales staff a commission on these supposed sales. Consequently, the percentage of commissions paid to sales should decline.
- *Deferred charges comprise a large part of total assets.* The assets reported on a balance sheet may contain a large proportion of deferred charges, such as prepaid rent, advertising, and so forth. When this proportion is unusually high, it can mean that management is trying unusually hard to keep from recognizing certain expenses.
- *Delayed start to the audit.* The management team might request an unusually long delay before the start of the annual audit. This could be to give the

management team sufficient time to prepare fake documents to support their financial statements.

- *Earnings increase after a policy change.* When a new accounting policy is implemented, watch for an immediate increase in earnings. If that occurs, it is quite likely that the accounting policy was implemented specifically to generate additional earnings.

- *Extended streak of beating analyst expectations.* When a publicly-held company is large enough, it may attract quite a following of analysts, who all issue projections for their future expectations for company earnings. When a company has a lengthy streak running of having matched or beaten these expectations, there is a good chance that management has been manipulating the numbers.

- *Financing is provided by seller.* When a seller-provided financing program has just been implemented, the reason may be an aggressive push to bolster sales that would otherwise be flagging. If the economy tanks at this point, the seller should recognize a large reserve for bad debts. If not, financial results are probably overstated.

- *Free cash flow is declining.* Free cash flow is the net change in cash generated by the operations of a business during a reporting period, minus cash outlays for working capital, capital expenditures, and dividends during the same period. This is a strong indicator of the ability of an entity to remain in business. When free cash flow is declining, a desperate management team will be more inclined to present better-than-actual results in the financial statements.

- *High leverage.* A business is using a large amount of debt to finance its operations. In this situation, breaching loan covenants could be catastrophic, since the loans would be called by the bank, and the firm would fail. In this situation, management can be expected to generate results that never breach the covenants.

- *High pay combined with low qualifications.* When an accounting person is being paid an inordinate salary in comparison to his skill set, it is possible that the senior management team is paying this person to enter their fraudulent journal entries into the general ledger.

- *Increased foreign sales.* It is more difficult for auditors to confirm sales to customers in foreign countries. So, when sales unexpectedly increase in this area, it could be because the sales are fake.

- *Journal entries at odd times.* It is suspicious when journal entries are date stamped with weekend or holiday dates, or postings late at night. These indicate that someone is trying to make adjusting entries when no one else is there to see them.

- *Journal entries by management.* The use of journal entries should be restricted to the general ledger accountant, who can then control the posting of entries. When members of management have been given password access to the general ledger, this indicates that they could be making adjusting entries to alter reported results.

- *Key metrics no longer reported.* A publicly-held company usually reports a standard set of key metrics over many reporting periods. When one of these metrics is dropped, it may mean that the metric reveals an unusual decline in the business that management is trying to hide.
- *Long closing period.* When the closing process required to produce the financial statements is a long one, it is more likely that management is deliberately extending the closing period in order to keep shipments running into the next reporting period while recording them within the preceding period; a longer closing also gives management time to make any number of alterations to the accounting records in order to manage earnings. Conversely, if the closing process is quite fast (such as one day), this is a strong indicator that management is not "cooking the books," for the same reasons.
- *Offer of extended payment terms.* Management may offer extremely extended payment terms to its customers in order to accelerate sales into the current period. This is especially likely to be the case when the offer has a termination date. If the offer is instead open-ended, the arrangement may simply be a form of competition to attract lower-income customers.
- *Policy change.* When a business changes its accounting policies and assumptions to be more aggressive, this represents a change in tone by management that indicates the willingness to be more aggressive in other areas of accounting. When several policies are altered to be more aggressive, this is an especially strong indicator.
- *Reduction in number of accounts.* When there are many accounts, a fraud examiner can conduct a fine-grained review of changes in the balances of each account. When management wants to hide its alterations of the financial statements, it can merge accounts, so that there are more transactions in each account for the examiner to sort through, making it more difficult to discern any patterns. This is especially likely if problematic accounts that have attracted audit attention in the past have been rolled into other accounts.
- *Restructuring charges occur regularly.* Restructuring charges are intended to be one-time events, when management charges off a large expense to address losses from a specific issue. If restructuring charges are instead occurring regularly, it probably means that management is using them to create reserves that can be drawn against later to manipulate earnings.
- *Pace of change.* When a change occurs, it accelerates quickly over time. For example, if someone is engaged in the manipulation of profits by falsely increasing the ending inventory balance, one can reasonably expect that there will be an initial relatively small increase in the account, followed by a series of ever-increasing account balances. This indicates that the organization's reported results are falling further behind actual results, which calls for more drastic action to boost account balances.
- *Photocopied documents.* There should be very few photocopies of supporting documents, since nearly everything should have originated with a customer,

supplier, or internally. The presence of photocopies when large customer orders and invoices are involved is a particularly telling red flag.

- *Proportion of reserves.* A business may maintain any number of reserves, which it replenishes each month as specific items are written off. For example, there is likely to be an allowance for doubtful accounts, as well as reserves for sales returns, obsolete inventory, and warranty claims. Each of these reserves should be maintained at about the same proportion of sales, inventory, or some other measure on an ongoing basis. If the proportion changes (and especially when it changes in the same direction for multiple reserves), management may be manipulating the amount of expense recognized.

- *Drop in expenses.* When a business routinely makes all normal expense accruals from period to period and then does not do so at year-end, the raw total of these expenses will decline; the change is readily apparent when tracking expenses on a trend line for every month of the year.

- *Payments to attorneys.* When there are payments to attorneys for no obvious reason, it can indicate that these individuals are dealing with litigation on behalf of the company that has not been recorded on the books.

- *Response delays.* When requests are made to produce supporting documentation for various transactions, the response may be delayed – usually until the next day. This gives the management team enough time to falsify the supporting documents.

- *Restricted access.* Management restricts access to certain filing cabinets, locations, customers, suppliers, employees, and so forth. The intent is to make it as difficult as possible for an examiner to dig into the best information sources that would normally indicate the presence of fraud.

- *Shipping cost percentage is declining.* When goods are shipped, there should be a consistent proportion of shipping costs that are incurred to transport the goods. When the cost of shipping declines as a percentage of sales, it can indicate that some sales have been faked.

- *Significant new suppliers.* If fake inventory is being recorded, a thorough perpetrator will want to show where the inventory originated, which means creating records for one or more new suppliers. These suppliers can be spotted by focusing on new suppliers that do not appear to have ever been paid.

- *Spikes and trends.* When sales figures are being manufactured, the offset to the sales entry is an increase in accounts receivable. This results in a sudden spike in the receivables balance. Or, if management is more deliberate about falsifying sales, there will be a consistent upward trend in receivables.

- *Time pressure.* Management imposes pressure to complete any analysis of the financial statements as soon as possible. By doing so, they hope to achieve a much skimpier review that will not detect any issues.

- *Transactions with related parties.* Any transaction with a related party is suspect. It may be motivated by a desire to shift assets or liabilities off the books, or to engage in sale-and-buyback transactions, or other events that are essentially designed to create falsified financial statements.

- *Type of audit.* When a company's financial statements have been reviewed instead of audited, this means that a substantially less significant amount of audit work was performed by the auditors, which makes it much easier for management to engage in fraudulent activities.
- *Unapproved purchases.* The purchasing department should approve new suppliers. When a fake supplier is used as background documentation for the "acquisition" of fake inventory, there will be no documentation of approval by the purchasing department.
- *Unapproved sales.* In some businesses, all larger customer orders must be run through the credit department, where someone signs off on the order. When fake customers are created, there may be no supporting review documents from the credit department.
- *Unbalanced subledgers.* The detail for sales and cash receipts may be stated in subledgers, with the totals rolled forward into the general ledger. When the totals in these subledgers are less than the totals stated in the general ledger, it could mean that someone manually overstated sales and cash receipts by making journal entries directly to the general ledger.
- *Unrecorded liens.* When lenders have filed liens against certain company assets that are not reflected in the debt liability, there may be unrecorded loans outstanding.
- *Unusually high interest expense.* When a business is reporting an unusually high interest expense in relation to the amount of debt, a possible reason is that not all debt has been recorded on the books.

When one or two of these red flags appear, there may still be valid reasons for their existence. However, when there are a number of red flags, the probability that fraud is occurring increases drastically.

A Note of Caution

An analysis of the financial statements might generate one or more red flags, indicating the possible presence of fraudulent statements. Do not automatically assume that the presence of a red flag means that there is fraud. There could be valid reasons why the financial results or financial position of a business has changed, or there may be an underlying accounting error that has not yet been corrected. Here are several examples of situations that can cause a red flag, but which have an alternative reason:

- Revenue unexpectedly jumps. This can happen when there are intercompany sales between the various company divisions that have inadvertently not been backed out of the accounting records as part of the closing process.
- Expenses unexpectedly drop. A key supplier may not have sent in an invoice by the closing date, and the accounting staff forgot to record an accrued expense to take the place of the invoice.

- Margins suddenly increase. A business could have dropped a money-losing product and replaced it with one that generates a higher margin. Or, it could have dropped an entire subsidiary that was losing money.
- The days of receivables figure has lengthened substantially. This could be caused by a demand by a large customer for longer payment terms.
- The days of inventory on hand has lengthened substantially. This could be caused by the purchasing department taking advantage of several volume purchase discounts, or perhaps there was an unwise purchase of inventory in anticipation of sales that did not occur.
- The amount of assets has increased substantially. The company may have engaged in an acquisition that brought a large amount of assets into the business, or embarked on a large capital construction project.
- There are unrecorded liens. There may be liens against company assets that are not reflected in the outstanding loan liabilities. This could be due to a loan that has already been paid off, but for which the lending institution has not yet withdrawn the lien.

In short, the presence of a red flag does not automatically indicate the presence of fraud. There are valid reasons for some issues, or they were caused by innocent mistakes.

The Auditor's Approach

Much of the preceding text has focused on how to use various ratio-based analyses to detect the possible existence of financial statement fraud. Doing so may result in indicators of fraud, but this is only an indicator. The best way to find hard evidence of fraud is for the auditor to search for it. This is not a simple task, for the management team already knows the audit procedures that were used in the past, and will build its ongoing financial statement adjustments to avoid those procedures.

Instead, when a ratio analysis indicates the possibility of fraud, the auditor must understand that a game is being played with the management team, where managers are trying to outwit the auditor's procedures. This calls for the use of different procedures that are focused on areas that management does not expect. Ideally, this means that audit procedures will be rolled out that the management team has never seen before, and so will not have a prepared defense.

The audit procedures employed in this situation should be targeted at the type of fraud that the auditor suspects is occurring. For example, if the red flags indicate that revenue appears to be too high, a new set of audit procedures could focus on a detailed examination of a large proportion of customer contracts, or an expanded confirmation process for accounts receivable, or an additional review of new customers to see if they exist and are truly independent of the company.

As another example, red flags indicate that the gross margin has increased, resulting in net profits that allow the management team to earn a massive bonus. What types of fraud could management be engaged in to manufacture the additional gross margin? An obvious prospect is to artificially increase the amount of ending inventory, thereby driving down the cost of goods sold. The auditors could spring a surprise inventory count on the company prior to the scheduled date, or send people to outlying locations to personally inspect consigned inventory.

The auditor should also consider making inquiries among employees positioned below the management team. In many cases, managers cannot engage in financial statement fraud without others knowing about it. For example, if managers are making massive journal entries to artificially boost sales, the general ledger accountant may have knowledge of it. Or, if management offers customers absurdly low payment terms in order to boost sales, the credit manager will probably know. Possible questions to ask these people include the following:

- Has anyone talked to you about managing earnings?
- Have you been asked to make any unusual accounting entries?
- How closely does the management team follow financial controls?
- Should I pay attention to any specific accounts?
- Which parts of the financial statements are you most concerned about?

Direct questioning of this kind can be quite effective, especially when talking to people who are not willing to take the initiative on their own to point out that there may be a problem.

A particularly fine area in which to question the staff is in regard to excessively old inventory. The warehouse staff has the best knowledge of which inventory items are turning over (or not), and so can provide valuable insights into which items should have been classified as obsolete and dispositioned.

In addition, auditors should routinely direct their inquiries toward those members of management who are most likely to be engaging in fraud. The auditor may be able to catch a person lying about the reason for a transaction. Though there may be no associated admission of guilt, one or more obvious lies tells the auditor that there is a problem, and could point toward the best audit procedures to use that will uncover more information.

Other Factors to Consider

When determining whether financial statement fraud exists, one should consider the situation from all perspectives, to see if the environment within a business makes it particularly conducive to fraud. In the following sub-sections, we describe several issues that can make this type of fraud more likely.

The Management Team

The past actions of a manager can be used to predict his current and future actions. To this end, it can be useful to conduct an examination of the backgrounds of each member of the management team – especially the chief executive officer, chief financial officer, and controller, since they are in the best positions to influence the financial statements.

This examination can be a simple Internet search on a person's name, to locate where they worked in prior jobs and what happened in those positions. At a more detailed level, consider hiring a private investigator to dig more deeply into their backgrounds. Another good source of information if a business is publicly-held is to look in its most recent Form 10-K annual report or proxy statement to view a brief summary of each manager's background.

If there is evidence of financial mis-reporting at previous companies or any other type of fraud in which the individual might have been involved, one should consider this a strong indicator that the person will engage in the same type of behavior again.

The Organizational Structure

When a business is organized in a "flat" structure, where responsibility is spread widely through the organization, it is more difficult for management to engage in fraud, because too many people are involved in the compilation and reporting of financial statements. Conversely, when the organizational structure is strongly hierarchical, with power centralized at the top of the organization, it is much easier for senior management to take control of the financial statements.

When an organizational structure is unusually complex, the reason may be that management is intentionally obfuscating transactions. For example, sales to a customer could be made from one subsidiary and then funded by a different subsidiary, which loans the required funds to the third party. In total, this is clearly not a sale, but an investigator might have quite a difficult time matching up both sides of the transaction, since they originate in different subsidiaries. To make things even more difficult for an investigator, a canny management team can insert a significant time delay into the two parts of the transaction. To continue with the example, the loan sent to the third party might not happen until several months after the sale, and might be broken up into several pieces and issued by multiple subsidiaries.

The Size of the Organization

It is much more common for financial statement fraud to occur in smaller organizations, since so few people are involved in the preparation of financial statements in these entities. In a much larger organization, there are so many people involved in the process, as well as more controls and auditors, that it becomes more difficult to perpetrate fraud.

The Board of Directors

The board of directors is supposed to provide an oversight role for an organization. When the board is active, their ongoing oversight makes it more difficult for financial statement fraud to occur. However, the oversight responsibility can be abrogated when the board members are not truly independent. If they are instead members of management, close friends of the president, or family members of the management team, they are much more likely to ignore any hint of wrongdoing within the organization.

Another warning flag is when there is a high level of turnover on the board. It can take several years for a board member to fully understand how a business operates, so when most of the board is new, the management team can more easily engage in fraud without being detected.

The board should have an audit committee that is comprised entirely of independent board members, and preferably with a high level of finance and accounting knowledge. The outside auditors report to this committee, and the committee is directly informed of any fraud hotline messages. The audit committee can be highly effective in detecting fraud. Consequently, it is a bad sign when there is no audit committee, or the qualifications of its members are subpar.

The Auditors

A change in the outside auditors used by a business can be a red flag. The old auditors might have disagreed with the accounting practices of management or been uncomfortable with the financial statements for other reasons, and so elected to not renew their annual audit contract with the company.

In addition, the replacement auditors will require some time to build up their expertise with the client, and so will be more likely to miss any evidence of financial statement fraud in the first year or two of their engagement.

Legal Issues

When a business issues fraudulent financial statements, it is possible that some investors or lenders will suspect what is going on, and will sue the company for the return of their funds and damages. If so, the entity is supposed to reveal these lawsuits in its financial statement disclosures. If a public records search reveals the existence of lawsuits that were not included in the financial statement disclosures, there is a strong possibility that management is attempting to prolong a fraudulent situation for as long as possible.

Short Selling

Some investors make money by borrowing the publicly-traded shares of a business from stockbrokers and then selling these shares at the current market price; they later buy back shares on the open market and return the shares to the original owner. This practice is called short selling, and is predicated on the assumption that share prices will fall when the market learns of financial troubles at the company that issued the shares. For example, a short seller could borrow and then sell 1,000 shares of ABC Corporation at $10 each for a total of $10,000. The short seller then issues negative statements about the company to the investing public, and watches the stock price decline to $3 each. The short seller then buys the 1,000 shares on the open market for $3 and returns them to the entity from which they were originally borrowed, pocketing a $7,000 profit.

It can be useful to review the statements made by short sellers, since they are highly motivated to spot anomalies in a company's financial statements, and so could be the first to identify fraudulent statements.

Related Entities

An organization may do business with any number of related entities. These entities could be controlled by members of management, the board of directors, investors, or their families. These entities could engage in legitimate business transactions (such as the main investor in a business leasing it the building in which its operations are housed). However, there is a potential for related entities to be used for the fabrication of fake transactions. For example, a sale could be made to a related entity that is used to book just enough sales for the management team to earn a bonus, after which the sale is written off as a bad debt. As another example, one subsidiary could loan enough funds to a third party to allow it to buy an asset from a different subsidiary; in effect, the company is engaged in both sides of a sales transaction.

Footnotes

When a business releases audited financial statements, the accounting standards require that certain footnote disclosures accompany the statements. When the management team is falsifying the financial statements, look for them to observe the letter of the law by issuing footnotes, but to also make the footnotes difficult to understand, thereby masking their activities.

One way to detect this issue is to compare footnote disclosures over time, and see which ones have become more obscure in the more recent reporting periods. These disclosures are the ones most likely to be in the areas where reporting fraud is occurring. In addition, look for changes in accounting policies from period to period. For example, when an earlier accounting policy noted that depreciation was calculated on the straight-line basis and the most recent version states that accelerated depreciation is used, this is an indicator of a change to a more aggressive accounting policy.

Industry Analysis

In most industries, competitors build relatively similar products, use similar distribution channels, buy from the same suppliers, and so forth. Therefore, their price points and cost structures should be roughly the same. The market leaders will likely have somewhat of a pricing advantage that translates into a higher profit margin. However, the bulk of all competitors will probably report similar results. This being the case, a reasonable red flag to investigate is when a business reports sharply better results than its competition. This situation is particularly suspicious when the economy is declining, since every company in the industry should be reporting declining results that approximate the general market.

Summary

In order to detect financial statement fraud, the fraud examiner must have a deep knowledge of how a business operates, how it is governed, the pressures imposed on management, and the nature of its industry. With this information, one can better understand the ways in which financial statements can be altered, and how the fraud can be detected.

Once the examiner has the requisite level of knowledge, the general approach to detecting financial statement fraud is to focus on changes or comparisons that are unusual when compared to historical information. For example, a sudden jump in sales when a business has no new products or sales regions is a red flag. Or, a business that reports robust earnings in the midst of a general industry downturn should certainly engender some suspicion. This approach is nearly the only way to detect fraud, since a larger organization may generate hundreds of thousands or even millions of transactions per year – and the fraud examiner cannot be expected to review all of them.

When the managers of a company engage in financial statement fraud, they will likely focus on changing just one or two items in the financial statements, not realizing that there is a ripple effect that spreads through all of the financial statements. An alert analyst can spot these differences, which provide indicators of what might be going on. It may still require a substantial amount of effort to clearly identify the exact fraud being perpetrated, but financial statement analysis will be what provided the initial clue.

Chapter 4
Fraud Prevention

Introduction

In a typical organization, the general pattern of dealing with fraud is for a case of fraud to be discovered, followed by an investigation, after which action is taken to deal with the specific fraud, such as firing the offending employee and adjusting the control system to reduce the risk of having that specific fraud occur again in the future. And that is all. The organization proceeds on its current path without any further action being taken to combat fraud. The trouble is that the underlying factors causing fraud to occur have not been addressed, so the same level of fraud is quite likely to continue in the future. The exact type of fraud may shift, but there will still be fraud. In this chapter, we outline a different approach to dealing with fraud that addresses the underlying factors that cause it. When installed properly, this alternative approach creates a different environment that strongly discourages employees from even considering engaging in fraud.

In a previous chapter, we noted that perceived pressure, opportunity, and rationalization are needed for a person to engage in fraud. Many organizations work to reduce the amount of fraud by focusing solely on the opportunity aspect of this scenario. A better approach is to focus on reducing the effects of all three. Doing so can significantly reduce the incidence of fraud within an organization, though it may not be possible to completely eliminate all instances of fraud. Some people will commit fraud, irrespective of all preventive actions taken, so management must accept that it will not be cost-effective to keep layering on more prevention activities.

In the following sections, we describe ways to prevent the opportunity for people to commit fraud, while also addressing the issues of perceived pressure and rationalization.

Related Podcast Episode: Episode 34 of the Accounting Best Practices Podcast discusses fraud deterrence. It is available at: **accountingtools.com/podcasts** or **iTunes**

---

1. Combatting Perceived Pressure

A business can pay a third party to manage an employee assistance program (EAP). An EAP is designed to help employees deal with a number of issues, including substance abuse and other types of addictions, money management problems, health issues, and family-related concerns. When used by a sufficient number of employees, this service can have quite a positive impact.

Another program that can reduce certain types of perceived pressure is a corporate wellness program. This program focuses on the physical health of employees, offering dietary counseling, gym memberships, and incentives to maintain a healthy lifestyle.

Such a program can mitigate the risk of incurring unexpected medical bills, and relieves stress in general by promoting a healthier lifestyle.

Another way to combat perceived pressure is to actively encourage an open door policy. When employees are willing to discuss their personal problems with management, they bring up personal issues, which can then be talked about and perhaps resolved. For example, if an employee is having trouble paying for an unexpected medical bill, the company may be able to arrange for financing that will cover his immediate need, thereby mitigating perceived pressure that might otherwise result in a fraud situation.

2. Minimizing Fraud Opportunities

An organization could implement a broad range of multi-layered controls in order to reduce its risk of suffering from fraud losses. We cover many of these controls in the next chapter. However, the cost of these controls could be severe, and they may slow down the operations of the business. It is possible to arrive at a less-expensive and more streamlined approach to controls by evaluating the risks of fraud, and then designing controls to mitigate those specific fraud risks. This approach can allow a business to safely avoid a few of the more onerous and expensive controls.

Cultural Adjustment Activities

An essential component of any effort to minimize the opportunities for fraud is to adjust the corporate environment to impose a high level of ethics on all employees. This adjustment includes the activities noted in the following sub-sections. When a company integrates all of these activities, a corporate environment is created that is more likely to persuade those with a variable moral compass to adopt correct business practices.

Hire Correctly

Part of the hiring process must be a detailed background check on all employees, to weed out those that have a history of less than ethical behavior. Certain individuals have a higher need for cash and so are more likely to steal – for example, those with drug, overspending, and gambling habits. These individuals should not be hired. Further, examine *all* of the information on a submitted resume. If any of this information proves to be false or exaggerated, do not hire the applicant. A resume and background check can be time-consuming, since some sources may not be willing to divulge information. Nonetheless, the human resources staff should be persistent in investigating these issues, rather than approving a job applicant once a certain minimum effort has been made. When supporting information is difficult to obtain, a possible reason is that the applicant is trying to hide the information.

A customary practice is to ask a job candidate for a list of references. In addition, the prospective employer may contact the previous employer for more information. Though the concept is laudable, this process rarely uncovers any valuable information. The supplied reference list is carefully selected by the applicant to yield glowing references, while the former employer is too afraid of defamation charges to make any revealing comments. There are several ways to circumvent these issues. Consider the following options:

- *Waiver form*. Have job candidates complete and sign an authorization form that waives any claims that the candidates might otherwise make against anyone providing reference information.
- *More references*. Require the human resources staff to contact a much larger number of references than the three or four normally provided by a candidate. By requiring double or even triple the usual number of contacts, it is likely that more varied opinions will be forthcoming. One way to obtain this larger pool of contacts is to become a premium member on LinkedIn, and use the greater level of detail afforded by this access to locate other people who worked with the candidate in the past (especially prior supervisors). Another option is to ask each contact referred by the candidate for the names of more people who might have information. Also, the contacts among competitors in a smaller industry may be relatively congenial, in which case it may not be difficult to plumb the company's own network to gain a more broad-based set of references.

There may be cases in which the information provided by a candidate's basic list of references does not appear to be quite right. Here are several situations that can be considered red flags:

- *Non-current references*. The provided references are from a job held a long time in the past; there are no more current references from a more recent position. This implies that the candidate's recent performance was less than stellar.
- *Inadequate list*. The company asked for more references than the candidate could provide. This may be understandable for a junior position where a candidate has not been in the work force long enough to compile a long list of references. However, someone who has been working for a number of years should certainly be able to provide a sufficient number of references.
- *Distant references*. The references provided have not directly worked with the candidate, but are instead acquaintances. This implies that a candidate has to resort to using friends and family as references.

A major red flag is when a reference refuses to say anything about a candidate. There may be a company policy that prohibits giving references, but people will usually be able to convey a sense of approval, despite the policy. If a person absolutely refuses to provide any information, a likely assumption is that the candidate did not do well at all, which calls for additional reference checking. When multiple former employers refuse to provide commentary on a candidate, consider the red flag to be a massive one.

A thorough background investigation includes a detailed verification of the information in a person's resume, and then goes on to search for other information that an applicant might not want to be found. The investigation might encompass the following activities:

- Trace a claimed university degree back to the records office of the university
- Trace a claimed professional certification back to the certifying entity, and verify that the certification is still up to date
- Verify that the social security number supplied by a candidate is a valid one
- Verify citizenship
- Run a credit report to see if there have been financial problems (most important if the position being applied for involves access to company funds, or any management position)
- Examine litigation databases to determine the type and extent of legal disputes
- Examine criminal record databases to see if the candidate has ever committed a felony
- Examine sexual offender databases (critical if the position involves teaching or child care)

When a business wants to be *extremely* careful about hiring people into certain sensitive positions, it can fingerprint them as part of the background investigation process, and compare the fingerprints to law enforcement records.

Tip: As part of the job application process, have applicants certify that the information in their resumes is accurate. This can deter them from including false or inflated information.

Another source of information is social media networks. For example, a perusal of a person's Facebook page might uncover insulting comments or illegal activities, which might be considered inappropriate for an employee. While the legality of this type of search is still being debated, the information *is* in the public record, and so can be considered just one additional source of information.

Conducting a full background check represents a laudable level of prudence, but can also require some additional cost and introduces a delay into the hiring process. In addition, the company may need to obtain the permission of applicants before conducting such a check. Consider obtaining a release form from the company's attorney that integrates the requirements of any laws pertaining to the release of personal information.

A reasonable mid-way point in deciding when to conduct background checks is to require it for all management-level positions, on the grounds that these individuals must be held to a higher standard, given their outsized ability to influence other employees and the direction of the company.

Tip: Outsource background checks. Though more expensive than a check that is conducted internally, an experienced outsider is more likely to have access to the most reliable information, and can provide a detailed background check in less time than could be achieved by the in-house staff.

In addition, the interviewing process should include questions that are designed to test the honesty of job candidates. These questions are derived from commercially-available examinations that translate applicant answers into a psychological evaluation of an applicant's ethical predispositions.

In particular, the hiring staff is looking for individuals with a strong personal code of conduct, who can not only translate this code into correct business behavior, but also instill in fellow employees a high level of ethical awareness. These people should be seeded throughout an organization in order to spread a sense of strong ethical conduct.

> **Tip:** Conduct a credit check on employees in sensitive positions at least every five years. This may uncover declining financial circumstances that flag a person as being at more risk of committing fraud.

Communicate Expectations

The management team must create a set of the values that it wants to instill in employees, and thoroughly communicate the resulting code of conduct to employees. A code of conduct can be quite massive, but then suffers from being unreadable. A better approach is to compress the code into a short, readable document that expresses core values, and which may have addendums that expand on the basic concepts. Samples of the topics that may be found in a code of conduct are:

- *Confidential and proprietary information.* Employees are not allowed to use any of the company's confidential or proprietary information for personal gain, and must return this information upon the termination of their employment.
- *Conflicts of interest.* These are situations in which the personal interests of a person conflict with those of the employer, such as owning an interest in a supplier. These conflicts must be discussed with management.
- *Controlled substances.* Operating under the influence of controlled substances is prohibited.
- *Fair dealing.* Employees cannot take unfair advantage of fellow employees or business partners by abusing privileged information or the concealment or misrepresentation of information.
- *Financial reporting.* The contents of all financial reports issued internally and to third parties shall be accurate, and fully reflect the actual financial results and condition of the business.
- *Gifts.* Employees may not accept gifts from business partners, if the gift could be intended to influence a business decision. Immaterial amounts are usually excluded from this requirement.
- *Harassment.* All forms of harassment are strictly prohibited.
- *Illegal payments.* Employees are not allowed to make payments to foreign persons or entities that would be considered illegal under the laws of the governing country.

- *Insider trading.* Employees are not allowed to use their insider knowledge of company operations or financial results as the basis for trades in its securities.
- *Political involvement.* Illegal political contributions of company assets are not allowed.
- *Reporting complaints.* Employees shall report any code of conduct violations to a member of management, the internal audit department, or a notification hotline.
- *Use of company assets.* Company assets cannot be redirected for personal use.
- *Trade laws.* All employees shall observe the government's trade laws in regard to boycotts; this means the company shall not enter into trade deals with any prohibited business entities or governments.

A code of conduct can be vigorously brought to the attention of employees by specifying within it the disciplinary actions that the company will take if there are any violations of the code.

Discussions concerning the code of conduct, expectations for employees, and fraud-related training can be included in the introductory training program for new employees. The level of information provided concerning fraud detection may vary by the type of position. For example, a new warehouse employee might receive training on fraud detection related to the theft of inventory, while a new finance employee might instead receive fraud training targeted at cash transfers. A more detailed level of training may be provided for new members of the management team and anyone in the internal audit department. Additional topics assigned to these people may include contract and procurement fraud, bribery in international transactions, evidence of cash skimming, inventory theft detection tools, and so forth.

Any fraud training should define what fraud is, and discuss how fraud impacts the organization through the loss of assets and reputation. The training should then address how to spot fraud situations, as well as what to do when an employee suspects that fraud has occurred. In the latter case, employees can be given contact information on a card that they can retain for easy access. The card lists the alternative actions that employees can take when they spot a potential fraud situation. These actions may include:

- Call a fraud awareness hotline
- Contact a member of management
- Contact the internal audit department

The communication of expectations regarding fraud should not end with the hiring process for new employees. Instead, this information should be periodically included in other communications to employees, such as the annual edition of the employee manual. Another option is to periodically run an anti-fraud campaign, using discussions, videos, and posters to bring the issue to the attention of employees.

> **Tip:** Require employees to confirm in writing – every year – that they have read, understand, and will abide by the corporate code of conduct. Otherwise, they are more likely to ignore the missive as just another corporate communication.

Provide an Example

The entire management team must set an example for the organization by always taking the most ethically correct course. Any members of management who deviate from this strict standard must be disciplined and/or fired. Otherwise, employees will see a permissive environment in the management ranks, and mimic that environment when engaged in their own activities.

The management team should also have high expectations for the ethical performance of everyone in the organization. By regularly communicating these expectations through their words and actions, managers set a high performance standard that they expect will be met.

Establish the Work Environment

A work environment in which employees feel a strong sense of buy-in to the mission of the organization is ideal for preventing fraud, since they are not likely to steal from an organization that they support.

A sense of buy-in to a business can be particularly strong when management commits to a minimal level of employee turnover and couples it with a reasonable and fair compensation structure. In this environment, the key concerns of employees have been met, so there is no reason for them to engage in fraud. Additional adjustments to the work environment that can also reduce the incidence of fraud are:

- *Broad-based management.* The management team routinely asks employees for input on a variety of topics, which may include tactical and even strategic decisions. This likely means that the organization has a relatively flat management structure, with few levels of management. By doing so, employees have a better sense of contributing to the organization, and so are less likely to steal from it.
- *Customer focused.* The company is entirely focused on providing the best possible experience for customers, rather than trying to increase the amount of profits generated. Management understands that creating the best possible customer experience will eventually generate profits, as well as a rabid fan base among customers that ensures long-term profitability.
- *Employee interactions.* When there are issues, these items are addressed at once and openly, rather than being repressed. By doing so, it is more difficult for problems to fester, which could cause someone to "take it out" on the company by stealing from it.
- *Fair promotion criteria.* The company promotes based on the performance and abilities of its employees, rather than cronyism. When employees understand that they will be fairly considered for promotions, it is less likely that

they will feel aggrieved if someone else is given a plum assignment or promotion.

- *Long-range planning.* The company focuses the attention of its employees on attaining long-term goals. Conversely, it does not force them to achieve short-term goals (such as quarterly sales figures) which are more likely to spawn a culture of financial statement fraud in order to meet those goals.

- *Orderly flow of business.* The business is well-designed to handle customer orders on a timely basis. This usually means there is a carefully controlled scheduling system that releases new jobs only when the system is able to handle the additional work load. Otherwise, purchases and overtime are handled on a rush basis, usually with scanty authorizations, which yields more opportunities for fraud.

- *Performance recognition.* The company routinely recognizes a job well done. This may involve public recognition, perhaps coupled with a system of minor rewards. This activity nullifies any feelings that might fester when a person believes she has made a good effort and yet has not been recognized for it.

- *Positive feedback system.* The feedback system used by the organization emphasizes giving positive feedback to encourage employees to engage in certain types of behavior, rather than employing negative feedback to punish employees if they do not follow the mandates of management. The use of negative feedback tends to set employees against the company, making them much more open to the possibility of committing fraud.

- *Profit sharing.* When there is a generous profit sharing plan in place that makes significant payouts to employees, they will be more likely to watch over the company's operations and report suspicious activity, since fraud losses are cutting into their profit sharing payments.

- *Well-defined and robust systems.* In a business with well-defined systems, job descriptions and responsibilities are clear, as well as process flows. These systems should hold up well during times of duress, such as the handling of rush jobs for customers. This means there are no ambiguous areas in which someone can discern a weakness that can be exploited to commit fraud.

An anti-fraud work environment typically employs a viable open door policy that is actively encouraged by management. This policy states that employees are welcome to discuss any issues with management at any time. By encouraging this policy, employees are much more likely to bring up issues that could be indicators of fraud.

Handle Fraud Situations Correctly

One way to prevent the occurrence of fraud is to always prosecute someone who is found to have committed fraud. This is not the usual situation, since most organizations do not want their internal failings to be made public, and instead simply fire someone and move on. The problem with this behavior is that the penalty for committing fraud is quite light. A person whose employment is terminated simply moves on to his next job, where he commits fraud again. In fact, this individual may never tell anyone the real reason why he left a job.

Conversely, what if an employer instead chooses to prosecute to the full extent of the law? The firm will incur legal fees, but there are several beneficial effects. First, the employee may be sent to jail, where he can wreak no further harm. And second, being prosecuted is profoundly embarrassing for the employee. With these two outcomes, a perpetrator receives such a hard reminder of his failings that he is much less likely to engage in fraud again.

Another beneficial side effect of prosecution is that other employees see how the company reacts to being defrauded. When a perpetrator is pursued vigorously in court, employees will understand that there is a greatly reduced opportunity for fraud within the company, and so will be less inclined to engage in it. Further, when the company pursues restitution for the amounts stolen, this reduces the perceived gain that others might see from engaging in fraud. This impression can be enhanced by maintaining an ineligible for rehire list. This list is maintained by the human resources department, and prevents someone from being rehired by any subsidiary of the company – ever. As soon as a person is found to have committed fraud, they are entered on the list. All subsequent job candidates are matched against the list before they can be hired.

Tip: Yet another way to make life difficult for fraudsters is to issue a Form 1099 to them for the amounts stolen from the business. Since this form is copied to the Internal Revenue Service (IRS), it notifies the IRS of the amount on which these individuals owe taxes.

In addition, there should be a highly visible process for examining and evaluating the circumstances of each fraud, with corrective action to reduce the risk of fraud occurring again. Otherwise, employees will not see an improvement in the control environment, leaving them wondering when the next fraud will occur.

Minimizing Collusion

One of the more difficult types of fraud to uncover involves collusion, where two or more people jointly conspire to commit fraud. These situations usually involve a customer or supplier. For example, the buyer of a customer demands "gifts" in exchange for placing orders with the company. Or, a supplier's salesperson offers a kickback to the company's buyer in order to accept bids proffered by the supplier.

One way to minimize this type of collusion is to mail to the company's contacts at its customers and suppliers a letter that states the company's policy of not allowing its employees to accept gifts of any kind from its business partners. This letter is intended to give business partners a clear idea of what the company's acceptable practices are. A hopeful outcome of sending such a letter is that customers and suppliers will contact the company's management, pointing out situations involving the company's employees that diverge from the practices stated in the letter.

> **Tip:** Include in all purchase orders sent to suppliers a clause that gives the company the right to audit the supplier's books. This clause sends the message that an investigation by the company could locate kickback payments on the supplier's books, which would hopefully prevent them from offering kickbacks to company employees.

Engaging in Fraud Auditing Activities

An excellent way to minimize fraud opportunities is to make it well known that the company operates a fraud auditing team. This group cycles through all departments of the organization, regularly looking for any hint of fraud. When employees routinely see this investigative team going about their work, they will realize that there is a reasonable chance of being caught if they ever engage in fraudulent activities. The fraud auditing team may never actually spot a case of fraud; the key point, however, is that employees are deterred from engaging in fraud because they believe they *might* be caught.

A good way for a fraud auditing team to increase its effectiveness is to constantly juggle the timing and type of examinations that it conducts. By doing so, employees will always be uncertain about the next time an auditor might appear in their department, and which areas they might audit. Otherwise, employees might attempt to engage in fraud during the intervals when they do not believe an audit team will be on-site.

3. Combatting Rationalization

The use of a code of conduct makes it more difficult for someone to rationalize fraud, because the code specifically itemizes good and bad behavior. For example, if the code specifies that it is not acceptable to borrow funds from petty cash, then anyone administering petty cash would have a hard time justifying a "temporary loan" of funds from the petty cash box.

An additional approach to battling rationalizations is to be quite clear about the penalties that the organization will impose on fraud perpetrators, including publicity and prosecution. When the risks to be run are well documented, it takes a remarkable amount of rationalization to still convince someone to commit fraud.

Fraud Prevention for the Small Company

The owners and managers of a smaller organization might be unwilling to go through the fraud prevention steps noted earlier in this chapter. Instead, they believe that only a larger organization with substantial resources can engage in these activities. However, a small company typically has only a small amount of reserves that can support it in the event of a fraud, so it may fail as the result of even a single medium-sized theft. Conversely, a large corporation may be able to withstand multiple large frauds and still have sufficient funds to keep operating. Consequently, it makes sense if only from a risk management perspective to try to contain the possibility of fraud in a smaller organization.

Fraud Prevention for Outsiders

The perpetrators of fraud frequently get away with their scams because they have access to more information than their investors. For example, a company might sell shares to new investors, knowing that the company has lost a major contract with the government and therefore lost much of its value. Or, a company adjusts its books to generate more profits, and presents them to a lender in order to obtain a loan. If more information had been available to investors in these situations, they might have been able to detect the issues, and not lost money. There are several ways for investors to keep from losing out in these situations. For example:

- *Obtain audited financial statements.* An investor should never invest funds without first reviewing the audited financial statements of the entity. When the statements are audited, an independent third party that is certified as a public accountant (CPA) has reviewed the books of the organization, and presents a letter that attests to the accuracy of the financial statements. If there is no audit, one should assume that the business is hiding something.
- *Obtain background information.* Obtain background information about the senior management team and owners of the business. This may uncover a history of false statements and lawsuits, which are indicative of what the investors can expect in the future.
- *Understand the business.* A company may claim to be making money because it engages in highly complex business arrangements that a normal person could not begin to understand. This may be an attempt to mask a relatively simple fraud scheme. Consequently, the prudent investor should delve deeply into the underlying business model. If it actually proves to be impossible to understand, then invest elsewhere.

Tip: Investors should not accept financial statements that have only been reviewed by a CPA. A review requires far fewer procedures than a full audit, and so could potentially miss significant problems with a set of financial statements.

Summary

The most effective fraud prevention actions are those that stymie fraud activities on the front end, so that few instances of fraud ever occur. Once fraud has already occurred, a business can (and should) conduct detailed investigations of all fraud issues and prosecute the perpetrators; however, these later activities are quite expensive and are layered on top of the fraud losses that have already been incurred, so these late-stage actions are less cost-effective than earlier prevention steps.

A broad array of fraud prevention activities are essential, since employees must see that the company takes fraud seriously and will prosecute perpetrators vigorously. If potential fraud perpetrators do not see that prevention measures have been taken, then they will become bolder over time, likely resulting in continuing increases in the amount of assets stolen.

Chapter 5
Fraud Policies and Controls

Introduction

As noted in the preceding Fraud Prevention chapter, it is necessary to have an adequate set of controls in place to keep people from committing fraud. What constitutes an "adequate" set of controls will depend on the viewpoint of the individual. Some organizations consider controls to be impediments to the smooth functioning of their processes, and so are willing to pare back on controls in order to achieve more efficiency. Other organizations are intent on creating a fraud-free environment, and so will install every possible control, no matter how much extra work is required to operate the company. We cannot advise on the correct mix of controls to install. Instead, this chapter contains a selection of those controls most specifically targeted at fraud prevention – the reader can decide which ones are the most necessary, based on the circumstances.

In addition, we make note of several corporate policies that can be useful for fraud deterrence, ranging from a requirement to have annual audits to installing a reward program for whistleblowers.

Policies

Policies are used to set general guidelines for how an organization is to be operated. There may be several hundred policies in use, most having no impact on fraud deterrence. However, some can be employed with varying degrees of success to create a more robust fraud fighting environment. Those policies are noted in this section.

Audit Policy

Outside auditors who are independent of the company should be hired each year to audit the financial statements. Doing so creates an on-site presence that may keep employees from engaging in fraud. The auditors may also find evidence of fraud, which can lead to additional investigations.

Check Signing Policy

Require two signers for larger checks. Doing so mitigates the risk that an individual who is already authorized to sign checks can illicitly remove a large amount of cash from the business. Having a second person sign off cuts this risk, but only if the second person takes the time to understand the reason why the check payment is being made.

Employee Background Check Policy

There should be a requirement that all job applicant finalists (or at least those with access to company assets) have a background check conducted before they are hired. This should include not only an employment history check, but also a criminal check and a credit check. The last item is especially important, since a low credit score indicates that a person is under financial pressure, and so is more likely to commit fraud.

Employee Bonding Policy

The company should have bonding coverage for any employees who handle cash. Then, if these employees steal money, the company can file a claim for reimbursement with the bonding company.

Expense Receipt Policy

Employees are required to submit original paper receipts with their expense reports. If they have lost receipts, then they cannot claim reimbursement. This policy is used to keep electronic receipts or photocopies from being used as proof of a personal expenditure; these items are too easy to falsify.

Expense Review Policy

Employees are required to have their supervisors review and approve their expense reports. The supervisor has the best knowledge of where a person has traveled, and so is most likely to spot expense report irregularities. This policy can be enhanced by requiring periodic training for supervisors in how to spot anomalies on an expense report.

Employee Transfer Policy

A business could have a policy of switching everyone in at-risk positions into a new job once every few years. By doing so, it is more difficult for employees to maintain any ongoing frauds. For example, buyers could be given responsibility for a new commodity at regular intervals, thereby forcing them to terminate their relationships with their existing group of supplier contacts – and also ending any kickback schemes that might be in existence.

Missing Check Policy

If a blank check is missing, the standard policy is to issue a stop payment order to the bank at once, on the assumption that the check has been stolen and will be cashed.

Stock Sale Investigations

The board of directors should have a policy of investigating any stock sales made by members of the management team just prior to the release of bad news. This approach targets insider trading. If managers know that even the smallest sale of this type will be investigated, thereby putting their jobs at risk, they will probably be deterred from engaging in it.

Supplier Background Check Policy

Before an order is placed with a supplier or it is paid, the company should conduct a background check on the business. Of particular interest is who owns the business and whether it has a street address. A third party credit report can also be purchased. The intent behind this control is to ascertain whether the business is a sham entity that is simply submitting invoices without providing any goods or services, and whether it is owned by an employee of the company.

Vacation Policy

The corporate vacation policy should require employees to take the vacation time that they have earned. Once these people are out of the office, it is more likely that any frauds they are running will be uncovered. This control can be strengthened in the following ways:

- *No one-day vacations.* An employee should not be allowed to split his annual vacation into a multitude of one-day vacations. Doing so side-steps the spirit of the policy, which is to get employees out of the office for an extended period of time. When a person is only away for a single day, everyone else in the office will likely just defer any actions related to his work, so that frauds are never uncovered.
- *Require cross-training.* The intent of the policy is not served if the rest of the office simply defers all activities related to anyone on vacation until they return. Instead, require all employees to cross-train someone else in their job functions, and expect the replacement person to engage in these activities during the vacation period. This makes it much more likely that an ongoing fraud will be uncovered. If an employee refuses to provide cross-training, or only in certain areas, this is a red flag that should draw the attention of management.

The vacation policy should be most rigidly enforced in the accounting and finance departments, since the employees in these areas have the most access to funds. In other areas, such as production or engineering, there are fewer opportunities for fraud, so the vacation policy could be relaxed.

Whistleblower Rewards Policy

Institute a policy that whistleblowers will be given some type of reward if they notify the company of an actual case of fraud. The amount offered may vary – the main point is to send the message that forwarding information about potential issues is highly encouraged.

Control Activities

One of the principle methods used to prevent fraud is a strong system of controls. Before we delve into the specific types of controls that are available, we will first cover the general types of control-related activities that can be employed, which are noted in the following sub-sections.

Segregation of Duties

A key aspect of a system of controls that can have a profound impact on the occurrence of fraud is the segregation of duties. The risk of fraud declines dramatically if multiple employees are involved in different phases of a transaction, since fraud would then require the collusion of at least two people. For example, one person opens the mail and records a list of the checks received, while a different person records them in the accounting system and a third person deposits the checks. By separating these tasks, it is much more difficult for someone to (for example) remove a check from the incoming mail, record a receivables credit in the accounting system to cover his tracks, and cash the check into his own account.

Unfortunately, there is a major downside to the segregation of duties, which is that shifting tasks among multiple people interferes with the efficiency of a process. Consequently, only use this control principle at the minimum level needed to establish the desired level of control – too much of it is not cost-effective.

A variation on the segregation of duties concept is to have two or more people work together on the same task, which is called *dual custody*. For example, the counting of cash in a casino's count room is jointly conducted by a count team; this multi-person approach makes it much less likely that the group can conspire to steal cash. Similarly, two people in a typical business are usually asked to jointly open the mail and record all checks received.

Authorization Levels

A system of authorization levels limits the activities of employees, so that they can only engage in certain activities, and only up to a certain dollar level. These limits essentially place blocks on the risk of greater losses due to fraud. For example:

- An employee's password access only allows him to access the billing system in order to write invoices to customers. He has no access to the cash receipts module of the accounting system, so he is unable to commit fraud by intercepting cash receipts and hiding the stolen funds by altering the amounts billed to customers.
- An employee in the purchasing department is only allowed to make purchases with the company procurement card up to a maximum of $5,000 per day, so his fraud opportunity is capped at $5,000 per day.
- Two signatures are required for all checks that are $50,000 or greater. This requirement mitigates the risk of loss, since it is less likely that two people will conspire to steal funds.

Independent Reviews

Employees are much less likely to engage in fraud, and especially over the long term, if they know that their employer will examine their work from time to time. This can be accomplished in a number of ways. For example, there may be a periodic, unscheduled audit of certain activities. Or, a supervisor may go over a person's work at irregular intervals. Another approach is to require a certain amount of vacation time each year, with someone else performing the work during the vacation period.

A type of independent review is the annual audit. This is performed by a group of certified public accountants, and is focused on determining whether the information in the financial statements is fairly presented. While detecting fraud is not the main focus of auditors, it is possible that they will spot it. Consequently, having an annual audit acts as a deterrent to anyone contemplating whether to commit fraud.

The internal audit department can be tasked with any number of surprise audits, to be conducted throughout the company. Ideally, the bulk of these audits are conducted in areas where the company appears to be at the highest risk of fraud, though the audits should be spread far and wide in order to show employees that the company is investigating every area.

Of particular concern is to engage in surprise audits that cannot be detected based on the prior history of audits conducted. Instead, different types of surprise audits should be used in as random a manner as possible. Doing so makes it more difficult for perpetrators to hide their activities.

Physical Safeguards

There are a number of ways to physically protect assets. Doing so makes it much more difficult for someone to access assets, and doing so may trigger an alarm or cause them to be photographed or videotaped. Here are several examples of physical safeguards:

- The petty cash box is stored in a locked filing cabinet
- Undistributed paychecks are stored in the office safe
- The warehouse area is surrounded by a fence, for which the gate is locked at night
- Biometric access is required for anyone attempting to enter the server room
- All cash on the premises is locked in the company safe each night
- Maintenance tools are locked in a cage area

Documentation

There should be a strong audit trail for all transactions. This means there are supporting documents for each step in a process that justify the transaction. For example, a customer submits a purchase order, which creates a solid authorization for the creation of an internal sales order, which eventually triggers a shipment authorization to send goods to the customer. If anyone suspects fraud, they can dig back through these documents to see if there was an authorizing customer purchase order. If not, this would be evidence that someone improperly authorized a delivery of goods.

Preventive and Detective Controls

When considering the proper balance of controls that a business needs, one must also consider the types of controls being installed. A *preventive control* is one that keeps a control breach from occurring. This type of control is highly prized, since it has a direct impact on cost reduction. Another type of control is the *detective control*. This control is useful, but it only detects a control breach after it has occurred; thus, its main use is in making management aware of a problem that must be fixed. However, detective controls are not to be ignored, since they can still make management aware of a fraud in its early stages, before the amount stolen has increased in size. This is a critical point, for frauds tend to begin with quite small amounts, while the perpetrator waits to see if the theft has been detected. If not, they become greedy and are much more likely to steal increasing amounts. Thus, a detective control that points out a minor fraud could be an essential tool in keeping the loss from becoming larger.

When examining the information generated by detective controls, some advance consideration should be given to the types of results that are most indicative of fraud. For example, if the average historical level of product returns has never exceeded 0.2%, with occasional spikes to 0.3%, an outcome that breaks through the 0.3% threshold should be flagged as an indicator of a possible fraud situation. When there are a number of these thresholds built into the reporting system, it is more likely that fraud situations will be spotted earlier, thereby reducing the total fraud loss.

A control system needs to have a mix of preventive and detective controls. Even though preventive controls are considered more valuable, they also tend to be more intrusive in the functioning of key business processes. Also, they are installed to address specific control issues that management is already aware of. Management also needs a liberal helping of detective controls, which can be used to spot problems that management was not aware of. Thus, a common occurrence is to throw out a web of detective controls that occasionally haul in a new type of problem, for which management installs a preventive control.

In short, a mix of the two types of controls is needed, where there may be no ideal solution. There can be a range of possible configurations within which a controls auditor would consider a control system to be effective.

Manual and Automated Controls

If a control is operated by the computer system through which business transactions are recorded, this is considered to be an *automated control*. If a control requires someone to manually perform it, this is considered a *manual control*. Automated controls are always preferred, since it is impossible to avoid them. Conversely, manual controls can be easily avoided, simply by forgetting them. Examples of automated controls are:

- A limit check in a payroll data entry screen that does not allow a person to enter more hours in a work week than the total number of hours in a week.
- An address reviewer in the vendor master file that does not allow for the entry of an address without the correct zip code.

- An error checker in the inventory database that does not allow an inventory deduction that would otherwise result in a negative inventory balance.

Examples of manual controls are:

- Requiring a second signature on a check payment that exceeds a certain amount.
- Requiring the review of the final payroll register by a supervisor.
- Requiring the completion of a monthly bank reconciliation.

The best controls are ones that are preventive (see the preceding section) and automated, since they actively prevent errors from occurring, and are very difficult to avoid.

When to Add Controls

An overly enthusiastic management team could blanket a business with an inordinate number of controls, with the intent of making it exceedingly difficult for anyone to commit fraud. There are two negative effects resulting from an excessive number of controls, which are:

- *Operational effect.* An excessive number of controls can be a considerable burden on employees. When their work is constantly being interrupted or slowed down by an ongoing series of controls, their efficiency will undoubtedly drop, which can have numerous negative impacts, including the slower fulfillment of customer orders and a possible increase in error rates.
- *Cost.* When the efficiency of employees drops, more people are needed to complete daily tasks. The compensation of these additional people reduces profits. Theoretically, it would be possible for a comprehensive system of controls to wipe out the profits of a business.

Given these issues, it is not possible to apply every possible control to an organization. Instead, there should be an evaluation of all possible fraud risks, their probability, and the costs of each one – both in terms of the costs of controls and the losses from fraud. The likely outcome will be a strong focus on improving controls in areas where there is a risk of high-loss fraud, while giving lesser consideration to areas where fraud losses are low. For example, there is no real point in implementing tight controls over office supplies, since the aggregate cost of even a widespread amount of fraud in this area is minimal.

A variation on this concept is to focus on those specific positions within a company that are in the best position to commit fraud (such as the controller and chief financial officer), and build an especially robust set of controls around these positions.

When to add controls is an especially difficult problem in a small business, where there may be only one or two people in each department to whom different tasks could be handed off. In these cases, controls must be specially designed to accommodate the skills and experience of individual employees. In a smaller business, the owner may be called upon to approve payments and reconcile certain accounts, just because there is no one else available to do them.

Control Overrides

A system of controls is only effective if there is a commitment by management to abide by the controls. In many instances, managers override controls if the controls get in their way. This is a significant problem not only because managers are not observing controls, but also because employees see this behavior, and copy the managers' behavior – in short, management circumvention of controls translates into employee circumvention as well.

The issue with control overrides is less of a concern when controls are "baked" into the system – that is, the controls are so deeply interwoven into the operating procedures of the business that the controls *must* be completed. It may also be possible to shift responsibility for controls to third parties, so there are no controls within a business that anyone can breach.

EXAMPLE

Giro Cabinetry has had problems in the past with employees stealing checks from the incoming mail and cashing the funds into their own accounts – this despite the use of a two-person procedure for opening the mail. Rather than trying to keep correcting the process, Giro's controller decides to contact all customers and require them to mail all payments to a lockbox that is operated by Giro's bank. By taking this step, the entire cash receipts function is moved out of the company and over to its bank. There is no longer any concern with a control breach, since the control has been discontinued.

Fraud-Specific Order Entry Controls

It is not that common for fraud to arise in the order entry area, though it can be accomplished in small amounts with no-price sales orders, and in larger amounts by inserting fake or altered sales orders into a company's order processing system. The following controls can prevent or at least detect these problems:

- *Password-protect the order entry system.* In a computerized order entry system, always password-protect the system, and require that passwords be changed regularly. By doing so, an unauthorized person cannot access the system and alter the prices that customers are required to pay.
- *Lock up unused sales order forms.* A sales order is essentially an internal authorization to ship goods to a customer. Someone could therefore use it to ship goods to a fake customer. Thus, unused sales order forms should be stored in a locked location. It is particularly important to lock up sales order forms when there is no credit department, since there would then be no credit approval function that would otherwise spot a falsified sales order.

- *Pre-number sales orders*. If customer orders are written down manually, there is some risk that the resulting sales order will be processed more than once, with multiple shipments (and billings) being sent to the customer. Conversely, some sales orders may be lost, which results in lost sales. To avoid this, pre-number all sales orders, thereby uniquely identifying each document.
- *Review no-price sales orders*. Sales orders are occasionally issued with no price listed, usually because marketing samples are being issued. If the quantities on such a sales order are unusually large, it could indicate a fraudulent transfer to a third party.
- *Verify buyer*. If a customer has designated a particular person as its only authorized buyer, it is possible to keep a signature card on file for that person, and verify all incoming customer purchase orders against it. The order entry staff then initials or stamps the purchase order as having been approved. This control is rarely used, and is probably only needed in cases where a company sells high-value items.
- *Review unusual delivery locations*. Someone could pose as a customer and place an order for delivery to a location different from the default address used for that customer. To avoid this, the order entry staff should contact its normal contact person at the customer, using the stored phone number listed in the customer master file, to verify that the order is correct.

Fraud-Specific Credit Controls

There is a strong incentive for someone to fraudulently move a sales order around the credit department, or to falsify a credit limit, since doing so presents the opportunity to deliver goods to a customer who has no intention of paying. Controls that can prevent or at least detect such activity are:

- *Separation of duties*. Anyone who grants credit to customers should not engage in the issuance of invoices. Otherwise, someone could grant an inordinately large amount of credit to a customer who clearly cannot afford it, and then cover up the sale by issuing a credit memo to cancel the receivable.
- *Password-protect the credit management system*. In a computerized credit management system, always password-protect the system, and require that passwords be changed regularly. By doing so, an unauthorized person cannot access the system and alter customer credit levels or give an unwarranted acceptance to a sales order.
- *Lock up the credit approval stamp*. In a manual credit management system, the credit approval stamp is all that someone needs to fraudulently allow a sales order to be fulfilled. Thus, these stamps should be locked up when not in use.

Fraud-Specific Shipping Controls

Someone intent on committing fraud may try to fool the shipping manager by for-warding sales orders that have not been approved by the credit department, or by con-figuring sales orders to have no prices. Further, the shipping manager himself may commit fraud by backdating shipping documents to inflate revenues in a reporting period. The following controls deal with these issues:

- *Return sales orders with no authorization to the credit department.* If a sales order without a credit approval stamp is delivered to the shipping manager, the manager should forward it immediately to the credit manager. This is an excellent way to highlight sales orders that have circumvented the credit ap-proval system.
- *Specify no-price sales orders in shipping log.* Whenever the shipping staff is given a sales order for which there is no price, it should make note of this point in the sales log. If the system is computerized, the system will automat-ically populate the shipping log with this information. Highlighting no-price items makes it easier for someone to later investigate deliveries for which the company is earning no revenue.
- *Maintain an approved order log.* The credit department could maintain a log of all sales orders that it has approved, and periodically compare this docu-ment to the sales orders that have shipped. The analysis pinpoints any sales orders that were routed around the credit department.
- *Verify period in which shipment is reported.* The shipping manager may be pressured by management to backdate some shipments into the preceding pe-riod, thereby increasing the amount of revenue booked in that period. This issue can be identified by comparing shipping documents from third-party shippers with the dates on which shipments are recorded in the shipping log.
- *Report on early deliveries.* Create a report that identifies deliveries made prior to the delivery date requested by the customer. This may indicate situations where employees are attempting to artificially increase revenues in the short term by issuing goods before customers want them.

Fraud-Specific Billing Controls

The customer billings area can be used to commit fraud by altering invoices and issu-ing credit memos to hide the theft of cash receipts, or to hide the delivery of goods to fake customers. The following controls can prevent or at least detect these issues:

- *Separation of duties.* The billing clerk should not be able to apply cash re-ceipts from customers to the accounts receivable records. Otherwise, the bill-ing clerk could pocket incoming cash and alter the accounts receivable rec-ords to hide the receipt.
- *Verify shipping date.* Management may pressure the shipping manager into recording shipments as having occurred in the preceding accounting period, thereby inflating revenue in the preceding period. This can be detected by

comparing copies of the bill of lading to the shipping log. However, a continuing control weakness is that management may pressure the accounting department into also engaging in the same trickery.

- *Review cash receipts*. The billing clerk can commit fraud by increasing the prices on an invoice above those stated on the sales order, issuing a replacement invoice for the company's records at the correct prices, and sending the incorrect invoice to the customer. Then, upon payment by the customer, the billing clerk or a person working with the billing clerk pockets the difference and only records the expected amount of the receipt. To detect this type of fraud, the internal audit staff should periodically compare the amounts shown on the images of checks received (usually posted on the bank's website) to the amounts listed as having been paid in the accounting system.
- *Review credits on a trend line*. The credit manager or controller should periodically run a report that shows the dollar total of credits issued to each customer, by month, on a trend line. This information is useful for spotting unusually large credit amounts that may indicate unauthorized activity.
- *Audit revenue recognition*. Have the internal audit staff periodically review how well revenue recognition was handled in relation to a selection of revenue-generating activities. This may result in adjustments to the procedures the billing clerk uses to record customer billings.
- *Issue statements*. Issue a statement to customers at the end of each month, detailing the transactions that have occurred in their accounts. One reason for these statements is to nudge customers to pay any outstanding balances. Another reason is from the fraud detection perspective; customers might examine these statements and complain if they see any unusual activity in their accounts. To ensure that the issuance of statements has the maximum effect, make sure that the following items are addressed:

  o Contact information. All statements should prominently display a message that, if a customer has an issue with the information on a statement, they should contact a member of management (such as the controller), for which contact information is provided.
  o Statement preparation. The person who prepares statements should not be responsible for the preparation of customer invoices or the processing of customer payments. Otherwise, someone committing a fraud related to cash receipts and billings could remove or alter a customer statement.
  o Statement mailing. As soon as statements are prepared, they should be delivered directly to the mailroom for immediate mailing. Otherwise, someone engaged in fraudulent activities could intercept the statements and remove any that contain evidence of suspicious activities.

Fraud-Specific Cash Controls

There is a reasonable chance that fraud will occur in the cash receipts area, since cash is such an obvious target. There are many fraud controls, so we have segregated them into controls that apply in general to all forms of payment, to cash payments, and to credit card payments. The controls are:

General Fraud Controls

The following controls are useful for preventing or detecting fraud for all types of cash receipts:

- *Confirm cash receipts system access.* Only a small number of people should be allowed to apply cash to accounts receivable under the separation of duties concept. To see if this is the case, periodically examine the access log for the cash receipts module. Also require password access to the cash receipts system, and require regular changes to the password.
- *Endorse checks.* Endorse all incoming checks for deposit only, so that they cannot be redirected into an employee's account.
- *Frequent deposits.* If customer payments are made on-site, then ensure that the funds are deposited at a local bank the same day. The longer cash remains on the premises, the greater the number of opportunities for theft.
- *Lock up deposits overnight.* There will be cases where cash and checks are held on the premises overnight, perhaps because they were received too late on the previous day to make a deposit, or perhaps due to a banking holiday. These overnight deposits should always be stored in a locked location, preferably in a safe.
- *Reconcile the bank statement.* The bank statement can be a treasure trove of information regarding possible cash thefts, so ensure that it is completed regularly (even daily) by someone who does not handle cash or have check-signing authority.
- *Request ACH payment.* The best preventive control of all for cash receipts is to have no cash to receive. This can be done by asking customers to pay with direct deposit (Automated Clearing House) transactions that shift funds directly into the company's bank account.
- *Separation of duties.* To reduce the risk of cash theft, have one person open the mail and record cash receipts, another person record the cash in the accounting records, and (if possible) a third person deposit the cash at the bank. Where possible, anyone involved in the handling of cash should not have access to the customer billing system, since someone could steal cash from a customer and then hide the theft by issuing a credit to the customer to cancel their related receivable.
- *Trace check images back to the cash receipts journal.* If there is not a sufficient separation of duties, it is possible that the person recording cash receipts could claim that a customer took an early payment discount or some other

108

type of discount, and then pocket the difference. This can be detected by tracking check images back to the cash receipts journal.

- *Use a lockbox*. The best single control that a business can install over the handling of cash is to install a bank lockbox. Under this arrangement, customers send their payments directly to a post office box that is managed by the company's bank. No cash payments from customers ever enter the premises of the business, so there are far fewer opportunities for employees to steal cash.
- *Verify checks from unknown buyers who want immediate delivery*. When a new customer is willing to pay with a check for immediate delivery of a product, this could be a scam, since the check might be counterfeit or drawn on an account that has insufficient funds. Thus, always verify these checks prior to delivering goods.

Cash-Related Fraud Controls

There are a number of additional controls that can reduce or at least detect fraud when cash is being paid. The following controls include several reports that can indicate the presence of fraud, as well as make sales clerks think twice before taking cash from their cash registers:

- *Run gross margin trend analysis*. There may be cases where employees are taking cash at the point of sale, and destroying the evidence of the sale. The possible presence of this theft can be detected by running a trend line of the company's gross margin. The cost of goods sold should be increasing in proportion to sales, since goods are still being sold, but the related sales are not being recorded.
- *Supervisors approve cash refunds*. A supervisor should be required to override a cash register to allow cash refunds to customers. Otherwise, a sales clerk could create a fake refund transaction and pocket the cash. This tends to be a relatively weak control that is only perfunctorily observed by supervisors, but it must be used to act as a deterrent.
- *Run cash refunds trend analysis*. Compile information about the proportion of cash refunds to sales for each sales clerk or cash register. This may spot unusually high proportions of refunds to sales, which can indicate cash being removed from the register by the sales clerk and hidden with a refund transaction.
- *Limit cash register access*. Ideally, only one sales clerk should operate a cash register between reconciliations, since any cash shortfalls will then be the clear responsibility of the clerk. This is difficult from a practical perspective, since clerks need to take breaks, and someone else will likely operate the cash register in their absence. Thus, responsibility for a register can be somewhat diffused.
- *Install cash register video surveillance*. Sales clerks will be less likely to attempt to pocket cash from a sale if they know they are being observed with a video camera. It may not be necessary to monitor the video at all, since it is

both unutterably dull to do so and unlikely to spot any activity. However, it provides a historical record that may be useful for researching potential fraud after the fact, and also acts as a deterrent to sales clerks if they know they are being monitored.

Credit Card-Related Fraud Controls

The following two controls are designed to prevent unauthorized access to customer credit card information that the company has used to charge customers. They are not part of the normal cash receipts process flow, but are necessary to protect customer interests. The controls are:

- *Shred or secure credit card numbers.* If the accounting staff writes down customer credit card numbers in order to charge the cards for sales, it needs to either shred the documents containing the card numbers or lock them in a secure location. This is a particular problem when the staff takes down *complete* card holder information, since this can be used to make fraudulent purchases.

> **Tip:** Some customers want their monthly billings to be charged to the same credit card, month after month. While this is fine from a cash collection perspective, it does present a security risk. Be especially careful to lock up this information, not only to prevent its theft, but also to avoid a breach of faith with the customer. After all, customers are not likely to make credit card purchases again if the company's actions result in fraudulent use of their cards.

- *Password-protect the customer master file.* If the company stores customer credit card information in the customer master file, ensure that access to the file is password-protected, and that the password is changed regularly.

Fraud-Specific Inventory Controls

There are so many places in a business where inventory can be stolen that it can be difficult to build a reasonable set of controls that has any chance of working. Consequently, we only provide a few of the more useful controls, which are:

- *Assign responsibility.* Assign each warehouse employee responsibility over a section of the warehouse. Each person is then held accountable for inventory shortfalls. This approach improves the odds that discrepancies will be noted and investigated more quickly.
- *Fence in the warehouse.* Access to the warehouse should be strictly controlled, with fencing and a monitored gate. Doing so requires all inventory removals to go through a gate, where manual reviews or video monitoring can be applied.
- *Count inventory.* If employees know that the inventory will be counted regularly, they will be less likely to steal it and have the removal discovered.

Fraud-Specific Fixed Asset Controls

Fixed assets may have a considerable resale value, which makes the more portable ones subject to theft. Here are several controls that can be of assistance in preventing or at least mitigating asset losses due to theft:

- *Use prenumbered approval forms.* Someone may try to forge the signatures on a fixed asset approval form, so consider using prenumbered forms. Also, store them in a locked cabinet, and keep track of all forms taken from the cabinet. This control may be overkill – after all, the presumed penalties for being caught with a forged approval form would likely deter most people.
- *Segregate fixed asset responsibilities.* It is easier for an employee to steal an asset if that person is given complete responsibility over all aspects of asset purchasing, recordation, and disposal, since they can alter documents at will. Consequently, the person who receives a fixed asset should not be the same person who records the transaction, while the person who disposes of an asset cannot also record the sale. Further, the person who audits fixed assets should not be involved with fixed assets in any other way.
- *Lock out the fixed asset master file.* Depending on the nature of the accounting systems, there may be a fixed asset master file in which detailed information about every fixed asset is kept. If someone were to steal a fixed asset, they could cover all traces of the act by removing the asset from the master file, or at least altering it. Consequently, require password access to this file.
- *Restrict access to assets.* If some assets are especially valuable and can be easily removed from the premises, restrict access to them with a variety of security card access systems, gates, security guards, and so forth.
- *Assign assets to employees.* Assign responsibility for specific assets to employees and tie some portion of their annual performance appraisals to the presence and condition of those assets. This control works best at the department level, where department managers are assigned responsibility for the assets in their areas. Issue a periodic report to each responsible person, detailing the assets under their control, and reminding them to notify a senior manager if any assets are missing. Also, if responsibility for assets is shifted from one person to another, there must be a process for doing so, where the newly-responsible person formally evaluates the condition of the asset and takes responsibility for it.
- *Look for duplicate serial numbers.* Though rare, it is possible that employees may be stealing fixed assets from the company and selling them back through a dummy corporation. To detect this, enter the asset serial number in the fixed asset record for each asset, and then run a report that looks for matching serial numbers. If a duplicate number is found, this means that an asset was stolen and sold back to the company.
- *Conduct a fixed asset audit.* Have an internal auditor conduct an annual audit of all fixed assets to verify where they are located, the condition they are in, and whether they are still being used.

- *Affix an identification plate to all assets.* Solidly affix an identification plate to any fixed asset that can be moved, so that it can be clearly identified. Better yet, engrave an identification number into the asset, which eliminates the risk of someone removing the identification plate. Another alternative is to affix a radio frequency identification (RFID) tag to each asset, so that they can be more easily located with an RFID scanner. If any form of identification tag is used, be sure to record the unique number on each tag in the appropriate asset record, so that the information in the record can be traced back to the actual asset.
- *Link RFID tags to alarm system.* Install an RFID scanner next to every point of exit, which will trigger an alarm if anyone attempts to remove an asset that has an RFID tag attached to it.

Fraud-Specific Payable Controls

The disbursement of funds presents a major opportunity for fraud, so there needs to be a correspondingly large number of controls to prevent that fraud. There are so many controls that we have split them into groups, separately noting those used for payables, expense reports, procurement cards, and petty cash.

Payables-Related Controls

- *Lock up check stock.* Both unused check stock and any signature stamps or signature plates should be locked up – and in separate locations. Otherwise, someone could steal a check, make it payable to them, and use a signature stamp to sign it.
- *Use positive pay.* A positive pay system detects fraudulent checks at the point of presentment and prevents them from being paid. This means that checks that have had their payment amounts altered or which are derived from stolen check stock will be flagged by the bank. The basic positive pay steps are:
  1. The issuing company periodically sends a file to its bank, in which are listed the check numbers, dates, and amounts of all checks issued in the most recent check run.
  2. When a check is presented to the bank for payment, the bank teller compares the information on the check to the information submitted by the company. If there is a discrepancy, the bank holds the check and notifies the company.

- *Run a credit report on new suppliers.* Someone within the payables department could create a vendor record in order to pay fraudulent invoices to it, with the payments being routed back to the employee. It is possible to detect this by running a credit report on all new suppliers to verify their existence. From a practical perspective, this is an expensive way to locate potentially fraudulent activity.

112

- *Search for purchase authorization avoidance.* Run a search through the payables records to see if the company received multiple invoices from a supplier during a period. If so, investigate to see if the invoices should have been aggregated into a single invoice for a large-dollar item that would otherwise have required a higher level of purchase authorization. This indicates possible chicanery within the company to obtain assets.

- *Match supplier addresses to employee addresses.* An employee may be directing supplier payments to his or her home address, or may own a supplier that does business with the company. To detect these payments, periodically run a comparison of employee addresses to supplier addresses to see if there are any matches. From a practical perspective, a reasonably knowledgeable employee will simply set up a post office box and have payments sent there, so this may not be an overly productive control.

- *Review vendor master file change log.* An employee could access the vendor master file, change a payment address to his or her home address, then cut a check that is mailed to that address, and then re-enter the file and switch the address back to the supplier's real address. This can be detected by periodically reviewing the change log for the vendor master file. Less expensive accounting systems may not have this feature.

- *Review direct deposit change log.* Some high-end accounting systems store supplier direct deposit information in a separate file. If so, conduct a periodic review to see if anyone has altered the direct deposit information. This is one of the easier ways to route money into an account owned by an employee.

- *Set check printing to avoid blanks.* Set the check printing methodology in the accounting software to insert characters into the blank spaces on the amount and payee lines of checks. This makes it more difficult for someone to fraudulently alter checks.

- *Make check reproduction difficult.* There are a large number of anti-fraud features built into check stock that make them more difficult to reproduce. This can hardly be called a control anymore, since many of the features are provided automatically by check stock printers.

- *Destroy check stock for inactive accounts.* If a checking account is no longer being used, shift out any residual funds, close the account, and shred any remaining check stock. Otherwise, someone could clear out any remaining funds with one of the unused checks.

> **Tip:** It is especially common to eliminate bank accounts following an acquisition, so include a work step in the acquisition integration procedure to close the accounts and shred the related check stock.

- *Reconcile the checking account daily.* It is extremely useful to conduct a complete account reconciliation of the checking account every day. By doing so, any problems with fraudulent checks will be immediately apparent.

- *Install a debit block.* Someone can create an ACH debit transaction that removes funds from the company's bank account. It is possible to set up a debit block with the bank that prevents ACH debits from being enacted. Under this approach, the company must notify the bank when it authorizes a debit from a specific supplier. Also, it may make sense to set a daily cumulative limit for ACH debits; this keeps even an approved supplier from withdrawing an inordinate amount from the bank account.

Expense Report-Related Controls

- *Review employee expense trends.* There may be an unusual blip in the expenses charged by an employee in a particular month that was not caught by any of the in-process controls. Once investigated, the system can be modified to catch similar offending transactions in the future.
- *Review detailed hotel billings.* Employees can pile a number of additional expenditures onto their room charges, such as meals and in-room movies and games, so have employees submit the detailed hotel bills for examination.
- *Review for excessive miles.* Given the high mileage reimbursement rate, someone might take advantage of the situation by reporting an excessive number of miles. When there seems to be a clear overage, use an Internet search engine to estimate the miles that should have been driven, and point out the issue to the employee.

> **Tip:** If the company has common travel destinations, such as from the company headquarters to specific customers or suppliers, create a table that lists the miles that will be reimbursed for these standard trips, and issue it to employees.

- *Review actual receipts.* Many expense reporting systems allow employees to submit scanned copies of their expense receipts. If so, consider adding a requirement that they retain the original receipts for a few months following the expense report date, in case the internal audit staff wants to see the originals. This may reveal that some of the receipts were doctored to show larger expense amounts.
- *Look for fake airfares.* Look for airfares to locations for which there are no corresponding hotel or car rental bills. This indicates that an airfare was faked.
- *Look for large cash payments.* Since a cash payment is more difficult to investigate, a significant cash amount can indicate a fake payment.
- *Look for rounded numbers.* See if receipts from certain suppliers contain consistently rounded off numbers or numbers for the same amounts. If so, these receipts might have been forged by a lazy employee.
- *Look for sequential receipt numbers.* An employee may have purchased a block of blank receipts from an office supply store and is using them to create fake receipts for fraudulent claims. If so, the receipts may be consecutively numbered, so look for the numbering across several consecutive expense

reports. This control is a manual one, since no expense report systems track receipt numbers.

- *Look for unusual locations*. A receipt may originate in a place where an employee has not been on company business; these are likely to be personal expenditures that the person is trying to have the company pay.
- *Match to company credit card*. Compare the statements for the company credit card to the amounts listed on employee expense reports, to see if employees are trying to be reimbursed for items for which they did not pay.

In general, look for any employee whose travel expenses are consistently higher than those of other employees engaged in the same type of work. This is an indicator of expense report padding, even if the exact method used has not yet been identified.

Procurement Card-Related Controls

- *Terminate lost cards at once*. The company should mitigate its liability by having a system in place to terminate lost procurement cards as soon as possible. The easiest method is to plaster the contact information for the procurement card administrator on every document sent to card users, so that they know who to call.
- *Retrieve procurement cards as part of terminations*. The human resources staff should have an item on its employee termination checklist to retrieve any procurement cards held by terminated employees, to prevent them from making purchases after they have left.
- *Cancel the procurement cards of terminated employees*. The person responsible for procurement cards should cancel the card of any person who leaves the company, even if they have turned in their cards. The problem is that the terminated employees may still have access to the card numbers, and so can still pay for items without the physical cards (for example, using Internet stores).

Petty Cash-Related Controls

- *Eliminate petty cash*. The best control over petty cash is to not have petty cash. This completely eliminates the risk of loss. A reasonable replacement for a petty cash system is a combination of company procurement cards and requiring employees to pay for items themselves and then request reimbursement from the company by check or direct deposit. If there is a continuing need for petty cash, then at least consider reducing the number of petty cash boxes in use.
- *Conduct random audits*. It is fairly common for the petty cash custodian to use petty cash as a bank, pulling out funds for personal use from time to time. This issue and others can be spotted by conducting a series of random audits. Even if no issues are ever found, the mere presence of these reviews will encourage the custodian to keep a tightly-run petty cash box.

- *Track reimbursements by person on a trend line.* It is entirely possible that a few employees will figure out that they can falsify receipts and obtain a small amount of cash by making submissions to the petty cash custodian at relatively long intervals. If reimbursements are tracked by person over time, it may be possible to detect these submissions.
- *Bolt down the petty cash box.* One of the easier ways to steal from the petty cash box is to steal the entire box. This risk can be eliminated by bolting down the box. A variation on the concept is to install a contact alarm under the petty cash box that is triggered as soon as the box is lifted out of direct contact with the alarm device.
- *Require receipts to spell out sums issued.* If employees are required to fill out receipts with fully spelled-out amounts, it is less likely that someone can later alter the amounts. Thus, a $30.00 receipt would be submitted as "Thirty Dollars."

Fraud-Related Purchasing Controls

There is a reasonable chance that fraud will occur in the purchasing area, since it involves the creation of a document that is a legal authorization to buy from a supplier. If someone can gain access to a company's purchase orders, they could order goods for which the company would be liable to pay suppliers. Accordingly, consider implementing the following controls to prevent or at least detect fraud:

- *Prenumber purchase orders.* If a company prepares purchase orders by hand and uses them as the primary authorization to pay suppliers, the purchase order document itself becomes quite valuable. Someone could fraudulently use a purchase order to order goods for themselves. To avoid this issue, prenumber all purchase orders and lock them up.
- *Password-protect purchasing software.* If the company creates purchase orders on-line and uses them as the primary authorization to pay suppliers, someone accessing the purchase order database can fraudulently order goods. To prevent this, use passwords to restrict access to the purchasing software.
- *Password-protect the vendor master file.* A supplier could offer a kickback to an employee for altering the terms of payment listed in the vendor master file, or an employee could create a fake supplier and use it to pay himself. These problems can be mitigated by using passwords to restrict access to the vendor master file.
- *Review the vendor master file change log.* There are a number of ways that the vendor master file can be altered for fraudulent purposes, such as changing a payment address to that of an employee, and then changing it back. To detect these changes, review the change log on a regular basis. Change logs are usually only available in higher-end purchasing software.
- *Review expense trends.* There may be an unusual blip in an expense line item in a particular month that was not caught by any of the in-process controls.

Once investigated, the system can be modified to catch similar offending transactions in the future.

Fraud-Related Receiving Controls

There is a chance that goods could be fraudulently recorded as having been received. The following controls are designed to prevent or detect this issue:

- *Password-protect receiving software.* If someone working with a supplier could access a company's receiving software and fraudulently log in a delivery as received, the company would pay for it even though it never arrived. To reduce this risk, use passwords to protect access to the receiving software.
- *Use a transaction log to record receiving transactions.* If someone accesses the receiving software to fraudulently log in a delivery as received, this can be detected with a transaction log that is attached to the receiving database. The log should record the identification of the person making the entry, as well as the nature of the entry.
- *Separation of duties.* The person who authorizes the purchase of goods should not also receive it. If this were allowed, someone could authorize a purchase, log it in as having been received (so that the company would pay for it), and then remove it from the premises.

Fraud-Related Payroll Controls

This section contains many controls that can be used to either prevent or at least detect fraud. It would be burdensome to install all of the controls noted here, but it may be useful to install those few that appear most applicable to the particular circumstances of a business. Consider installing at least a few of these controls, since payroll is a tempting area for someone intent on committing fraud, and preventing it can potentially save a great deal of money. The controls are:

- *Lock up all payroll documents.* Payroll files contain a large amount of sensitive information, including pay rates and social security numbers. These files should be stored in locked filing cabinets. It may be necessary to store the cabinets in a locked room.
- *Shred old payroll documents.* Never throw out or recycle old payroll records without first shredding them thoroughly. Otherwise, sensitive social security number and pay rate information may be left exposed for general viewing.
- *Only pay employees after an employee number has been assigned.* Give the human resources department sole control over the assignment of employee numbers to new employees, and make it impossible to pay an employee without an employee number. As long as the human resources staff only assigns employee numbers after conducting background checks and conducting drug tests, it should be much more difficult for someone to create a ghost employee.
- *Only allow direct deposit for employees with company e-mail addresses.* This control makes it much more difficult for someone to create a ghost employee

117

and send money to it, since they must also obtain authorization from either the human resources or information technology departments to create an e-mail account.

- *Match security badge file to employee file.* The security staff should only issue security badges to employees who are physically present, so comparing the badge file to the employee file in the payroll system is a good way to spot ghost employees.

- *Obtain a direct deposit authorization signature.* Have employees sign a form, stating their authorization for the company to pay them by direct deposit, to which is stapled a copy of a cancelled check for the designated account. This makes it more difficult for someone to fraudulently alter bank account information.

- *Lock up direct deposit information.* Since direct deposit authorization forms include an employee's bank account information, lock them in a secure location, probably with the employee personnel folders.

- *Change passwords.* There is a risk that someone could obtain a password that permits access to the payroll software, and use it to alter payment amounts. To reduce this risk, mandate a relatively frequent password change, such as on a quarterly basis.

- *Restrict access to on-line records.* Use password protection if employee payroll records are stored on line. This precaution is not just to keep someone from accessing the records of another employee, but also to prevent unauthorized changes to records (such as a pay rate).

- *Monitor change tracking log.* If payroll is being processed in-house with a computerized payroll module, activate the change tracking log and make sure that access to it is only available through a password-protected interface. This log will track all changes made to the payroll system, which is useful for tracking down erroneous or fraudulent entries. The log should also track the user identification number under which changes were made.

- *Review payments without deductions.* If a payment has no tax deductions or other types of withholdings, there is an enhanced risk that this is a payment issued to a ghost employee, since these items would reduce the amount paid. Thus, run a report that searches for these payments and investigate them.

- *Approve negative deductions.* When an employee receives a negative deduction through the payroll system, it means that he or she is receiving additional cash. While a negative deduction can be used to correct an excessively large deduction in a prior period, it can also be used to fraudulently increase wages. Consequently, either require supervisory approval for negative deductions or at least run a report that highlights these items.

- *Look for double endorsements.* If someone is cutting checks to ghost employees, a good way to spot it is to look at the back of each deposited check to see if there are two endorsements. The first endorsement will be a forgery in the name of the ghost employee, while the second endorsement is the name of the employee cashing the check.

- *Match addresses.* If the company mails checks to its employees, match the addresses on the checks to employee addresses. If more than one check is going to the same address, it may be because a payroll clerk is routing illicit payments for ghost employees to his or her address.
- *Identify simultaneous deposits to the same account.* If an employee has created multiple ghost employees and pays them by direct deposit, it is likely that the payments will all be sent to the same bank account. Create a custom report that searches for this evidence of fraud.
- *Require pay change authorizations.* Consider requiring not just one approval signature for an employee pay change, but two – one by the employee's supervisor, and another by the next-higher level of supervisor. Doing so reduces the risk of collusion in altering pay rates.
- *Mark voided checks.* When a check is voided, do so not only in the accounting software, but also on the check itself, so that no one can cash it. This involves writing "Void" across the face of the check and cutting away or tearing the signature line.
- *Limit remittance advice information.* The remittance advice is the informational tear-away portion of a pay check. Employees routinely throw away their remittance advices without shredding them, so limit the information recorded on them. In particular, replace the social security number with the company-assigned employee number.
- *Separation of duties.* Have one person prepare the payroll, another authorize it, and another create payments, thereby reducing the risk of fraud unless multiple people collude in doing so. In smaller companies where there are not enough personnel for a proper separation of duties, at least insist on having someone review and authorize the payroll before payments are sent to employees.

Fraud-Specific Journal Entry Controls

Hundreds or even thousands of journal entries may be created each year by an organization. The volume of these entries makes it quite difficult to sort through them to see if they are all valid. It is possible to reduce the examination workload by creating an automated routine that searches through the journal entries and extracts just those few that are flagged based on certain criteria. This routine could be run as a standard control at regular intervals.

For example, the routine could flag journal entries with the following criteria:

- Entries are made just prior to or as part of the closing process
- Entries are made on weekends or holidays
- Entries are made to accounts that contain the more complex transactions
- Entries are made to seldom-used accounts
- Entries are made with rounded numbers
- Entries are made without completing the description field

With such an analysis tool, it is easier to spot possible instances of fraud. However, those committing fraud may become aware of these search criteria and so will alter their journal entry patterns. Outwitting them may require a many-layered set of highly detailed search criteria.

General Controls

We include in this section a few additional controls that can be used more generally to locate or prevent fraud losses. They are:

- *Install a shared services center.* A shared services center moves all key accounting and finance activities to a central location, from which these activities are handled on behalf of all corporate subsidiaries. A key advantage of a shared services center is that the people working there are less likely to be influenced by local management, and so will probably not engage in any financial statement fraud. It is also easier to maintain tight controls when these functions are aggregated into one place, which further improves the control environment. A shared services center is particularly recommended when acquisitions are conducted frequently; doing so may eliminate pre-existing frauds at the acquirees.
- *Review customer complaints.* A useful control is to ensure that all customer complaints are examined at a sufficient level of detail to see if fraud may be present. For example, a salesperson may be overcharging customers, recording a reduced sale amount in his ordering paperwork, and pocketing the difference. In this case, a customer complaint about being overcharged leads to a finding of fraud.

Oversight Capabilities

A business that has an above-average control environment likely has an oversight capability, which means that certain groups within the organization are specifically tasked with maintaining an environment that is not conducive to fraudulent activities. The following two groups are especially important in this effort:

- *Audit committee.* A group of people that can bolster the policies and controls of a business is its audit committee. This group is comprised of members of the company's board of directors, and so sits apart from the management team. The outside auditors report to the audit committee. The committee also reviews all fraud hotline comments that have been received. If this group is comprised of people with a deep understanding of finance and accounting, and they actively monitor financial information, then there is a good chance that they can direct audit activities toward the discovery of fraud.

- *Internal audit department.* An internal audit team is used to investigate high-risk parts of a business, as well as to evaluate the reasonableness of existing controls and to recommend whether additional controls should be added. This group is especially useful for conducting surprise audits and generally being so visible that their mere presence deters people from engaging in fraudulent activities.

Incentive Systems

The incentives that a business offers to its employees are not usually considered a control over fraud. Nonetheless, the types of incentives offered can have a powerful impact. In particular, the incentives should not offer major rewards in exchange for unrealistic boosts in sales or profits. When such systems are in place, employees are essentially being compensated to come up with new ways to generate money – possibly falsely.

One might view such a recommendation with a snort of derision, since aggressive compensation plans are sometimes needed to spur a work force in the direction of rapidly growing a business. Nonetheless, there is a difference between valid attempts to grow a business and setting goals so improbable that fraud or speculative activities are realistically the only way that they can be reached. Thus, management must take care to stay firmly on the side of encouraging actual growth, not false or highly risky growth.

EXAMPLE

A new management team is brought into Feedlot Enterprises, which holds and distributes agricultural commodities, because the firm's sales have been flat for the last two years. The new team offers managers massive bonuses if they can double sales within two years. This compensation plan is clearly impossible in the existing market, so managers embark on a speculative commodities trading plan to generate the sales. Doing so gives the company a much higher risk profile. Further, when trading losses inevitably arise, there will be few controls over this new business area, so that management can also engage in financial statement reporting fraud in order to cover up the losses.

Small Business Controls

In a small business, there are too few employees to allow for a proper segregation of duties. Instead, a few employees may have to take on multiple tasks that would be considered control breaches in larger organizations. The owner of such a business can pursue a few simple controls to still maintain a reasonable level of control over the business. These controls are:

- *Never pay in cash.* All payments to all parties should be by check, so that a record is kept of each payment. In addition, by not paying in cash, there is no reason to keep an inordinate amount of cash on the premises, which reduces the risk of having the cash stolen.

121

- *Sign all checks.* Since all payments are being made by check, the owner can then require that he sign all checks. This allows the owner to examine all payments before they are released.
- *Reconcile the bank statement.* The monthly bank statement should be delivered directly to the owner (or better yet, mailed by the bank directly to his home), after which the owner reconciles the bank statement without "assistance" from anyone else. Doing so keeps others from hiding fraudulent transactions that may appear on the bank statement.

These three controls are hardly comprehensive, but they represent a good starting point for small business controls that may prevent a significant number of frauds.

The situation can be especially difficult when a small business is growing rapidly. In this case, management might want to keep the number of controls as low as possible in order to maintain a low level of bureaucracy. In these cases, be sure to observe at least the most essential controls with no exceptions. Further, consider hiring a controls consultant who can observe the growth of the business from an outsider's perspective and make recommendations for when additional controls need to be added to the organization as it becomes larger and more complex.

Summary

A broad-ranging set of policies and controls targeted at fraud will likely eliminate some instances of fraud entirely. In other cases, fraud may still occur but will be detected more quickly, thereby mitigating the amount of losses. Despite the value of policies and controls, some perpetrators will be so determined and ingenious in their pursuit of theft that significant losses will still be incurred. To locate these last items, it will be necessary for the oversight groups to maintain a careful watch over all types of fraud indicators and examine all employee hotline tips, to see if there are problems being missed by the controls. As each successive issue is addressed, the mix of controls will probably change, eventually resulting in a complex and multi-layered set of controls that is effective in dealing with the fraud environment that a business is currently experiencing.

Chapter 6
Fraud Detection

Introduction

The prevention of fraud can be highly effective, but the level of prevention achieved will not be absolute. It is also necessary to engage in detection activities to spot fraud after it has begun to occur. Detection is a critical activity, for fraud is rarely a one-time event; it is more likely that someone will continue to steal from the company if there is no indication that the initial theft has been spotted. In this chapter, we cover the many symptoms of fraud that one can search for, data analysis techniques for spotting fraudulent transactions, and several related topics.

Fraud Symptoms

Fraudulent activities can be quite difficult to spot directly, since they may be concealed and the proportion of fraudulent transactions is likely to be quite low. An alternative way to identify fraud is indirectly – by being alert for the symptoms of fraud. These symptoms can come in many forms, such as:

- *Accounting anomalies*. A key supporting document for a large expenditure is missing or has been altered.
- *Analytical anomalies*. A routine analysis of trend lines and ratios detects an odd spike or decline in the data.
- *Lifestyle symptoms*. An employee arrives at work one day with a sports car that he should not be able to afford.
- *Unusual behavior*. An employee starts working much longer hours.

In the following sub-sections, we explain the nature of these fraud symptoms.

Accounting Anomalies

The typical organization uses a certain set of accounting transactions that do not vary much over time, requiring roughly the same accounts and calling for the same types of supporting documents. When there are differences from these baseline transactions, there is a good chance that the anomalies are indicators of fraud. Here are a number of examples of accounting anomalies that could be symptoms of fraud:

- *Altered documents*. There may be an unusual number of instances in which accounting documents have been manually altered with crossed-out figures that have been replaced by different amounts. This could indicate that someone in the accounting department is modifying documents to hide the theft of assets.

- *High-volume credits*. When there are many credits in the accounts receivable records, it can indicate that the accounting staff is intercepting payments from customers and then covering their tracks by creating credits to reduce the balances in the customer accounts.
- *Increase in aged receivables*. When the collections department appears to be unable to collect on an increasing proportion of receivables, it is possible that some of those invoices are fakes. They may have been constructed internally to create sales that never actually occurred.
- *Increased expenses*. Someone could steal cash and then charge the amount to expense. This approach works well for fraud, since expense accounts are flushed out at year-end, so that the record of the theft does not persist in the account past year-end. When fraud occurs, charges are usually made to large-expense accounts, such as the cost of goods sold, so that a few thousand dollars of expense will not be detected through an analytical analysis.

DISCUSSION

When someone steal assets from a business and wants to hide the theft in the accounting records, the best place to do the hiding is indicated by the *accounting equation*, which is:

$$Assets = Liabilities + Equity$$

This equation is duplicated in the organization's balance sheet, where the total of all assets equals the sum of all liabilities and all equity.

So, if a person steals assets, how can the theft be hidden, so that the accounting equation in the balance sheet still balances? If assets decline due to theft, the choices are:

- *Reduce liabilities*. Reducing liabilities would continue to balance the balance sheet, but creditors would complain when the company does not pay its bills.
- *Reduce equity*. Reducing equity would continue to balance the balance sheet, but there are very few transactions within the equity area, so an adjusting entry in this area would be immediately obvious.
- *Reduce sales*. If sales are artificially reduced, this decreases profits, which in turn decreases equity, and thereby keeps the balance sheet in balance. However, a reduction in sales is usually investigated, since this area is subject to trend line analysis.
- *Increase expenses*. An increase in expenses decreases profits, which in turn decreases equity, and thereby keeps the balance sheet in balance. If the expense account chosen for this entry is a large one, the percentage change in the account will be small, and so may never be investigated.

In short, the best way for someone to hide an asset theft is by charging the amount of the expense to an expense account.

- *Last-minute entries*. Management may be targeting a specific profit figure to report at the end of a reporting period. If so, they may mandate that a journal entry be created that ensures that the target figure is achieved. This journal entry is likely to be one of the last journal entries in a period, since all other entries must first be made before it is possible to determine the shortfall for which fake profits must be manufactured.

- *Missing documents*. There may be no supporting documents that explain why a transaction occurred. For example, there would normally be a customer purchase order associated with an internal sales order. If not, it is possible that an employee made up the sales order, with the intent of having goods shipped to a dummy corporation.
- *Old reconciling items*. Most reconciling items on a bank statement will clear out within one or two months, such as uncleared checks or deposits in transit. When items linger on the reconciliation for a longer period of time, it could indicate a problem. For example, if a check paid to a supplier is not cashed for several months, it is possible that the supplier does not exist.
- *Rewritten records*. Employees may claim that they are rewriting records in order to eliminate errors or make the documents easier to read. What they may actually be doing is completely altering the documents in order to cover up a fraud.
- *Unsupported journal entries*. Someone could alter an account balance in order to bring the actual amount of assets on hand into agreement with the amount stated in the books. If so, they will have a difficult time creating any kind of supporting document that states the reason for the journal entry, and so may provide no supporting documentation at all.

The bulk of the issues underlying accounting anomalies have their origins within the accounting department, since few others have access to the accounting records. This means that someone within the department is engaged in fraud. Consequently, anyone investigating accounting anomalies will have to be exceedingly careful in their investigations, since the person engaged in fraud could be sitting next to them.

Analytical Anomalies

An excellent way to detect fraud is to keep track of a variety of financial and operational metrics over a long period of time. The activity level of almost any measure should not vary all that much over time, so when there is a sudden change in a measure, this is certainly grounds for an investigation. Here are several examples of analytical anomalies:

- *Bad debt reductions*. A company that focuses hard on its profitability is reporting very low bad debts as a percentage of sales. The accounting department achieves this low figure by not keeping the reserve for bad debts at an adequate level, and also by delaying the recognition of bad debts. The result is a low bad debt expense, coupled with an inordinately high accounts receivable balance (since bad debts have not been flushed out of it).
- *Budgeting perfection*. A company consistently budgets aggressively for more sales and profits, and has an amazing ability to almost perfectly meet those

125

numbers, period after period. Further investigation reveals that the management team is using whatever type of reporting fraud it takes to meet the budgeted targets in every reporting period.

- *Commodity price differs from market.* A business uses a large amount of plastic pellets as direct materials in its plastic molding operations. A routine comparison of commodity market prices to the prices paid to the company's pellet supplier finds that there was a modest divergence between the market price and actual price paid, starting one year ago. This could indicate a kickback situation between the supplier and the company's buyer assigned to the acquisition of plastic pellets.

- *Comparison of inventory value to volume.* The auditors of a wood products company evaluates the amount of finished boards that were supposedly in stock at year-end by calculating the approximate volume of boards that would be required to match the amount of ending inventory valuation that the client claims. This calculation reveals that the amount of inventory claimed would overwhelm the existing storage facilities. Clearly, management has been overstating the amount of ending inventory.

- *Excessive expense reports.* A company has a large sales department, which travels constantly. This group submits a large number of expense reports to the accounting department each year, from which the payables manager has developed a good idea of the average amount of expenses that a sales person should submit per week. When she plots these reports on a trend line by salesperson, she notes that Mr. Abrams routinely submits reports that are at least 50% higher than those of the next salesperson. This may be an indication of expense report padding, so she requests a detailed audit of the reports that he has submitted in the past.

- *Fixed asset increases.* The auditors of a manufacturing firm routinely calculate the ratio of fixed assets to sales, to see if the proportion changes significantly from year to year. They discover that this proportion has spiked in the past year, indicating a surge in fixed assets. Further investigation reveals that the controller has been capitalizing expenditures that would normally have been charged to expense, resulting in an increase in profits just sufficient to earn the management team a hefty performance-based bonus.

- *Industry comparison.* A business continually reports increasing sales and profits, despite an industry-wide slump. In this situation, competitors are likely to be cutting prices in order to preserve their market share, which means that everyone in the industry is just trying to maintain sales levels while also reporting lower profits. For someone to both increase sales *and* profits in the face of such competitor actions is quite unlikely.

- *Inventory count corrections.* A company uses an incremental daily inventory count (cycle count), which is resulting in a large number of adjustments to the book balance of the inventory. The preponderance of these adjustments are downward, and almost entirely in the area of finished goods; that is, counts are verifying that the book balances of raw materials items are accurate most of the time. The situation indicates that someone might be stealing finished goods from the warehouse.

- *Low quality materials*. A company has been experiencing a number of product failures in the field, so it traces the issue back through the production process, eventually finding that a supplier is delivering low-quality raw materials. By tracing the customer complaints back in time, the internal audit manager believes that the low quality goods began to be shipped at about the time a new receiving manager was hired. This may indicate that the supplier has been paying kickbacks to the receiving manager to overlook low-quality deliveries.

- *Management turnover*. A business has a history of running through its senior management team at a rapid clip, with new chief executive officers being hired at the rate of one per year. Shortly thereafter, many types of fraud are discovered throughout the business. An analysis reveals that the lack of consistent management oversight led to a highly permissive culture where many people took advantage of the situation to steal assets from the company.

- *Petty cash replenishment*. The controller is accustomed to replenishing the petty cash box in the production department about once every three months. Suddenly, the replenishment rate increases to once a month. Since the box holds $300 of cash, this means that the petty cash usage rate has jumped from $100 per month to $300 per month. Some kind of fraud involving the use of petty cash seems likely.

- *Rapid rollouts in emerging markets*. Emerging markets have a well-earned reputation for being rife with corruption. This means that any organization wanting to do business in one of these countries will likely need to pay bribes in order to achieve a rapid rollout of their operations. Thus, when a rapid rollout *does* occur, it could be due less to the business acumen of the local manager and more to the size of the bribes paid. This red flag is especially true when a business miraculously obtains permits and licenses in short order.

- *Small amounts of overtime*. A review of overtime records finds that most employees incur overtime only at long intervals – except for one person, who routinely charges a half-hour of overtime, once or twice a week. This small amount falls below the overtime approval threshold for the business, so there is a possibility that the employee is reporting the overtime without actually working the extra hours.

- *Spike in expenses*. A trend line analysis of legal costs finds that legal expenditures jumped two years ago by 20%, and have stayed at that level since. There have been no unusual lawsuits or public company filings during that time, so it is possible that one or more law firms are overbilling the company.

- *Supplier billings too low*. A review of invoicing volumes by supplier finds that there are ten suppliers whose billings to the company never exceed $99. Since the invoice approval threshold for the business is $100, these smaller invoices are always paid automatically. Further investigation reveals that eight of the ten suppliers were added within the past year. The circumstances indicate that an employee might have set up a series of dummy corporations, and is using them to fraudulently bill the company at a level that will not be detected.

Analytical anomalies cannot always be detected if a fraud has been running for a long time. The reason is that a fraud auditor might be looking for unusual changes in a trend line, but if the fraud has been running for the entire duration of the trend line, the data will appear to be quite normal.

Another issue with analytics is that managers know these analytics will be run by their auditors, and so may alter the financial information to conform to the expectations of the auditors. Consequently, it may take a detailed analysis of analytics in multiple areas to discern whether there may be a problem.

Lifestyle Symptoms

Employees who are engaged in fraud would require an immense amount of self-control to steal from their employer and not spend the money in some visible way. Instead, there is usually some evidence of a change in lifestyle. Here are several examples of lifestyle symptoms:

- Gambling trips to Las Vegas
- The replacement of an older car with a much nicer one
- Upgrades to an employee's house, or shifting to an entirely new one
- Taking up an expensive hobby, such as sailing or heli-skiing
- Stories of gifts made to friends and family

A common excuse given for a suddenly more profligate lifestyle is that a person has inherited wealth. If so, a reasonable question is why the person continues to work at the company. This is a particular concern when the individual refuses to take any vacation time or refuses to be promoted, which can indicate that they are covering up a fraud situation.

A change in lifestyle is one of the easiest indicators of fraud, and yet many people do not notice changes, or do not equate them to possible fraudulent activities. Consequently, it is necessary to include a discussion of lifestyle changes in fraud training for employees.

Certain types of fraud, such as kickback schemes, do not leave a record on a company's books, since the employees engaged in the scheme are being paid by a supplier. In these cases, the most immediate evidence of fraud could be a lifestyle change. Consequently, this should be an essential part of a fraud investigation.

The search for information about lifestyle changes usually involves an examination of public records to find evidence of asset purchases or debt payments.

Unusual Behavior

When a person commits fraud, he will be under an increased level of stress. This can lead to changes in the person's behavior in the office, which may be extreme enough to be clearly visible to co-workers. Examples are:

- More variable mood swings
- A high level of suspicion of others
- Defensiveness
- Uses intimidation to keep others from investigating
- Using excuses to an excessive degree
- A higher level of security, such as locked filing cabinets or office doors
- Working longer hours
- Extensive amounts of drinking, smoking, and drug use

Combinations of several of the preceding items can be particular indicators that a person is engaged in some kind of fraud.

Assistance in Spotting Fraud

A person does not have to work alone when attempting to spot instances of fraud. Other people both within and outside of the organization can be encouraged to assist, as noted in the following sub-sections.

Assistance from Employees

One way to detect fraud is to rely upon fellow employees to spot issues and bring them to the attention of management. Employees are in the best position to see someone engaged in fraud, or attempting to cover it up, or spending the proceeds, since they are on-site year-round. For example:

- An employee may return to work late at night and see someone engaged in a suspicious activity.
- Employees have access to all company records at various times, and so have an excellent opportunity to notice when supporting documentation is incorrect or missing.
- Employees will notice changes in the lifestyles of their fellow employees, such as vehicle or clothing upgrades.

In short, employees are ideal fraud witnesses.

To maximize the use of employees for fraud detection, it is necessary to educate the staff regarding indicators of fraud, so that they will be more inclined to notice suspicious activity. They must also be provided with a means of contacting management that does not result in any negative repercussions for themselves. In addition, the general environment for forwarding information should be made as easy as possible. Employees could fear reprisals for being whistle-blowers, so every effort should be made to mitigate these concerns, with a particular emphasis on keeping all tips private. As noted next, one of the best ways for employees to leave tips is the hotline.

The Employee Hotline

An essential ingredient in a system that relies upon employee input is a fraud hotline. This is usually the best single method for detecting fraud. These hotlines do not require an employee to identify himself, which greatly reduces the risk of adverse consequences for the whistleblower. Ideally, the person receiving a hotline contact should be an independent third party, such as a company that specializes in providing hotline services. This supplier then reports issues to the company's board of directors or its audit committee. By using an outsider, there is no risk that the person receiving the call will be the individual committing fraud. Other best practices related to the use of a hotline are:

- Create a multi-lingual capability, so that tips can be left in those languages used by employees, customers, and suppliers.
- Ensure that the hotline is available 24×7, so that people can contact it at any hour.
- Maintain several different avenues by which employees can contribute tips, such as a phone number, e-mail address, and mailing address. Doing so allows employees to leave tips via whichever means is most comfortable for them.
- Manage each tip received through a case management system, so that each one is properly examined and resolved, and to ensure that an audit trail is maintained that shows the sequence of follow-up steps taken.
- Publicize the actions that have been taken as a result of hotline tips. Doing so encourages employees to continue using the hotline. If there is no publicity regarding the results of the system, employees will assume that their tips are being ignored.
- Publicize the fact that tips can be left anonymously, which makes people more willing to forward information.
- Regularly post reminders that the hotline is available, and reinforce the availability of the hotline in communications with employees.

The operator taking a call through a hotline system should record a significant amount of information as the basis for an investigation. The following information should be taken down:

- Time and date of the call
- Whether the caller is an employee, customer, vendor, or other
- The nature of the violation
- The names of the people involved
- The dates and locations when the violation occurred
- How long the violation has been conducted and whether it is ongoing
- Comments regarding the existence of any documentary evidence

Assistance from Suppliers and Customers

The preceding discussion of an employee hotline can certainly be extended to suppliers and customers. By doing so, an additional pool of people is accessed that may be able to comment on unusual activity, such as kickback schemes between these entities and the company's employees.

Assistance from Auditors

Outside auditors are not good at spotting fraud, since they are on-site for only a short period of time, during which frauds usually stop. Also, auditors only conduct sample tests, which are not designed to detect fraud; instead, auditors are only looking for material misstatements in the financial statements. Consequently, they are far less likely to detect fraud than employees. Nonetheless, auditors may occasionally make note of puzzling transactions that turn out to be evidence of fraud, or are approached by employees with tips. Thus, though auditors are not the best source of information for fraud, audits should certainly be conducted at regular intervals in hopes of uncovering an occasional case.

Records Examination

Another way to detect fraud is to engage in an ongoing review of transactions and account balances to see if there are any unusual trends or anomalies that could indicate the presence of fraud.

A detailed records examination that is focused on locating instances of fraud will go well beyond checking for the mere existence of supporting documents. In addition, this examination will review documents in detail to see if:

- The documents are authentic
- The nature of the expenditures is reasonable
- There are any aspects of the paperwork that are unusual, such as missing or different signatures, dates that fall on weekends, or addresses listed as post office boxes

Publishing Activities

Various parties within a business may be called upon to assist with the detection of fraud, but they may not attend to this task with much vigor, especially if they do not believe that fraud is much of a threat. One way to combat this mindset is to publish a memo within the company whenever a fraud has occurred. It is not necessary to identify the perpetrator (especially if the investigation is ongoing) – just noting the fact that a fraud was uncovered and describing the general circumstances of the situation should be sufficient to increase the level of alertness throughout the organization.

The publication of such a memo is particularly useful in a larger organization where there are many locations. In this environment, news of a fraud might not otherwise travel to the various locations.

Data Analysis

It is much more common to find anomalies in the records of a business than actual cases of fraud. Anomalies may have many causes, such as poor employee training, equipment failures, and faulty procedures. These instances should appear with a fair amount of uniformity throughout the business records. Fraud, on the other hand, is entirely intentional, and may only arise once or twice. Consequently, a certain proportion of anomalies will be expected in any sample of transactions, whereas instances of fraud will occur much more rarely.

When analyzing data within a business, the number of transactions involving fraud is so small that a sampling approach will not work. That is, it is not reasonable to expect a five percent sample of all invoices paid to unerringly locate the one invoice that was fraudulently submitted by a fake supplier. Instead, it is necessary to examine the entire data set. This can be accomplished automatically with data analysis tools.

The basic process for using data analysis tools to search for fraud is as follows:

1. *Knowledge acquisition.* Develop an understanding of how the business operates, including the processes used. It is not sufficient to assume that all businesses are subject to the same types of fraud; for example, the processes used by a casino (with its massive cash flows) are quite different from those used by a retail store (which is more concerned with controlling inventory levels). Several activities could be employed to gain the appropriate level of understanding, such as:

   - A plant tour
   - Interviews with key personnel
   - Observe procedures being conducted
   - Discuss company processes with its internal and external auditors
   - Review the financial statements and related disclosures of the business

2. *Potential fraud identification.* Have a basic understanding of the types of frauds that might be perpetrated within or upon a business, as well as the symptoms that will be caused by those frauds. The outcome should be a listing of potential frauds, as well as which individuals might commit them. To do so might require the following activities:

   - Discovering the types of fraud afflicting this industry
   - Discovering the types of frauds that occurred in the past
   - Discovering the types of people and business partners engaged in business transactions
   - Speculating about the types of frauds that could be perpetrated by employees or business partners

3. *Potential symptom identification.* Identify the types of fraud symptoms that may be found, as described earlier in the Fraud Symptoms section. In

particular, try to identify specific fraud symptoms that may be associated with the potential types of fraud identified in the preceding step.

DISCUSSION

A data analysis team is conducting an analysis of possible fraud situations that might occur. One possibility is that the mailroom clerk might intercept check or cash payments that are sent in the mail. If so, the team surmises that the following fraud symptoms might result:

- Accounts receivable increase, since payments are not being applied to outstanding invoices
- Complaints from customers that their payments are not being credited against outstanding receivables
- The mailroom clerk becomes less chatty and more suspicious of anyone in his area
- The mailroom clerk's lifestyle expenditures begin to increase
- The mailroom clerk resists having a second person participate in opening the mail

---

4. *Data collection.* The data analysis team gathers data about the fraud symptoms catalogued in the last step. The focus is on those symptoms for which data *can* be collected. In the preceding discussion of symptoms, the most obvious data collection activity would relate to increases in accounts receivable. Better yet, the analysis could focus on changes in accounts receivable by subsidiary, to see if there is a fraud situation going on within a specific mailroom.

   A significant issue with data collection is that the first pass may result in a multitude of possible fraud indicators. The analysis team will need to go through several iterations, applying filters to the data, before it excludes a sufficient number of extraneous factors to arrive at a small set of items that could be real fraud symptoms.

5. *Investigative activities.* Once all possible data analysis activities have been concluded, the analysis team works with the internal auditors or other investigative personnel to gather additional information pertaining to an identified item. These additional actions might include interviews and the examination of paper documents.

A particular advantage of data analysis is that it is commonly run using a company's own databases. This means that a fraud examination team could be searching for fraud while in an off-site location, so that wrongdoers have no idea that a search is even being conducted. Thus, they may continue to engage in fraud without knowing that their actions are being examined elsewhere.

Once a data analysis routine has been created, it can be run repeatedly over time as a standard routine. By doing so, it can highlight additional anomalies that could indicate other fraud situations. This is highly useful, since the automated analysis may be able to highlight frauds that have only just begun, while the amounts being stolen are still relatively small.

Data Analysis Techniques

There are a number of data analysis techniques that can be used to extract relevant information from a data set. Entire books have been written on this topic, so we will focus on just some of the more common techniques.

Benford's Law

Benford's Law states that, in a naturally occurring set of numbers, the smaller digits appear disproportionately more often as the leading digits. The leading digits have the distribution shown in the following table, where the number 1 appears slightly more than 30% of the time as the leading digit, and the number 9 appears as the leading digit less than 5% of the time (which is a difference of 6x).

Numeric Distribution in Benford's Law

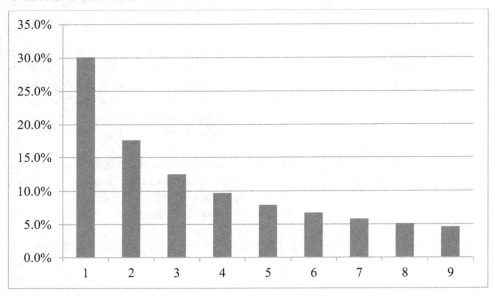

If all digits were to appear as the leading digit in a uniform manner, then each one would appear about 11.1% of the time. Since there is quite a disparity between the distributions stated in Benford's Law and what a uniform distribution would indicate, this disparity can be used to locate instances of fraud.

The analysis involves calculating the distribution on the first digit in a series of numbers. If the distribution varies from the proportions indicated by Benford's Law, then it is possible that someone is engaged in fraud. The reason for the difference is that someone committing fraud will create randomly generated numbers, rather than following Benford's distribution.

EXAMPLE

The data analysis team of Nuance Corporation wants to use Benford's Law as the basis for an examination of the invoices submitted to the company by its suppliers. The analysis is run for two suppliers, Supplier A and Supplier B, where the first digit is extracted from the total amount billed on each invoice. The results of the analysis are shown in the following two tables.

Supplier A Comparison to Benford's Law

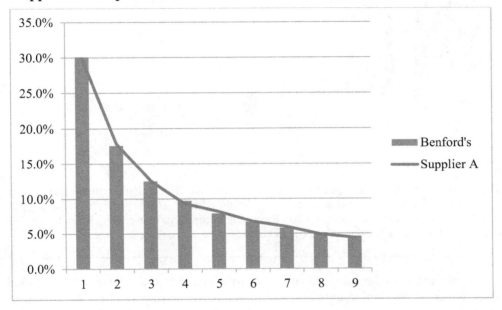

Supplier B Comparison to Benford's Law

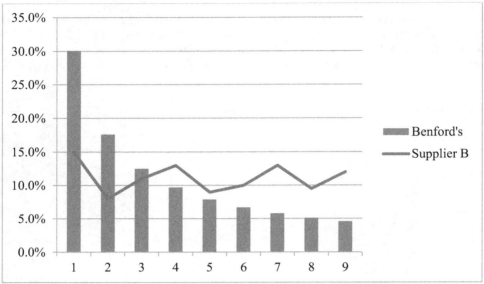

The analysis for Supplier A appears to be quite normal, with the actual numeric distribution closely following the proportions indicated by Benford's Law. This is not the case for Supplier B, where it appears that the supplier has been making up random numbers to be billed. The latter situation certainly calls for a more detailed review.

It is important to understand the situations to which Benford's Law can be applied. The frequency distribution only occurs for naturally occurring numbers. In a business, examples of these numbers are the grand total billed on an invoice, the compiled cost of a product, or the number of units in stock. It does not apply in situations where numbers are assigned, such as a sequentially assigned check number or invoice number. Also, it is more applicable to larger data sets than to quite small ones. When the data set contains less than 50 numbers, it is quite possible that the distribution of numbers will differ significantly from what is indicated by Benford's Law, and yet will not be an indicator of fraud.

The preceding example might make it look as though Benford's Law can be used to locate all kinds of fraud in short order. This is not really the case. Instead, the analysis works only if the analysis team drills down deeply enough into the data to locate a potentially fraudulent situation. For example, an examination of every supplier invoice received by a company in the past year might not have spotted the issue in the preceding example, because the suspicious behavior was lost in the much larger volume of invoices. Another concern is that this technique only indicates the possible existence of fraud; someone still needs to find out exactly how fraud is being perpetrated, which calls for a significant amount of additional investigatory work.

Cross-Matching Analysis

Cross-matching analysis involves matching information from different parts of the company to find a match that could point toward a fraud. Common examples are:

- Matching employee addresses to the addresses of suppliers, to see if employees have set up dummy entities that are billing the company.
- Matching employee bank accounts to supplier bank accounts, for the same reason just noted.
- Matching employee bank accounts to the bank accounts of other employees, to see if any fake ("ghost") employees have been created, to which payments are being sent.
- Matching employee social security numbers against the national social security database to see if employees have mis-represented themselves.
- Matching of invoices received to the purchase order database, to detect invoices that were not authorized by a purchase order.
- Matching of invoices received to receiving reports, to see if there is no record of receipt of certain billed items.

The analysis can also involve any number of analyses within a single data set to search for anomalies. For example:

- Duplicate invoice numbers submitted by the same supplier
- Sequential invoice numbers submitted by the same supplier
- Multiple invoices submitted by a supplier that contain the same billing description
- Equipment charges associated with a contract when no labor hours were charged

Outlier Analysis

An outlier is a value that lies outside the other values in a set of data. Data analysis can be used to focus on outliers, which are sometimes associated with fraudulent activity. Examples of activities that could be the focus of an outlier activities analysis are:

- Unusually large price increases by a supplier
- Unusually large cost overruns on supplier contracts
- Unusually large numbers of goods returned to a supplier
- Unusually large overtime payments

The main issue with the analysis of outliers is deciding when a data point is really an outlier, or falls within the main cluster of values. To do this, a data analyst compiles a z-score, which is a statistical measurement of a data point's relationship to the mean of a set of data points. The calculation of the z-score is:

$$\frac{(Value - Mean)}{Standard\ deviation}$$

A z-score of zero indicates that the score of a specific value is the same as the mean of the data set to which it is related; such a score is certainly not an outlier. As the score becomes larger (either negative or positive), the related value is more likely to be considered an outlier. A score of one indicates one full standard deviation from the mean, while a score of two represents two standard deviations from the mean, and so forth. Each incremental standard deviation represents the following values:

- 68.2% of all values lie within one standard deviation
- 95.4% of all values lie within two standard deviations
- 99.6% of all values lie within three standard deviations

Thus, a z-score that is approaching two should certainly draw the attention of a fraud auditor, while a z-score of three or more will raise a considerable red flag.

Trend Analysis

Many types of fraud can be found by examining a trend line of data over a period of time. For example, when a purchasing agent starts taking kickbacks from a supplier in exchange for buying too expensive goods, the unit cost paid to that supplier should jump when the kickback begins, and remain high thereafter. A variation on the concept is to generate a trend analysis of raw material returns; if the quantity of returns increases and then stays at a higher level, a kickback situation could have been entered into, where the price remains the same but the supplier is allowed to ship lower-quality goods. Here are several other situations in which trend analysis could be used:

- Trend line of labor rates charged by a contractor
- Trend line of equipment rental rates charged by a supplier
- Trend line of price increases by a supplier for raw materials and components

A sample trend analysis appears in the following exhibit, which states the trend line of foodstuffs missing from a grocery store warehouse. The amount missing is derived from a comparison of the book balance of units on hand to the amounts actually counted as part of an ongoing cycle counting program.

Trend Line of Warehouse Losses by Week

The exhibit shows a gradual increase in the amount of losses, as the perpetrator waits to see if anyone spots the issue, and then becomes more emboldened over time. The complete absence of losses during weeks 6 and 7 coincides with the arrival of an audit team, which conducts a standard set of audit procedures in the warehouse. Once they leave, the fraud begins again, except at a higher level as the perpetrator becomes bolder.

Discovery Sampling

The problem with auditors collecting documentary evidence is that they normally test a sampling of the total population of documents. If the selected sample does not reveal fraud, then they may conclude that fraud does not exist. If fraud is suspected and it is possible that fraudulent documents are only a small proportion of the total amount, auditors would need to conduct an analysis of the entire population of documents in order to be assured of collecting documentary evidence that clearly points toward the existence of fraud. This can involve a vast amount of work.

An alternative to testing the entire population of documents is discovery sampling. Under this approach, sampling is used to determine whether there is at least one error in a sampling of documents, assuming a certain population error percentage. In essence, the auditor calculates a sample size based on the amount of risk he is willing to assume. For example, to be 98% confident that the fraud rate within a total population is no more than 1%, it might be necessary to review a sample of 400 documents. In essence, to reduce the risk of missing an instance of fraud, one must increase the sample size. If the auditor is willing to assume some risk of having missed a fraudulent document, then the sample size can be reduced.

There is still a risk that discovery sampling will not detect a case of fraud, because the documentation involving a fraudulent transaction was not selected. This is called *sampling risk*. Sampling risk can be reduced by increasing the sample size, as well as by using a random number generator as the basis for selecting documents. For example, a random number generator could be used to randomly select customer invoices for examination; if the auditor had simply selected a block of invoices for review, this would reduce the probability of finding a fraudulent transaction.

It is also entirely possible that the correct document was selected, but the auditor did not realize that it indicated a fraudulent transaction; this is called *non-sampling risk*. Non-sampling risk is quite possible when an auditor is inexperienced or the perpetrators have done a good job of altering documents.

Access to Documents

It can be difficult to obtain access to certain documents. For example, it may be necessary to access the private banking records of an individual as part of a fraud examination. One way to obtain these documents is by voluntary consent. In this case, a fraud suspect is simply asked for access to the documents. If the person agrees, he signs a consent form that states the documents that he is allowing the investigators to examine. This is a common technique as part of the initial confrontation with a suspect, and will frequently result in being granted access to the required information.

Another approach for obtaining documents is the *subpoena*. A subpoena is issued by a court or grand jury, and requires the recipient to produce the documents listed in the subpoena. If the recipient does not produce the documents, the issuing entity can punish the person. Subpoenas can only be served by law enforcement authorities, so this implies that law enforcement has been called upon to assist with an investigation.

Yet another way to obtain documents is via a *search warrant*. A judge issues a search warrant when there is probable cause indicating that documents have been used to commit a crime. Again, a search warrant can only be acted upon by law enforcement authorities, so a business must be willing to notify the authorities in this situation.

Nonfraud Factors

Just because an issue has been detected does not mean that fraud is actually present. For example, there could be a good reason why funds are being wired to a Grand Cayman bank account, or why the company controller is now driving an expensive new sports car. Or, there may be a valid reason why an anonymous tip identifies the purchasing manager as taking kickbacks. In the first case, for example, the company may be operating a captive insurance company in Grand Cayman, while in the second case the controller might have just received a large inheritance. And in the third case, the person leaving the tip may want the purchasing manager's job. Consequently, one cannot assume that every indicator of fraud will actually result in a fraud finding.

The investigation of fraud within a business can be highly disruptive, since the targets of an investigation might conclude that they are suspected of engaging in criminal behavior. When these individuals are doing nothing of the sort, they will view their loyalty to the business as having been called into question, which can have catastrophic consequences. Consequently, investigations need to be as discrete as possible up until the point when it appears to be quite likely that fraud has indeed taken place, at which point it may be necessary to engage in a more detailed investigation that is difficult to shield from the view of employees.

Another reason for circumspection is that there may actually be an ongoing fraud, in which case the perpetrators will be alerted by unusual investigatory activities in the office. If so, they will likely attempt to destroy or hide evidence, making it more difficult to prove a case against them.

Where Fraud Does Not Occur

We have focused in this chapter on those areas of a business in which fraud can be found. It is also worth noting where fraud is unlikely to be found, so that fraud examiners will not waste too much of their time in these areas. Here are several places in which fraud is unlikely to occur:

- *Small-balance expense accounts.* When an expense account has a small balance, a sudden increase in the balance (such as might be used to hide a fraud) would be spotted at once through a trend line analysis.
- *Liability accounts.* Altering a liability account in order to hide a fraud would be quite unusual. However, it is possible that management might attempt to reduce the reported amount of liabilities in order to improve the financial ratios that outsiders are using to track the financial stability of the business.
- *Equity accounts.* It makes no sense for anyone to alter equity accounts, for several reasons. First, changes in equity are usually tracked in detail in a statement of retained earnings, so fudging the amounts would be immediately obvious. And second, most equity transactions require board approval (such as for dividends and stock sales), and so can be readily proven – any residual entries in these accounts would stand out at once.

Though fraud is unlikely to occur in these areas, it is not impossible. A person could alter these accounts purely out of ignorance that doing so will be highly visible, so it makes sense to continue to monitor these areas – just not very frequently.

Undetectable Fraud

What kind of fraud would not set off any of the triggers noted in this chapter? The ideal fraud would have the following characteristics:

- *Very small.* The amount of the fraud must be so small that the detection levels employed by the organization would never spot it.
- *Inconsistent timing.* The person engaged in the fraud only perpetrates it at irregular intervals, so there does not appear to be any reason for a loss.
- *Inconsistent amount.* The perpetrator always varies the amount of the fraud, so no pattern emerges that could lead to a solid conclusion that fraud is present.

- *Inconsistent location.* The nature of the fraud changes continually, perhaps jumping from inventory losses to bad debt write-offs to petty cash losses, and back again.

Under these circumstances, someone engaged in fraud detection work would have an extremely difficult time pinpointing the existence of any fraud. However, this situation would require an exceptional amount of planning by the perpetrator, and in exchange for a relatively small amount of money. It would also require someone in a relatively responsible position to be perpetrating the fraud, so that the losses keep jumping around among multiple locations. The only persons who could carry off this type of fraud would be a bookkeeper, assistant controller, or controller, because they have access to the accounting records and widespread access to numerous parts of the accounting systems.

Role of the Auditor in Fraud Detection

Audits conducted by a firm's external auditors are specifically designed to determine whether the financial information in its financial statements is fairly presented. The procedures and tests directed toward this result will not necessarily detect fraud. Nonetheless, there are a few ways for the auditor to arrive at a condition that is more likely to achieve fraud detections. These options are:

- *Rotate in staff.* There is a tendency to continually bring back the same auditors from the year before, on the grounds that these people already know the client, and so will conduct a more efficient audit. This is certainly true. However, a high level of familiarity tends to decrease the professional skepticism of the auditor, which might otherwise lead to questions about certain transactions that might be indicators of fraud. Instead, consider rotating in a certain proportion of different audit staff each year that do not know the client, and so may make more inquiries.
- *Base procedures on fraud risk.* The audit manager for the most recent audit is likely to copy forward the audit plan used last year. It is familiar, the audit staff already knows how to complete it, and the outcome will be a more efficient audit. However, the client already knows which procedures will be conducted, and so will be more likely to engage in fraudulent activities that will not be detected by any of these procedures. Instead, the audit partner and manager should consider in advance those areas in which fraud is most likely to occur, and explore the use of new audit procedures each year that will cover these higher-risk areas.
- *Inquire on-site.* When e-mail is used to make inquiries of client personnel, the auditor cannot pick up on any visual cues from interviewees. In addition, a person can craft a technically correct answer to an e-mail that sidesteps an issue, which is more difficult to do when the auditor is making inquiries on the spot. Consequently, try to keep the audit staff on-site as much as possible

over the course of an audit, rather than pulling them back to the office prematurely and relying on e-mail to settle all remaining issues.

Summary

Fellow employees can be of great assistance in detecting fraud, for they may spot issues that are not being addressed at all by the ongoing examination of records. They may also spot situations in which the fraud level is so low that it is falling below the detection limits set by the company's automated detection systems. Consequently, it makes a great deal of sense to actively engage the entire workforce in the pursuit of fraud.

No matter what system is used to detect fraud, someone must act upon it as soon as possible. Otherwise, the amount of fraud committed will continue to occur, and probably at an increasing rate. Once the evidence becomes overwhelming, the amount stolen will likely be much higher than the amount of the loss if action had been taken when fraud indicators first showed the presence of a potential problem.

Chapter 7
Fraud Investigation

Introduction

When fraud is suspected, a fraud examination team does not just leap into action, scouring the organization for clues. Doing so may not be cost-effective, could lead to the loss of key evidence, and will probably alert the perpetrator that management is coming after him. A more logical flow of events is discussed in this chapter, where a decision must first be made whether to investigate, followed by an orderly process that initially operates quietly and very much in the background to build a case.

Whether to Investigate

When there is a strong indication that fraud exists, a fraud investigation does not necessarily follow immediately thereafter. Instead there are several factors to consider, not least of which is the cost-benefit of the investigation. A full investigation can be quite expensive, possibly involving outside investigators as well as the human resources, legal, and internal audit departments. Offsetting these costs is the benefit of savings from no longer having anyone stealing assets. Another factor is the strength of the evidence pointing in the direction of fraud. If the evidence is relatively weak, it could make more sense to wait and collect more evidence that fraud really exists, especially if the amount of the presumed theft is relatively small and unlikely to get much larger.

There are also several "soft" issues to consider when deciding whether to investigate. One is the impact on employees. If they see that an investigation has been conducted, they will be less inclined to perpetrate fraud themselves. Conversely, if they *do not* see an investigation, this can also be taken as a signal – that one can get away with fraud in this company. Another "soft" issue is that an investigation may exonerate the person who had been suspected of fraud. Otherwise, the person might have had a black mark against him within the company that could have prevented further advancement, just because of the suspicion of fraud.

Investigation Policies and Procedures

An organization should be able to deal with reported fraud incidents promptly, which calls for a set of policies and procedures that can be used as a framework for these investigations. The following policies should be in place:

- The position that is responsible for the investigation
- When a fraud situation is to be referred to the police
- How news of the fraud is to be communicated, both internally and externally
- What actions the company will take against perpetrators

The following procedures should also be in place:

- The investigative techniques to be used
- The procedure to use to deal with tips coming through the hotline

Fraud Investigative Techniques

One way to investigate fraud is to delve into the motivations of a suspect, looking for any perceived pressures, fraud opportunities, or rationalizations that the person might have mentioned to a third party, or which anyone might have observed. For example, a person might have mentioned the pressure of coming up with enough money to pay for a child's college education, or he might have expressed dissatisfaction with having been passed over for a promotion.

An alternative approach is to focus on the fraud itself. One option is to try to catch the person in the act of committing fraud. This can be quite difficult, so an alternative is to examine those records that an individual might have altered in order to hide the evidence of their activities, and then reconstruct how the fraud was perpetrated. A third approach is to examine the lifestyle and personal records of the suspect to determine how any stolen funds or other assets might have been used.

The investigative method chosen should be tailored to the type of fraud that appears to have been committed. Some methods are especially effective when applied to certain types of fraud, as noted in the following example.

EXAMPLE

An anonymous tip reveals that there is a ghost employee in the company – specifically, in the maintenance department. Mr. Jones retired from the maintenance department a year ago, and yet he appears to still be drawing a paycheck. Since there is no physical loss of assets, consulting surveillance will not be helpful. Instead, the fraud investigation team determines the account number into which paychecks for Mr. Jones are being deposited, and works with the local bank to determine the owner of the account – which turns out to be one of the payroll clerks.

EXAMPLE

Mule Corporation, maker of Bad Ass motorcycles, is suffering from losses in the tool area of its maintenance department. The tool storage area is locked and only three people have the key, so the list of suspects is gratifyingly short. The fraud investigation team elects to install a microscopic video camera in the cage to monitor tool check-outs and returns, and finds that the newest hire into the department has been making off with a few tools during the third shift.

EXAMPLE

A routine review of commodity prices finds that there has been a suspicious increase in the prices paid for certain commodities above their normal market prices. All of these commodities are under the control of Q.T. Smythe, one of the senior buyers. There is no direct evidence that a kickback scheme may be in progress, so the fraud investigation team instead decides to compile evidence that Mr. Smythe's lifestyle has increased substantially since the presumed start of the kickback scheme. This includes a before-and-after examination of mortgages and other loans being paid off.

The team also works with the local law enforcement authorities to have wiretaps installed on his phone. They examine his prior e-mail records to see if there are any incriminating conversations with suppliers, interview both current and former buyers who have worked for the company, and interview suppliers unrelated to the current investigation to see if they have been solicited for kickbacks.

The type of investigatory techniques used should initially be restricted to those that will not trigger suspicion by the subject of the investigation, so that the team can collect information without fear of having any evidence destroyed. For example, e-mail records can be examined from the information technology department, while public records can be reviewed over the Internet or at a local government facility.

Once the team has accumulated more information and there appears to be a solid case, the team can engage in more visible activities. This may first involve interviews with people who no longer work for the company or who work for other companies, since they are least likely to warn the suspect. Once information has been collected from the less-visible sources, the investigation escalates to include an interview with the person under suspicion. By the time the interview takes place, the team should have a solid case that does not allow the suspect any room to wriggle away from the accusation.

A key step in deciding upon the course of an investigation is to first develop an overview chart that summarizes what might have been stolen, who had an opportunity to steal the assets, and other speculations, such as:

- How the assets might have been stolen
- How the theft might have been concealed
- How the assets might have been converted into cash
- What types of fraud symptoms might be displayed by a suspect
- What kinds of pressure the suspects might be under to trigger the theft
- What types of rationalizations the suspects might have employed

Having all of this information in one place makes it easier to scan through the possible perpetrators, how they engaged in fraud, and why they did it. One can then more easily determine the best course of action for the fraud investigation. A sample fraud overview chart for a theft of consumer goods inventory is noted in the following exhibit.

Fraud Overview Chart

Item Stolen	Who had Opportunity	How Stolen?	How Concealed?	Conversion to Cash?	Fraud Symptoms?	Triggering Pressures?	Possible Rationalizing
Cell phones	Warehouse staff	Removed from boxes in warehouse	Re-tape boxes	Fenced on eBay	Incorrect inventory records	New car	Greed
	Shipping staff	Removed during palletization	Hole in center of pallet loads	Same	Customer complaints	Tax liens	Not promoted
	Delivery staff	Extracted while in transit	Claim theft from truck	Same	Customer complaints	Student loans	Feels underpaid

As an example of the logic used in the preceding fraud overview chart, one possible suspect is the company's shipping staff. Several of them have tax liens outstanding against them (for which the garnishment information is available from the human resources department), and there was a recent promotion in the group that could have annoyed several people who were passed over for the promotion. To engage in the theft, they could have repositioned boxes of cell phones on the pallets, so there is a hole in the center that is not readily discernible. This represents a complete scenario for how and why a fraud might have been perpetrated.

Documentary Evidence

Documentary evidence is collected from physical and electronic records. This usually involves the manual examination of documents, but can also include automated searches of electronic records to look for anomalies or other indicators of fraud. Documents can also be subjected to a variety of analyses, such as examining financial statements to see if there are indicators that the underlying accounting records have been altered.

Personal Observation

Investigators may engage in the direct surveillance of suspects or other similar activities to collect information. These activities usually involve either viewing or listening to suspects or the activities that appear to be related to a suspected fraud. The key types of surveillance are:

- *Electronic observation*. This most commonly involves the use of video recording equipment, which is a common emplacement in areas where there is a high risk of theft. Wiretapping is only allowed for duly authorized law enforcement personnel.
- *Following the persons in question*. This involves tailing the individuals in question, with the intent of identifying additional individuals who may be involved in a fraud.
- *From a fixed location*. This involves having one or more people set up at a location from which they can observe the activity in question. They then take

notes or record the activity. Notes should include a complete time log of what was observed. A sample time log follows.

Sample Time Log

June 30, 20X3 [Time]	Event
7:00 p.m.	Surveillance begins at Rummy's Bar & Grill, 123 Main Street, Denver CO.
7:05 p.m.	John Matthews and unidentified black male enter bar area and order drinks.
7:15 p.m.	Unidentified black male pays for drinks with credit card.
7:20 p.m.	Unidentified black male passes manila folder to Matthews, who places it in his briefcase.
7:25 p.m.	Both parties leave the premises.
7:30 p.m.	Bartender is interviewed. The name on the charge slip for the drinks is Arnold Masterson, card number xxxx-xxxx-xxxx-xxxx.

When someone is engaged in personal observation, the intent is to catch a perpetrator in the act. There is no intent to investigate how a fraud is being concealed or how the proceeds are spent because there is no need to do so – witnessing a fraud is far better evidence than compiling circumstantial evidence about it.

Personal observation is an expensive technique, so its use may be limited by the investigatory budget. Given its cost, this approach is usually limited to situations in which the amount of loss is suspected to be high, or when other alternative approaches have failed.

Physical Evidence

The collection of physical evidence includes an examination for fingerprints, identification numbers on stolen property, tire tracks, and any other types of tangible evidence related to fraudulent activities. The collection of physical evidence is relatively rare in fraud cases, with the exception of the theft of fixed assets or inventory. In other cases where cash is stolen or financial results are manipulated, there is little physical evidence to obtain.

One type of physical evidence that *is* used in many fraud investigations is searches of electronic records, which is called computer forensics. In particular, e-mail records may be searched for communications between colluding parties that contain allusions to any prior or ongoing frauds. When the information needed for a search of electronic records is located on a hard drive, the fraud team should follow these steps as part of the process of gaining evidence:

1. Ensure that there is a legal right to seize the hardware.
2. Have witnesses on hand when seizing the hardware.

3. Copy the entire contents of the hard drive to a second storage device. This should be a bit-for-bit copy, so that even deleted files on the hard drive will be copied. These deleted files can later be recovered.
4. Validate that the data on the clone device matches the data on the original hard drive.
5. Seal the original hard drive as legal evidence.
6. Search the data on the clone device. This can include examinations of Internet activity logs, chat logs, bookmarks, on-line data storage, and the trash can, in addition to the usual file searches. An automated search can also be used that peruses the entire hard drive for keywords.
7. Extract deleted files with a recovery utility.

It is especially important to clone the hard drive, since there is a good chance any investigative techniques performed on the drive could damage or alter the data. Also, working on the original hard drive would introduce the suspicion in legal proceedings that the data on the drive might have been altered.

Testimonial Evidence

One form of evidence is testimonial, where a fraud investigator interviews individuals to obtain information. Interviews are addressed in the Fraud Interviewing Techniques chapter.

Invigilation

There are situations in which fraud is suspected, but the best efforts of the investigation team cannot tease out the nature of the fraud. If so, a possibility is to use invigilation, which means that a tight watch is kept over the area in which fraud appears to be occurring. For example, a warehouse could be flooded with security personnel, or a CPA firm could take up residence in the accounting department. When invigilation is used, whoever is committing fraud will presumably stop doing so in order to avoid detection. This means that a proper baseline can be established for the results of the area when fraud is *not* present. Then the additional oversite is removed, so that operations return to normal and the fraud presumably returns. The operations in the area can then be compared to the baseline results when the high level of oversite was present, which may allow the investigative team to spot the nature of the fraud.

EXAMPLE

The owner of an outboard motor company has seen the profit level in his business drastically decline over the past few years. A CPA friend suggests that he tell his employees that the company is looking into a factoring arrangement with a local lender, so there will be an auditing team in the accounting department, examining receivables.

A local CPA firm is hired to pose as the audit team. Once they have left, the owner examines the financial statements and finds that customer returns declined during the invigilation period from 4% of sales to 0.2% of sales. Further investigation reveals that the warehouse manager has been dating one of the billing clerks. The warehouse manager was stealing motors, while the billing clerk covered up the theft by issuing credit memos to document the return of supposedly defective motors from customers.

Clearly, invigilation is quite expensive, since it involves a large amount of manual oversite for a period of time. To control the cost, it should be used only within very specific parts of a business, thereby reducing the associated labor cost. Before using it, the investigation team should devote a considerable amount of time to measuring every possible aspect of the target area, so that the before-and-after analysis will be most likely to pick up anomalies that are indicators of fraud.

The Need for Objectivity

A fraud investigation can be quite a tense undertaking. It can impact the investigators, co-workers, those committing the fraud, and their families and friends. Consequently, those conducting the investigation should be quite sure of their facts before taking the additional step of making allegations to a suspect. Up until that point, investigators must be guarded in their discussions with anyone, since rumors will permeate the organization in short order. In addition, the investigators must focus on obtaining evidence that clearly indicates the name of the crime and who perpetrated it; this calls for a high level of objectivity in examining evidence, understanding where there are weaknesses in the case, and calling for additional activities to build a solidly facts-based case. Further, all information collected should be independently corroborated, thereby ensuring that the information is accurate and complete.

When the investigators issue a report regarding the outcome of their investigation, they should not only include information pointing to the guilty party, but also any evidence indicating that the person might *not* be guilty. Doing so results in the most objective fraud investigation, showing that all possible alternatives were considered, including an examination of other possible causes of a fraud.

The Need for Investigation Secrecy

One reason for circumspection in conducting a fraud investigation is that the perpetrators will be alerted by unusual investigatory activities in the office. If so, they will likely attempt to destroy or hide evidence, as well as manufacture alibis, making it more difficult to prove a case against them.

Involving the Police

It is not sufficient to simply notify the police when a fraud has been uncovered, and hand off the remaining investigatory and prosecution work to them. The police may have many other crimes to investigate, and so may not have the resources to devote to the situation. If so, the police may elect to not pursue the matter further. Instead, the company's investigative team should engage in a thorough investigation and fully document its findings before handing the matter off to the police. Ideally, this may include a signed confession by the perpetrator, thereby giving the police an open-and-shut case that consumes the minimum amount of their resources.

Signed Confessions

It is particularly important to obtain a signed confession whenever possible. Not only does this make it easier to convince law enforcement to participate in the investigation, but it also assists greatly with obtaining payments under an employee dishonesty insurance claim. Otherwise, an insurer may require an exorbitant amount of additional investigation being paying, or may try to force settlement for a much smaller amount.

Summary

It should be evident from the discussion in this chapter that the bulk of all fraud investigation work is conducted as quietly and discretely as possible. By doing so, the fraud examination team can methodically work its way through piles of information, accumulating documents, testimony, and physical evidence before finally taking the step of interviewing the suspected perpetrator. By the time this final interview takes place, the team should have assembled a solid case that the interviewee cannot wriggle away from. A discussion of how to engage in this final interview is included in a later chapter.

Chapter 8
Investigation of Concealment and Conversion

Introduction

A particularly difficult aspect of fraud detection is attempting to locate it when the person committing fraud is actively attempting to conceal the activity. A perpetrator usually conceals fraud by altering or destroying the documentary evidence that would normally be used to identify the fraud. Since documents form a key part of the case against anyone accused of fraud, it is essential for a fraud investigator to understand how a document trail works, how these documents should be organized when preparing a case, how to research a persons' background and assets, and several related topics. We cover these issues in the following sections.

The Chain of Custody

The chain of custody is the concept that a record must be maintained that notes the receipt of each document, as well as every transfer of that evidence from person to person. This record should include the following:

- The conditions under which the document was gathered;
- The identity of all handlers of the document;
- The duration of the custody period;
- The security used when handling and storing the document; and
- The manner in which the document is transferred to each subsequent custodian.

It should also be provable that no one outside of this group could have had access to the evidence. From the perspective of maintaining the purity of the documentation, it therefore makes sense to minimize the number of transfers.

When a document is received, a copy should be made that can then be used as part of the investigation and subsequent trial. The original should be preserved in a transparent envelope, with the date of receipt stated on the outside of the envelope. The original may be used during the trial.

Photocopies are considered secondary evidence, behind original documents. This is because photocopies are subject to manipulation, which is especially common when a perpetrator is intent upon concealing his or her fraud. They are only used when the originals were lost or destroyed, in the custody of a third party that refuses to produce them, or being held by a government entity.

Organizing the Evidence

There can be a vast number of documents associated with a fraud case, especially when the fraud was running for a long period of time. One way to deal with these documents is to store them in a document depository. To keep track of these documents, a few keywords are extracted from each document and entered into an index, along with a unique document number that traces back to the underlying document. Then, when information is needed, a user can peruse the index for applicable keywords, which leads back to specific documents. A more advanced form of a document depository is to scan all applicable documents and then use optical character recognition to index every word on all documents, resulting in the ultimate searchable database.

With a completely searchable database, it is much easier to peruse the information, looking for connections between the various documents. Link analysis software is available that can automatically scan electronic documents, looking for linkages that can assist in a fraud investigation. The output from these packages can include timelines for when documented actions took place, linkages between different people, documents that center around certain locations, and so forth.

When creating a document depository, metadata (which describes other data) should be recorded for each document. This metadata can be used to better identify the documents. Examples of useful metadata are:

- A summary of the document contents
- The date on which a document was created
- Identification number of the document
- The date on which a document was obtained
- The location from which a document was extracted

The identification number assigned to a document may be derived from the *Bates numbering* system. Bates numbering is a method used to label legal documents with unique numbers. These numbers were originally designated using Bates stamps, which were stamping devices that automatically advanced the stamp number by one digit every time the device was used to stamp a document. When Bates numbering is used on Portable Document Format (PDF) files, each file is tagged with an arbitrary unique identifier. This identifier may be solely numeric, or alphanumeric. Software can also create an electronic identification stamp that superimposes a unique numeric or alphanumeric value on an electronic document.

Document Examination

Documents can be closely reviewed by document examiners to determine whether they have been tampered with. This investigation may be warranted when there is evidence of damage to or alteration of a document, such as an erasure, disguised writing, torn pages, several ink colors, inconsistencies within the document, and so forth. This review can be used to reach a number of conclusions, including the following:

- The identity of the forger
- The nature of the copy machines used to make a photocopy
- Whether a document has been altered by adding or deleting text or graphics
- Whether a signature has been forged
- Whether an envelope was opened and re-sealed
- Whether copies of the document were made
- Whether identification photos were adjusted or replaced
- Whether pages have been substituted
- Whether printing was added after a document was signed
- Whether the age of the paper matches the date of the document
- Whether the writing in a document is genuine

Conversion and Incarceration Information Sources

When a person uses stolen assets to acquire goods or pay down debts, this leaves a paper trail. In addition, there are several databases in which one can search for evidence that a person has been incarcerated in the past, which can provide a clue that the person may engage in fraud. In the following sub-sections, we describe a number of these sources of information.

National Crime Information Center

The NCIC is operated by the Federal Bureau of Investigation (FBI). The NCIC database is massive, covering many topics pertaining to fraud, including the following:

- *Boat file*. Contains records about stolen boats.
- *License plate file*. Contains records about stolen license plates.
- *Securities file*. Contains records about stolen, embezzled, or counterfeit securities.
- *Vehicle and boat parts file*. Contains records about stolen vehicle and boat parts.
- *Vehicle file*. Contains records about stolen vehicles and vehicles that may be seized based on a federally issued court order.

The NCIC can only be accessed by law enforcement authorities, so they must be involved in a fraud investigation in order to access the database.

Interstate Identification Index

The Interstate Identification Index (III) is a national index that contains the criminal histories of offenders within the United States. The system is maintained by the FBI. The system is intended for use by all state justice agencies, which can verify the states in which a person has a criminal history. A researcher can then access the databases of the applicable states via the National Law Enforcement Telecommunications System for more detailed information. In addition, the index contains millions of fingerprint identification cards for those persons who have been jailed in the past.

The III can only be accessed by law enforcement authorities, so they must be involved in a fraud investigation in order to access the index.

Federal Inmate Database

There is a good chance that someone suspected of having committed fraud has served time in a federal prison or correctional institution. To see if this is the case, access the Federal Bureau of Prisons (www.bop.gov) and run a search by inmate name or identification number. The database contains records for inmates going back to 1982. For information about incarcerations prior to 1982, contact the National Archives Records Administration (www.archives.gov), which will conduct a manual search of the records.

When searching for inmate records at state or local prisons, the governing entity must be contacted for information, rather than the Federal Bureau of Prisons.

Tax Returns

Someone engaged in fraud will probably not record stolen assets on a tax return. Instead, tax records are more useful for proving the falsification of a tax return because it did *not* contain income from the theft of these assets. The Internal Revenue Service (IRS) does not release tax returns to the public. However, they can be accessed by law enforcement officials; again, this means notifying the police of the existence of a fraud in order to gain access to records.

State-Level Information

A significant amount of information is maintained at the state level that can be used in a fraud investigation. The attorney general's office in each state stores records about anyone who has been convicted under the state's laws. This information could be fairly basic.

Another good source is the secretary of state's office in each state. These offices manage publicly-available online databases of information about all of the business entities registered in their state. This information includes the bylaws, articles of incorporation, and registered agent of each entity. Depending on the information provided, these databases can be used to establish who owns a business, and the names of people serving on its board of directors. This information can be used to establish the existence of dummy corporations that are being used to hide assets, as well as situations in which a person has a conflict of interest. For example, a records search might indicate that a company's buyer is the owner of a key supplier.

A seller may create a security agreement between the buyer and seller that states the rights of each party in regard to the asset. The seller then files a UCC-1 financing statement with the required government office (usually the secretary of state) to publicly reveal the presence of a lien on the asset. Doing so gives the seller seniority over other creditors who might also file liens against the asset at a later date; this is known as *perfecting* the lien. When conducting research, consider reviewing all applicable UCC-1 filings to see if any assets held by an individual are being used as collateral on a loan or lease. This information may be available on-line through the office of the applicable secretary of state, or on physical records at the local county clerk's office.

For a small fee, the state departments of motor vehicles (DMVs) will issue basic information about a driver and any vehicles registered to that name. However, information requests may have to be made in person, and DMV responses may be quite late. Given the low cost-benefit of this approach, it could be limited to more protracted investigations where it is necessary to determine the rightful owner of a vehicle to be repossessed.

County-Level Information

Many fraud-related crimes result in a recordation in a criminal database at the county level. These records are not necessarily uploaded into a state-level database. Since there are more than 3,000 counties in the United States, it is not efficient to conduct searches for all counties in order to find out whether a person has any prior convictions. A better approach is to use a person's social security number to search for the past addresses at which the individual has lived. Then conduct a search of the county criminal records for just the counties in which those addresses are located.

Divorce Information

Though not always available to the public, a divorce filing can be a treasure-trove of information, since it contains a net worth statement that describes all assets.

Probate Court Information

Probate court records can provide details about inheritances received. When a suspect claims that his or her suddenly extravagant lifestyle was supported by an inheritance, probate records can be examined to see if the claimed inheritance actually exists.

Professional Licensing Information

If a suspect is certified by a state organization, the certifying agency should have contact information, assuming that the person has an interest in continuing to use his or her certification. The following table contains a sampling of professions for which licenses may be required.

Professions Requiring Licenses

Architect	Dentist	Pharmacist
Barber	Doctor	Private investigator
Beautician	Engineer	Public accountant
Chiropractor	Financial planner	Real estate agent
Construction contractor	Insurance agent	Real estate appraiser
Cosmetologist	Nurse	Therapist

Where this information can be especially useful from a fraud investigation perspective is that complaints may have been filed with the certifying organization against a person who is registered with the organization. This gives the investigator a better idea of the propensity of a suspect to engage in fraud over a period of time. If investigations were conducted by the certifying organization in the past, this information might be available for review.

Rental Information

Contact the individual's former landlord. When applying to rent an apartment, the landlord probably required the person to fill out a credit application, which could contain a variety of useful information.

SEC Filings

The Securities and Exchange Commission (SEC) monitors publicly-held companies, and posts all of their filings on its website at www.sec.gov. The site contains a vast amount of information, but only for companies that are current in their filings as publicly-held companies.

A publicly-held company is required to issue the Form 10-K to report the results of its fiscal year. The Form 10-K includes not just the financial statements, but also a number of additional disclosures. The Form 10-Q is used to report quarterly results, and contains a subset of the information found in the Form 10-K.

In addition, any material events that arise during the year must be filed on the Form 8-K within four business days of each event. Depending on the size and activity level of a business, there may be quite a large number of these forms available for examination. Examples of the events that may be covered within a Form 8-K are:

- A change in the certifying accountant used by the entity
- Bankruptcy or receivership of the business
- Entry into or termination of a material agreement
- Material impairments of assets
- Material modifications to the rights of security holders
- Non-reliance on previously issued financial statements or a related audit report
- The creation of a direct financial obligation
- The departure of directors or officers
- The disposition of assets
- The submission of matters to a vote of security holders
- Triggering events that accelerate or increase a direct financial obligation

The SEC requires corporate insiders to file periodic reports with the SEC, disclosing their holdings in the company and any changes in that ownership. Form 3 states the initial ownership of company securities by a corporate insider, while Form 4 is used to reveal changes in ownership of a company's securities. These forms identify each security, the amount and price at which they were acquired or sold, and the nature of the ownership situation. This information can be quite useful for determining the net worth of a suspect. Also, tracking the timing of purchases and sales can be used to generate a case that a person illicitly acted on insider information for personal gain.

Tax Assessor Information

The county tax assessor may have records of the owners of property that has been assessed. This information is not always available in on-line databases, and so may require more time-consuming on-site research to obtain. A fraud examiner could use these records to estimate the value of the real estate holdings of a suspect, which could be used to determine the individual's net worth. The records may also indicate when liens were removed from real estate, which may indicate a large loan pay down by a suspect.

Title Information

A title company may allow paid inquiries into the existence of property held by an individual, possibly for an entire state.

Voter Registration Information

The local city or county government maintains a list of registered voters, stating names, addresses, and birth dates. Though it may be necessary to access this information in person, the resulting information could be quite worthwhile, since it indicates where a person lives, and possibly their social security number.

Acquaintances Information

A suspect tends to be much less guarded in sharing information with friends, relatives, business associates, and neighbors. Though it can be difficult to extract information from this group, it can also result in valuable leads, such as the existence of additional assets or admissions of guilt made to the acquaintances.

Trash Analysis

It is legal to inspect a person's trash once it leaves the premises of the individual's home. If a suspect does not shred key documents, it is entirely possible that valuable tax records, bank statements, credit card statements, and other documents can be extracted from a trash bin.

Fee-based Search Tools

The Internet is full of search tools. A few are entirely free, in which case expect the amount of information provided to be more limited, and the sites to be full of ads. Better search information is available from on-line databases that charge fees on either a per-report or subscription basis. The following table contains some of the more popular sources of information.

On-Line Sources of Information

accurint.com	experian.com	microbilt.com
cbcinnovis.com	inetcreditexchange.com	peoplefinders.com
dnb.com	intelius.com	transunion.com
equifax.com	lexisnexis.com	whitepages.com

Investigations Related to Mail Fraud

When engaged in investigations, it is useful to consider how a perpetrator might have employed the U.S. postal system. When anything related to a fraud situation passes through the postal system, the perpetrator is violating one or more mail fraud statutes, and so can be prosecuted under those statutes. For example:

- A kickback payment is sent through the mail from a supplier to a buyer.
- An employee creates a fake "ghost" employee, and uses the mail system to send payments to the ghost employee.
- An employee steals a check sent in by a customer, and redirects it into her own bank account – by mailing it to her bank.

When determining whether mail fraud has occurred, it can be useful to contact the U.S. Postal Inspection Service (www.postalinspectors.uspis.gov). This service describes itself as follows:

> U.S. Postal Inspectors are federal law enforcement officers who carry firearms, make arrests, execute federal search warrants, and serve subpoenas. Inspectors work with U.S. Attorneys, other law enforcement, and local prosecutors to investigate cases and prepare them for court. Inspectors throughout the country enforce roughly 200 federal laws related to crimes that adversely affect or entail fraudulent use of the U.S. Mail, the postal system, postal employees, and customers.

> The Postal Inspection Service operates a National Forensic Laboratory crime laboratory staffed with forensic scientists and technical specialists. They assist Inspectors in analyzing evidentiary material needed for identifying and tracing criminal suspects and in providing expert testimony for cases brought to trial.

Calculating the Amount Stolen

A key focus of the preceding data collection activities is to formulate an estimate of how the net worth of a suspect has changed. Net worth is the assets owned by a person, minus all liabilities owed by the individual. For example, if a person owns a $500,000 house and owes $350,000 under the terms of an outstanding mortgage, then her net worth is $150,000. What is of particular interest to the fraud examiner is the extent to which a person's net worth has changed since the fraud is suspected to have begun. When the change in net worth is combined with a suspect's estimated annual living expenses, this results in an estimate of the amount of income that the person realized.

The amount of income realized is then reduced by her take-home pay from the company to arrive at the amount of income that must have been earned from other sources. These other sources are presumed to be the amount stolen, unless other sources (such as dividend income, gifts, or an inheritance) can be proven. Thus, the series of calculations used to determine the amount stolen is as follows:

1. **Net worth** = Assets − liabilities

2. **Change in net worth** = Net worth in year 2 − net worth in year 1

3. **Income generated** = Change in net worth + estimated living expenses

4. **Other sources of income** = Income generated − take-home pay

---

EXAMPLE

Mr. Snyder is the controller of Kelvin Corporation. He is suspected of having stolen funds from the company for the past year. A fraud examiner is discretely hired and charged with developing an independent calculation of the amount that may have been stolen by Mr. Snyder.

A record search indicates that Snyder's assets one year ago were approximately $480,000, while his liabilities were $310,000, resulting in a net worth of $170,000. His present net worth has ballooned to $600,000, which represents a $430,000 change in net worth in one year. In addition, an analysis of his current lifestyle indicates that he has committed to a golf club membership and taken up polo lessons, resulting in estimated living expenses of $300,000. When the change in net worth and estimated living expenses are combined, this results in an estimated amount of income generated of $730,000.

Mr. Snyder's take-home pay is $80,000, which leaves other sources of income of $650,000. He is then presented with this information, and validly shows that he generated an additional $10,000 of income from dividends, as well as $25,000 from gambling winnings. This leaves unexplained income of $615,000. He then confesses to stealing funds from the company.

The calculation of the amount stolen tends to yield a conservative outcome, because many purchases are difficult to document. For example, a person could spend an inordinate amount on jewelry or fine dining, and yet leave little trace of these purchases that an investigator can find.

Summary

When documents relating to a fraud investigation are found, they must be properly handled, identified, and stored, or else they may not be allowed in court, thereby damaging the prosecution of a case. It is especially important to properly show how documents may have been altered so that perpetrators could conceal their actions.

A vast amount of evidence may be found within a company, including such documents as purchase orders, credit memos, invoices, and cancelled checks. Nonetheless, an investigation may call for an examination of information located *outside* the business, residing in any number of online, federal, state, and local databases, some of which may only be available through in-person searches. These searches are particularly useful for locating newly-acquired assets or debt payments that a person has only been able to afford as the result of an act of fraud. This information can then be used to make estimates of the amount of assets that may have been stolen.

Chapter 9
Fraud Interviewing Techniques

Introduction

An interview is used in many fraud investigations to obtain information. This approach involves a considerable amount of preparation to ensure that the correct topics are covered. When used appropriately, interviewing can result in the collection of highly specific information pertaining to a fraud investigation, including:

- Information about the motivations of the suspect
- Information about how a fraud was conducted
- Leads that can be used to collect additional information elsewhere

Sometimes, interviewing can result in a direct confession by the perpetrator of a fraud. We discuss all aspects of interviewing in the following sections.

The Ideal Interviewer

Some fraud examiners have an exceptional ability to dig into data and extract evidence of fraud. This focus on documents, common among introverts, does not necessarily translate into an ability to conduct interviews. Instead, the ideal interviewer needs a completely different set of characteristics, which are:

- *Sets people at ease.* Discussing fraud is a difficult topic that can cause people to tighten up and be unwilling to make comments. The ideal interviewer is able to settle down a nervous person, which allows the interviewee to impart more information. The ability to calm a person can include acting in a low-key and informal manner. For example, the interviewer is relaxed and nods when the interviewee makes a statement.
- *Draws people out.* Even a willing interviewee may only be prepared to pass along a certain amount of information. The ideal interviewer listens carefully to what they say, and is then able to develop additional questions on the spot that are designed to extract even more information.
- *Shows interest.* An interviewee is more likely to dredge up additional information if the interviewer expresses interest in them. This involves listening intently and asking questions or making comments at pertinent times in order to show that the interviewer is closely following what is being said.
- *Unbiased.* An interviewee will stop talking if it appears that the interviewer is merely trying to confirm what he already believes regarding the case. Consequently, the ideal interviewer must appear as nonjudgmental as possible.

Within the structure of the preceding characteristics, the ideal interviewer should also be businesslike. This means being polite and professional, without talking down to the interviewee. Once the interview has been completed, the interviewer expresses appreciation for the time spent by the interviewee, and for the information given.

Types of Interviewees

Many people may be interviewed as part of a fraud investigation, since even those with a seemingly distant association with a crime can still provide valuable information. Examples of people who could be interviewed are:

- The victims of the fraud, since they can provide details about how the fraud was conducted.
- Informants, since they have worked closely with the suspect, and so have the most detailed information about how the fraud was perpetrated.
- Expert witnesses, whose experience can be drawn upon to form a picture of the control weaknesses that may have allowed a fraud to occur, as well as details about how the fraud was conducted.
- Coworkers can be excellent interviewees, since they may have worked with the suspect for a long time, and have a deep understanding of his habits, motivations, and so forth.
- The friends and family of the suspect may be interviewed in order to determine the motivations that could have triggered a fraud situation, as well as to understand the lifestyle changes resulting from the fraud.
- The suspect can be the most critical person in this list of interviewees, since it may be possible to elicit a confession, as well as the details of how a fraud was conducted.

The Ideal Interview

Interviews can provide valuable information, but only if they are conducted in a certain way. The fraud examiner should strive to engage in interviews that have the following characteristics:

- *Duration.* The interview should be long enough to collect all relevant information. This means that the examiner should block out quite a long period of time for each interview, and be prepared to delve into every possible aspect of the fraud situation so that every nugget of information is uncovered.
- *Focus.* The interview remains focused on fact-finding, rather than allowing divergences from the key topics. An interviewee may engage in rants or explanations that are not needed, or may try to shift attention elsewhere. The interviewer must be able to shrug off these topics and remain focused on the key items.
- *Timing.* The fraud examiner needs to conduct interviews as soon as possible after the initial notification of a fraud event. By doing so, interviewee

memories of events are still relatively fresh, so that inaccuracies in their recollections are avoided.

Interview Planning

To obtain the highest-quality information from an interview, the interviewer should be as prepared as possible. This means reviewing all available information about the fraud as of the interview date, while also learning about the person to be interviewed. This includes understanding the type of crime committed, when it happened, and possible motives, as well as understanding the background of the interviewee and the person's attitude towards the investigation.

Another consideration is how to develop a roster of individuals to interview. One approach is to begin by interviewing people within the firm, and then shift to interviews of outsiders, using information learned from outsiders to confirm what was said within the firm. The reverse approach can also be used, starting with outsiders to gather background information. Another variation is to start with interviews of those most central to the investigation, and then talk to non-key personnel for confirming statements. This approach can be reversed by starting with non-key personnel to build up a baseline knowledge of the situation prior to engaging in any discussions with key personnel. Any of these approaches can work, depending on the circumstances, though it is generally better to talk to more peripheral people first to gather background information; doing so increases one's understanding of the issues before talking to those most closely associated with the targeted area.

The interviewer usually schedules interviews in the office of each interviewee. This is done to make the interviewee feel more comfortable, as well as to allow the person ready access to any documents that may be located in the office or nearby.

The Interview

There are a number of elements that an interviewer should consider when conducting fraud-related interviews. We discuss each one in the following sub-sections.

Interactions with Friendly Interviewees

The interviewer starts a conversation with a friendly interviewee by introducing himself and stating who he works for, and then spending a few moments to establish some level of rapport with the interviewee. The interviewer then states the reason for the interview in general terms, and asks if the person is willing to cooperate. The intent at this stage is to avoid making an interviewee feel threatened, while giving the impression that they can assist by helping the investigation. A reasonable statement that follows these guidelines is:

> **Interviewer:** [shakes hands] Hi, my name is ___. I work in the corporate department. They've sent me over here to work on a special project, and I need your help on part of the work. Can we chat about it for a few minutes?

Interviewee: Certainly.

Interviewer: Great, thanks. I'm looking into some paperwork issues involving shipments. Can you help me with this?

Interviewee: Yes.

In the preceding example, the interviewer uses the concept of a special project as the excuse for the meeting. Other possible reasons to provide to the interviewee are that the meeting is part of a special-purpose audit, a process improvement study, or an internal control study, or that the interviewer wants to understand further details about a specific transaction. In all cases, the intent is to provide a reasonably plausible excuse for the meeting.

The interviewer then proceeds to the gathering of facts about the case. This process takes the form of non-confrontational questions, so that interviewees will be more inclined to answer as fully as possible. The best way to structure these questions is in an open format, where more than a "yes" or "no" answer is needed to fully respond. By using open questions, the interviewer can collect a large amount of information within a short period of time. Examples of open questions are:

Please tell me about the process flow for how goods are shipped to customers.

Please describe how the petty cash custodian is supposed to handle requests for reimbursement.

Please go over the approval process for credit memos granted to customers.

Please tell me about the procedures you follow when an error is detected in a customer payment.

When you process payroll, what types of controls are built into the approval process?

Tip: Try to avoid using a prepared list of questions. Instead, allow the conversation to flow wherever the discussion leads. This approach tends to result in higher-quality information. However, it is acceptable to go into an interview with a list of the general topics to be covered, just to ensure that those topics *are* covered.

A less useful question format is the closed question, which can be answered with a "yes" or "no" response or some other very specific answer. Examples of closed questions are:

Is your name Helen?

According to your personnel record, you have worked here since May. Is that correct?

At what time of the day did you see him leave the counting room?

Whatever type of question is used, the typical interviewing sequence is to employ them first to collect a high level of general information, so that the interviewer can establish the scope of the information being covered. The next step is to drill deeper into selected topics that are of the most interest to the interviewer. This approach allows one to minimize the amount of time wasted talking about areas that are not related to the investigation.

This general-to-specific approach also applies to the use of sensitive questions. The interviewer should begin with non-sensitive, downright bland questions that will not cause offense, in an effort to get the interviewee to open up. Once this occurs, the interviewer gradually inserts more sensitive questions into the discussion. If the individual begins to look uncomfortable with these questions, back off and try to restate the question in a manner that is less threatening. Sensitive questions can be phrased carefully in order to avoid a negative reaction; the following table shows several examples.

Examples of How to Desensitize Questions

Instead of…	…use these words
Who do you think is stealing money?	Where do you think the company is wasting money?
Which managers are abusing their positions?	Are there any parts of the company where you think the control system can be overridden by management?
Do you think someone is stealing inventory?	Are there any areas in which you think controls are weak?

This process of going from non-sensitive to sensitive questions is also useful from the perspective of establishing a behavioral baseline. The interviewer closely observes the reactions of the interviewee when the mildest possible questions are being asked, in order to identify the person's normal behavior. The interviewer can then compare this baseline behavior to how the person reacts when more sensitive topics are covered. A person trying to deceive the interviewer is more likely to display different behaviors as the questions become more sensitive.

At the end of the fact-finding portion of the interview, the interviewer should summarize the information collected and verify that this information is correct. It is quite possible that the interviewee will make some adjustments to the recorded information at this point. If so, retain both the original and revised statements; it is possible that the interviewee's initial statement was correct, and that the restatement is an attempt to lead the interviewer down the wrong track.

Once all information has been collected, the interviewer asks a few closing questions that can be used to obtain additional information. These questions are:

- Is there anything I have not asked that could be relevant?
- Who else should I approach for information?
- Can I call you if I have any additional questions?

166

The interviewer can ask the person to keep the conversation private. Otherwise, the suspect could become aware of the investigation. Also, having rumors flying around the office could damage the reputations of people who are later proven to be innocent.

The interviewer's tone when closing out an interview should be a positive one. By doing so, the interviewee will feel less threatened if the interviewer needs to call the person later for more information.

Interactions with Unfriendly Interviewees

If the interviewer suspects that a person is providing incorrect or misleading information, the questions asked will shift to posing hypothetical questions that can then be used to assess his credibility. If the interviewer believes that the response indicates guilt, it may be acceptable to then ask if the person committed the fraud. To get to this point, it can make sense to encourage the person to talk as much as possible. By doing so, the person is more likely to make up false information on the fly, which can then be examined and challenged.

Assessment questions typically involve statements by the interviewer that an ethically challenged person would agree with, and with which a more honest person would disagree. The interviewer poses these questions and then asks the interviewee whether he agrees. While asking a series of these questions, the interviewer examines the behavior of the subject, both in terms of what they say and how they physically react. Based on the totality of this information, the interviewer may conclude that the person is indeed providing false or misleading information, which may lead to asking the person for an admission of guilt. The following table contains a number of possible assessment questions, along with a discussion of why each question is used.

Sample Assessment Questions

Assessment Question	Discussion
Most people do not want to steal. It's just that the company doesn't pay them enough, so they're forced to steal. What do you think?	A dishonest person would probably agree with this entire statement, while an honest one would point out that low wages do not justify theft.
What do you think is a justifiable reason for someone here to steal inventory?	A dishonest person would likely have a number of reasons that justify theft, since they have been pondering it for some time. An honest person would categorically deny that there is any reason to do so.
What do you think should be the company's response if it finds out that someone has been stealing?	A dishonest person would be more likely to say that the company should give the person a chance to redeem himself, while an honest person would be more likely to advocate firing and prosecution.
What would be your main concern if you were engaged in fraud and it was discovered?	A dishonest person would be more likely to focus on avoiding incarceration, while an honest person would reject the entire notion on the grounds that they have done nothing wrong.

The following verbal and nonverbal items are all indicators that a person may be lying to the interviewer:

- Their denials are not forceful
- Their denials tend to weaken over time
- Their pupils dilate
- Their stories contain conflicting statements
- Their stories are too perfect
- Their use of gestures decreases

- They are less cooperative
- They are more tense
- They blink more frequently
- They cannot remember important facts
- They complain more
- They speak more rapidly

Keep in mind that these indicators are only *possible* signs of deception. People react to stress in different ways, so a strong indicator of deception in one person might only be an indicator of being flustered in another person.

A liar is also more likely to issue qualifiers when denying involvement in a fraud. For example, if a person is asked whether he was in the building on the night of a theft, he might reply with "No, I was not in the building that Friday night," rather than a simple "no" response.

> **Tip:** Do not rely too heavily on the results of assessment questions. Pathological liars do not exhibit the normal reactions of people who are telling falsehoods, nor do children. Also, the cultural norms are different for other cultures, so someone who appears to be lying may simply be following how people in their culture normally interact with others.

There may be situations in which the person to be interviewed reacts poorly to questioning. If so, consider bringing in a second interviewer, so that there is strength in numbers. In a two-against-one situation, the interviewee is less likely to cause trouble.

If a person is likely to be difficult during an interview, consider posing questions in an unlikely sequence, in order to throw the person off what might be a prepared game plan for how to deal with the interview. Also, try not to formally schedule these types of interviews, since the interviewee is more likely to be well-prepared, and may bring legal counsel. Instead, try for a surprise interview with no warning at all.

When more than one person is suspected of engaging in fraudulent activities, it can make sense to interview them all at the same time, but separately in different rooms. By doing so, they will not have time to meet in between interviews to coordinate their stories with what was already said by one of them in an earlier interview. The result may be disparities in their statements that can then be investigated further.

Asking for an Admission of Guilt

If there is a reasonable probability that a person is the perpetrator of a fraud, the interviewer is justified in asking for an admission of guilt. This assessment is based on all of the information obtained thus far in the investigation, including the opinion formed during the preceding steps in the interview.

The initial query is an indirect one that is intended to prompt the suspect to make a statement. For example, the interviewer could hand a copy of a falsified credit memo to the suspect and simply ask if there is anything the person would like to say about it. Or, the interviewer could make a general statement, such as "Is there something you want to tell me about ___," and then wait to see if the person responds. Other variations on the concept use a questioning format that assumes the person committed the crime, thereby implying that the interviewer has absolute confidence in the guilt of the other party. Sample questions are:

- Is this the first time you forged a credit memo, or does it go back further?
- How did you take the inventory out of the building?
- Where did you take the payoff from the supplier?

Instead of a question, the interviewer can make a statement, such as "we have investigated the situation and established that you took money from a supplier," and then wait to see how the person responds.

An innocent person is more likely to strongly deny an accusation of this kind, whereas a guilty person is more likely to issue a weak denial or stay silent. If the latter reaction occurs, repeat the accusation. If the person continues to issue denials, interrupt him and continue with variations on the original accusation. Otherwise, once they have completed a denial, they are more likely to stick with it.

An innocent person will not accept the underlying assumption in these questions, that he is guilty. Conversely, guilty people will believe that there is no further point in hiding, since they have already been found out.

If a person continues to offer up denials, then it is time to start producing evidence. Start with relatively minor items and work up to larger and more damaging evidence, so that the person is gradually faced with a compilation of overwhelming evidence that refutes all possible denials. It is also possible to hint that there are witnesses available who will testify against the person in court. There is no need to continue presenting evidence past the point where the suspect stops issuing denials.

Once the interviewer has made an accusation and the suspect has stopped denying complicity, additional steps must be taken to bring the person to the point of making an admission. The interviewer should formulate some reasonably acceptable rationalization for why the person "did the deed" that allows them to face up to the situation. For example, the interviewer could say:

[sighs] I'm sure you would not have done this without a good reason. You deserved that promotion and didn't get it. If they had treated you fairly, you would not have done this. Don't you agree?

The legal bills from your divorce must have been ferocious. I know how it is when the bills pile up. You never would have done this if the divorce hadn't happened. Don't you agree?

You've been a great employee here for a long time, and I'll bet you worked hard to be so trusted. I don't think you would normally do this, it's so out of character. So you must have been forced into it. Don't you agree?

You are the best salesman in this company. I know that management has put you under a lot of pressure to increase sales – too much pressure, if you ask me. There is only so much pressure to perform that anyone can take. That's what triggered this whole incident, right?

You were so close to turning around the company from that bankruptcy a few years back, and then the board of directors cut off your additional funding. That must have been so frustrating. I would totally understand it if you decided to get back at them for what they did. That's what happened here, right?

It isn't like you took anything from a co-worker or a customer, right? I can see how you thought it was really just the government, and who cares about them? Isn't that right?

In the greater scheme of things, this must seem pretty minor. A few dollars from petty cash doesn't even come close to the financial shenanigans that bankers do every day, right?

I know there would have been problems for the company if you had not made those alterations to the financial statements. So, really, you were trying to protect a lot of jobs. Otherwise, the banks would have called their loans and that would have been it. So, you were trying to help the other employees, right?

At this point in the interview, the suspect may have fallen silent under the weight of the statement made and evidence presented. However, no admission has yet been made. One way to generate a statement of admission is to present a question that has either a "yes" or a "no" answer – and both of which state the guilt of the interviewee. For example:

Did you just want the money when you saw it lying there, or was it because you wanted to get back at them because of that bad performance review?

Did you just go ahead and take the inventory, or did your friends put you up to this?

Did you ask the supplier for money, or did they make the offer to you?

The worse of the two alternatives is stated first, so the suspect usually takes the second option as a "better" admission. Either way, the person has confessed to the crime. If this approach does not create a response, keep using variations on the concept to see if a different question will work.

The preceding steps will frequently result in an admission. If so, the interviewer needs to obtain the details of how the fraud was conducted. A good way to start is to first obtain a high-level view of the fraud, so the interviewer should focus on obtaining such information as:

- The amount of money or other assets that were stolen
- The motive behind the fraud
- Who else was involved in the fraud
- Where the funds or assets are now located

Gaining a reasonably accurate estimate of the amount of money taken can be particularly hard, since suspects tend to underestimate the amount. This may require an additional exchange with the person in order to narrow down the range of losses that the business has suffered. The interviewer should start with a high estimate and then work downward in response to the reactions of the individual. For example:

Interviewer: How much money do you think is now missing?

Suspect: I don't know.

Interviewer: Was it as much as $500,000?

Suspect: No, that is way too high.

Interviewer: How about $100,000?

Suspect: No, more like $10,000 to $20,000.

Interviewer: Are you sure about that?

Suspect: Well, no more than $20,000.

It is useful to learn about the person's motives for conducting the fraud, which fleshes out the documentation of the case. This information will not be forthcoming unless the interviewer asks. The following example illustrates how this information might be obtained.

So far, we've covered some possibilities for why you did this. But I need to hear it from you – why do you think you did this?

There may be instances in which several people conspired to engage in fraud. If so, the interviewer needs to know who else was involved, so that the entire group can be rolled up. There are several ways to ask about this, such as:

Did you talk about this with anyone else?

Who else knows about this?

Did anyone else work with you on this?

This range of questions may result in several names, including co-conspirators and people who took no action to halt the fraud.

Part of the discussion should cover where the funds or assets are now located. The theft usually involves cash, which means that the most likely storage place is the person's bank account. Accordingly, have him sign a written authorization that allows the examiner access to the suspect's bank records. A key question to ask is where the person maintains bank accounts, in case there are more accounts than the fraud examination team is already aware of. Depending on the types of assets stolen, additional inquiries may be necessary, such as:

What happened to the cash?

How much of the amount is left?

Once this general information has been obtained, the interviewer can work on filling in the details. This may involve having the person describe what happened in chronological order or by individual transaction, or a combination of the two. Use whichever method results in the most information. As more details are added, the interviewer may find that there are discrepancies in the admission, which could be lies that the person has inserted. If so, keep asking questions to resolve these issues and drill down to the truth. If the person has unclear memories of certain items, then produce whatever documentary evidence is needed to jog their memories.

If the suspect makes an admission, this is a legally binding statement. However, there is a risk that the person will later seek to back away from his verbal statement. Consequently, it is better to obtain a written statement, acknowledging that the person committed the fraud in question. The interviewer can prepare this document in advance, and present it to the person making a confession for a signature. If changes are made to the document, note them in ink on the document, and have all parties initial it. The best confession statements clearly acknowledge that the person knew the fraudulent action was wrong, and intended to commit the act. The statement should also include the date range during which the crime was committed, and the approximate amount stolen. A sample statement follows.

SAMPLE ADMISSION STATEMENT

January 15, 20X1
Kansas City, Missouri

I, Andrew Masterson, provide the following free and voluntary statement to Jeffrey Gaskins of Polio Containment. No threats or assurances have been used to prompt this statement.

I am a mail clerk at Polio Containment. Part of my duties include opening the mail, listing all cash and check receipts, creating a copy of this list, and then forwarding the list with the payments to the cashier's office. Beginning in late 20X0 and continuing through the present, I have appropriated roughly $5,000 in cash from the company.

Polio Containment is a nonprofit organization that receives small cash donations in the mail every day. Since donors did not expect an acknowledgment of their donations, I removed the smaller donations from their envelopes each day and destroyed the envelopes, prior to recording all larger cash receipts for use by the cashier's department.

No one knew of these activities. I understand that my actions are illegal and violate the policies of Polio Containment. I engaged in this behavior because I felt that I was severely underpaid, and wanted to bring my compensation up to an acceptable level. I am sorry for my actions and intend to repay the entire amount.

I deposited the cash in my savings account at the Currency Bank branch in Kansas City, Missouri, account number 102001017-014088. I hereby grant permission to representatives of Polio Containment to review the contents of the account for the period from September 1, 20X0 to the present.

I have read this statement. My signature below indicates that I believe this statement to be true and correct to the best of my knowledge.

_____   _____
Signature   Witness

_____   _____
Date   Date

Once the statement has been prepared, the individual should read the entire document and initial each page, indicating that he has read it. Otherwise, the person may later claim that he did not read what he was signing.

It is useful to have two witnesses observe the person when he signs a confession. This reduces the risk of the person claiming that he did not sign the document – that it was forged instead.

Here are several tips for how to conduct an interview when the intent is to seek an admission of guilt:

- Do not lock the door to the room, so that the suspect can leave. This means the person cannot later claim that he was detained against his will.
- Eliminate all extraneous items from the interviewing room, so there is no way for the suspect to distract the attention of the interviewer.
- Do not allow the suspect to sit behind a desk, since this barrier can be used as an emotional crutch.
- Try to avoid including other people, since the suspect is less likely to make a confession in front of a larger number of people.
- Display unshakeable confidence that the suspect is guilty; the suspect is less likely to confess if the interviewer appears uncertain.
- Do not use words such as "crime," "steal," "embezzle," or "fraud" when confronting a suspect, since that can result in a negative reaction.
- Do not show outrage or condescension when a person admits guilt; the intent is to obtain a confession, and condemning a person could interfere with that goal.

Additional Interviewing Rules

There are several additional issues to consider when engaged in interviews. By following these rules, one can achieve more consistent results. They are:

- Always conduct interviews with a high degree of privacy. Otherwise, interviewees will be concerned that their statements will be overheard by co-workers.
- Avoid the use of words that could close down an interviewee. For example, use "we are conducting an inquiry" instead of "we are conducting an investigation," or "we are looking into a paperwork issue" instead of "we are looking into a possible embezzlement scheme."
- Be firm in asking questions. If the interviewer is apologetic for asking certain questions, the interviewee will be less inclined to answer them.
- Delay the more difficult questions for later in the interview. This gives the interviewer more time to build rapport, and for the interviewee to relax.
- Do not interrupt when an interviewee is engaged in a free-flow narrative of events. Such a discussion can reveal a number of valuable items of information; an interruption could result in the person losing track of what they were talking about, so that some information is not revealed.
- Do not rush the discussion. Some interviewees need time to collect their thoughts before answering a question.
- Do not try to help a person remember the details. Doing so could plant false memories. Instead, try not to show any facial expressions or body language indicating that the interviewer is looking for a specific answer.

- Minimize the use of note-taking, since it can interfere with the interview. Instead, get permission from the interviewee to record the session, or only jot down key words related to the main points of the interview.
- Mix in questions that can be answered with a simple "yes." By doing so, interviewees are continually buying into the discussion.
- Only interview one person at a time. Otherwise, they may influence each other's statements.
- Set up a seating arrangement where the interviewee's entire body can be seen. This is useful for noting changes in his body signals as various questions are asked during the interview.

Activities Following the Interview

Once an interview has been completed, the interviewer should immediately write down all of the information received during the interview. Doing so ensures that the details are captured while her memories of the interview are still fresh. Conducting two interviews back-to-back is not recommended, since the interviewer might then mix up the information obtained in the two interviews.

The interviewer can also document the nonverbal actions of the interviewee. For example, a more defensive person might lean further away from the interviewer in order to put more space between them. Or, a person who is feeling ashamed will look down, rather than back at the interviewer. Another example is crossing the arms to indicate defensiveness.

Income Questions

When interviewing a suspect, one of the better topics to pursue is where a person's wealth comes from. If the person admits that his or her only source of income is a paycheck, this means there are no inheritances or funds that generate interest income or dividends – and therefore no outside sources of income. This admission can then be used to dig into how the person could have purchased expensive assets. Given enough pressure on this topic, the individual might confess to the theft of company assets.

Lifestyle Questions

It is useful to present a suspect with the fraud examiner's estimate of changes in the suspect's net worth and living expenses during the period of fraud. When the person's take-home pay is subtracted from this increase in wealth, the residual value is an estimate of other sources of income that the person must have. This discussion then feeds into the preceding topic, which is what types of other income sources the person has. If there is no other provable source of income, the suspect is more likely to confess to a theft of assets.

Interviewee Motivations

When interviewing people, be aware of the motivations that may be driving their willingness to impart information. By discerning the underlying motivation, the examiner will know whether the information received is more likely to be skewed or even false. For example:

- *Revenge.* A person might want to exact revenge upon the suspect, perhaps due to a perceived slight, such as negative performance review. If so, the information gleaned from an interview could be heavily skewed or even false.
- *Shifting attention.* The interviewee might be culpable, and wants to shift attention elsewhere. This could result in a range of statements, from slight adjustments to what actually happened to complete falsehoods.
- *Sincere assistance.* The interviewee might simply want to see a wrong corrected, and so is willing to supply every possible detail that might be of assistance to the examiner. These individuals can be quite helpful in providing unbiased information.

Reactions to Fraud

When people first learn about the potential existence of fraud, their reactions tend to pass through a series of predictable stages. The first stage is usually denial that a fraud could have taken place. People want to block out the possibility, and so will spend time exploring alternative avenues that could also explain the loss of assets. When people are in the denial stage, they are more likely to let a perpetrator's employment continue, which results in even more losses. Alternatively, if the perpetrator remains in his job at this point, there is a strong incentive for him to cover up the fraud by destroying evidence.

The second stage in the reaction to fraud occurs when the individual shifts from denying the existence of fraud to coming to grips with the situation – which results in being angry. This anger may be directed at the fraud examiners who are conducting the investigation, at the suspect, or anyone in the immediate vicinity. This can have serious repercussions on an investigation, because people who are angry may reach the wrong conclusion and fire an innocent employee, or fire the perpetrator without attempting to obtain additional information that would have revealed the full extent of the crime.

The third stage is a reversal of the preceding anger stage, where co-workers and managers attempt to rationalize what the perpetrator has done. They may feel that they understand the reasons for the fraud, and so will be more inclined to reduce the penalties that would otherwise be imposed on the individual, or even be willing to give him a second chance. The worst outcome is when a business actually attempts to hire back an employee who was fired during the preceding anger stage, in hopes of redeeming the person.

Next, employees begin to accept that a fraud has occurred and that the suspect did in fact commit the crime. At this point they tend to internalize the event, perhaps blaming themselves for not having prevented the fraud or detected it sooner.

Finally, individuals will accept the situation and be willing to move on from the fraud. At this point, they know what happened, why the perpetrator did it, and the approximate amount stolen. This stage is most easily reached if the fraud was a minor one, but may not be reached for some time if the amount stolen was significant.

An interviewer should be aware of these stages during the investigation of a fraud, since the information obtained during interviews will vary, depending on the stage. For example, if an interviewee is rationalizing what a suspect has done, the information gleaned during an interview may be more favorable toward the suspect. Or, if the person is in a state of denial, then the interviewer may be on the receiving end of a barrage of reasons why the suspect could not have committed the crime. If an interviewee has internalized the event, then he may not be willing to impart much information to the interviewer. It is only when a person has reached the end stage and accepted that a fraud has occurred that the interviewer can expect to have a complete discussion with an interviewee. The best interviewers will be able to nudge interviewees through these stages, thereby accelerating their progression toward accepting the event and cooperating more fully in the fraud examination process.

Integrity Testing

The most common investigative technique is the interview. Depending on the circumstances, it may also be useful to consider some form of integrity testing. The following are a sampling of the different types of integrity tests:

- *Overt tests*. These tests ask a person about their attitudes concerning theft and drug use, and also ask about their honesty and criminal histories. Questions can include the amount and type of theft that a person has engaged in in the past. The intent is to find any undesirable traits in a person. Examples of this type of test are:

  - London House Personnel Selection
  - Phase II Profile
  - Reid Report
  - Stanton Survey

- *Personality-based tests*. These tests identify those personality traits in a test taker that are most commonly associated with theft and other types of counterproductive behavior. The tests focus on the dependability of the test subject, his level of social conformity, conscientiousness, irresponsibility, and interest in engaging in thrill seeking activities. Examples of this type of test are:

  - Hogan Personality Inventory
  - Personnel Reaction Blank

Summary

We cannot place too much emphasis on the need for an experienced fraud interviewer. These types of interviews are difficult to conduct, and may be botched by someone who is unfamiliar with how information can be drawn out of a person during a detailed (and probably lengthy) interview. This is a clear situation in which a trained fraud examiner would be highly beneficial to an investigation.

The interviewing actions noted in this chapter are subject to the latest changes in federal laws or variations in existing local laws from those used at a national level. Consequently, it is essential to consult with legal counsel before undertaking any interviews, and especially before confronting a suspect and asking for an admission of guilt.

Chapter 10
The Fraud Report

Introduction

The next step after an investigation has been completed is to prepare a fraud report. This report includes the following topics:

- All findings of the fraud examination team
- The conclusions reached by the team
- Recommendations for control improvements that will mitigate the risk of having similar types of fraud in the future
- Any corrective actions that have already been made

In this chapter, we describe the contents of a fraud report, along with applicable examples.

Report Tone

The tone of a fraud report should be objective – the focus is on what happened, and does not attempt to be accusatory. All wording that may be construed as subjective or libelous must be purged from the report. Assigning blame is the job of a court of law, not the fraud examiner. This objective tone still allows the fraud examiner to state that an admission was obtained from the suspect, since this is a statement of fact.

The wording used should refer to purported or alleged actions taken, rather than stating the fact that actions were taken. For example:

The investigative team was called in when an informant called the company's fraud hotline with an allegation that inventory was being stolen from the warehouse.

From its review of associated documentation, the investigative team found reasonably credible evidence favoring the alleged activity.

Based on a review of the entire range of documents collected and interviews conducted, the team concludes that there is plausible evidence that supports the allegation.

Sample Text of the Report

In this section, we cover a number of pages that could be included in a fraud report. The report begins with a cover page that states the nature of the report, the name of the organization commissioning the report, and the case file number under which all related documents are indexed. A sample cover page follows.

SAMPLE COVER PAGE

INVESTIGATIVE REPORT
ON ZACH WEBB

HENDERSON INDUSTRIAL

Internal Audit
Case File 004209

The cover page is followed by a case file index that lists the page number on which each document in the investigative report can be found.

One way to begin the report is to state the circumstances under which the fraud situation was initially discovered and the investigation begun. The report is assigned a case file number. A sample of such a page follows.

SAMPLE DISCOVERY PAGE

To: Case File 004209
From: Tom Arrow
Date: January 12, 20X2
Subject: Discovery of Company Goods being Resold

On December 20, 20X1, Gerald Sanders, marketing director of Henderson Industrial, was conducting an Internet search on one of the company's products, the Diamax Oscillator. One link referred Mr. Sanders to a page on the eBay online auction site, which stated that ten of the units were for sale, without the original packaging, and in new condition. The units were selling for approximately $2,000 each, as compared to the normal retail price of $2,500.

These units are normally sold to customers on an individual basis and at a high price, so Mr. Sanders was curious about how many could find their way into the possession of a single seller. He talked to the sales manager, Katie Murdoch, who reviewed the sales records for the Diamax Oscillator. It had only been on the market for a few months, so she was able to verify every sales record. She concluded that it was impossible for one seller to accumulate 10 units if they had been acquired from the company's normal customers. This left the possibility that the units were being stolen from the company's inventory and then sold on the open market.

On December 27, 20X1, these findings were discussed in a meeting at which Tom Arrow (Henderson's internal auditor), Gerald Sanders, Katie Murdoch, and Danielle Liscano (Henderson's legal counsel) were present.

This group commissioned an investigation of the matter, which commenced on December 28, 20X1.

The fact-finding associated with a fraud investigation can cover many separate meetings, each of which should be documented in the report. In all cases, the participants in each meeting should be noted, as well as the date and the salient points covered. A sample interview document follows.

SAMPLE INTERVIEW PAGE

To: Case File 004209
From: Tom Arrow
Date: December 28, 20X1
Subject: Interview with Sandra Chan

Sandra Chan, controller of Henderson Industrial, was interviewed in her office at 123 Main Street, Cambridge, Massachusetts, on December 28, 20X1. Ms. Chan was told the identities of her interviewers, Tom Arrow and Danielle Liscano. Ms. Chan was asked if there were any ways in which multiple units of the Diamax Oscillator product could be removed from the premises without authorization.

Ms. Chan stated that, when the units are completed, they are run through a testing process to ensure that they are functioning properly. If not, a rework tag is completed and the units are sent to the rework shop. In the rework area, the goods are examined to see if they are repairable. If they are, the units are fixed and sent to the finished goods inventory area. If not, a product destruction form is completed and the units are scrapped. All finished goods are stored in a locked inventory area, which is also cycle counted regularly to ensure that the counts are correct. Different cycle counters are assigned to the area on a random basis. When a customer order is received, each unit is picked based on a pick sheet, logged out of the warehouse, and shipped to the customer.

Ms. Chan noted that, since the eBay units are being sold without the original packaging, they may have been removed prior to the packaging stage, which indicates that the removal may be occurring in the rework area. She then noted that someone could declare a rework unit to not be repairable, fill out a product destruction form for it, and then intercept the unit before it is scrapped.

Ms. Chan accessed her scrapped products report for the past year, and noted that the scrap percentage increased by 0.1% in October and then remained at that higher level in November.

Ms. Chan was advised to treat the information discussed during this interview as confidential.

The documentation of interviews should be presented in chronological order, so that someone perusing the information can better understand the trail of information followed by the fraud examiner. In the following sample interview, the reason for the meeting is derived directly from the information uncovered in the immediately preceding interview.

2nd SAMPLE INTERVIEW PAGE

To: Case File 004209
From: Tom Arrow
Date: January 2, 20X2
Subject: Interview with Dennis Johnston

Dennis Johnston, production manager of Henderson Industrial, was interviewed in his office at 123 Main Street, Cambridge, Massachusetts, on January 2, 20X2. Mr. Johnston was told the identities of his two interviewers, Tom Arrow and Danielle Liscano. Mr. Johnston was asked who was responsible for product destruction forms in the product rework area. Mr. Johnston noted that only the rework manager, Sean Farris, could sign off on the forms.

Mr. Johnston then pulled all submitted product destruction forms from storage and compared the signatures on all of the forms for the past 12 months. He confirmed that all of the signatures were the same. He photocopied one of the signed forms and gave it to Danielle Liscano.

Mr. Johnston was advised to treat the information discussed during this interview as confidential.

3rd SAMPLE INTERVIEW PAGE

To: Case File 004209
From: Tom Arrow
Date: January 3, 20X2
Subject: Interview with Stacey Cornelius

Stacey Cornelius, human resources manager of Henderson Industrial, was interviewed in her office at 123 Main Street, Cambridge, Massachusetts, on January 3, 20X2. Ms. Cornelius was told the identities of her two interviewers, Tom Arrow and Danielle Liscano. Ms. Cornelius was asked to match the signature on the product destruction form supplied by Mr. Dennis Johnston to the personnel records signed by the rework manager, Sean Farris. Ms. Cornelius confirmed that the signatures appeared to have been written by the same person.

The documentation can include an examination of federal, state, and local records of various kinds, both to collect additional background information about an individual, and to see if the person has paid off liabilities or acquired assets during the investigation period, as noted in the following sample documents.

SAMPLE RECORDS SEARCH

To: Case File 004209
From: Tom Arrow
Date: January 4, 20X2
Subject: Results of records search at the Massachusetts secretary of state website

The secretary of state database for UCC filings for the state of Massachusetts was reviewed on January 4, 20X2 for records pertaining to Sean Farris. The following information was found:

- A Harley-Davidson motorcycle was purchased for $19,000 at House of Harley on November 3, 20X1, with half of the amount paid in cash and the rest financed under the terms of a two-year loan.
- A house located at 400 Elm Street in Somerville, Massachusetts was purchased for $450,000, with a down payment of $45,000.

2nd SAMPLE RECORDS SEARCH

To: Case File 004209
From: Tom Arrow
Date: January 4, 20X2
Subject: Results of records search of the State Inmates Database

The Massachusetts database of inmates held at state penitentiaries was reviewed on January 4, 20X2 for records pertaining to Sean Farris. Record MA0452973 stated that Mr. Farris had been incarcerated in the Massachusetts Correctional Institution in Plymouth, Massachusetts for three years, serving a sentence for theft. He was released on August 10, 20X0.

A fraud report may also include an analysis of the available information to see if there are any trends or other indicators that would signal the presence of fraudulent activities. These analyses are intended to highlight information that can be used to estimate the amounts and types of funds or other assets stolen. A sample analysis report follows.

SAMPLE ANALYSIS REPORT

To: Case File 004209
From: Tom Arrow
Date: January 7, 20X2
Subject: Results of analysis of product destruction forms

A review of all product destruction forms for the Diamax Oscillator was conducted on January 7, 20X2, using the duplicate copies stored in the office of Dennis Johnston, the production manager of Henderson Industrial. The results of this analysis appear in the following table. Production of the Diamax Oscillator began in July 20X1, so there are no records from earlier periods. Mr. Johnston stated that the procedure used to examine products to see if they were repairable had been in place for at least the past three years, with no changes.

Analysis of Product Destruction Authorizations

	Jul.	Aug.	Sep.	Oct.	Nov	Dec.
Oscillators scrapped	12	14	10	18	22	26
Total produced	1,000	1,050	1,100	1,080	1,180	1,225
Scrap proportion	.012	.013	.009	.017	.019	.021

If the results of the first three months are to be considered a reasonable average product destruction rate, then the weighted average of these three months results in a 0.011 scrap proportion. When this proportion is applied to the production in the October through December time period, the number of units destroyed should have been 38, rather than the 66 that were reported to have been destroyed. This is a difference of 28 units.

When the 28 unit difference is multiplied by the $2,500 list price of the units, Henderson Industrial appears to have lost $70,000 of revenues. When the 28 units are multiplied by the $2,000 at which they are being offered for sale on eBay, the amount that could be potentially earned by the seller would be $56,000.

The preceding analysis establishes the scope of the likely theft, as well as the amount of the loss, and the amount obtained by the perpetrator. Given these specifics, it is now time to document the interview with the suspect. A sample admission report follows.

SAMPLE ADMISSION REPORT

To: Case File 004209
From: Tom Arrow
Date: January 9, 20X2
Subject: Interview with Sean Farris

Sean Farris, product rework supervisor of Henderson Industrial, was interviewed in his office at 123 Main Street, Cambridge, Massachusetts, on January 9, 20X2. Mr. Farris was told the identities of his two interviewers, Tom Arrow and Danielle Liscano, and was told that they were investigating an excessive number of products being withdrawn from the company's manufacturing process.

Mr. Farris stated that he was unable to find work following his incarceration, and so falsified his job application and used friends to provide false references. He then purchased a motorcycle and a home, which he was sharing with his friends as compensation for their assistance in helping him obtain a job with Henderson Industrial. Mr. Farris provided the following admission statement, which he freely and voluntarily signed.

If a written confession is made, it is also included in the fraud report. A sample admission statement follows.

SAMPLE ADMISSION STATEMENT

January 9, 20X2
Kansas City, Missouri

I, Sean Farris, provide the following free and voluntary statement to Tom Arrow of Henderson Industrial. No threats or assurances have been used to prompt this statement.

I am the product rework supervisor at Henderson Industrial. One part of my duties includes examining products that have been turned in for rework, to see if they can be repaired. Beginning in October 20X1 and continuing through the present, I have appropriated approximately 28 units of the Diamax Oscillator product from the company.

When a unit arrived for inspection, I completed a product destruction form for it and retained the unit, rather than scrapping it. I then sold it for a reduced price on eBay.

No one knew of these activities, other than my friends who provided false hiring references for me. I understand that my actions are illegal and violate the policies of Henderson Industrial. I engaged in this behavior because I felt that I could not otherwise obtain employment, and needed a way to compensate my friends for their assistance. I am sorry for my actions and intend to repay the entire amount.

I have read this statement. My signature below indicates that I believe this statement to be true and correct to the best of my knowledge.

Sean Farris	*Tom Arrow*
Signature	Witness
January 9, 20X1	*January 9, 20X1*
Date	Date

If warranted, the report may contain recommendations for control improvements that will mitigate the risk of having similar types of fraud in the future. A sample recommendation follows.

SAMPLE RECOMMENDATIONS REPORT

To: Case File 004209
From: Tom Arrow
Date: January 10, 20X2
Subject: Recommendations to Improve Controls

Following the completion of other activities related to this Case File, Tom Arrow and Sandra Chan met with the company's audit partner, Ms. Gina Jorgensen, to discuss how the controls of Henderson Industrial can be improved to mitigate the risk of this type of theft from occurring again. As a result of the discussion, the group recommends the following changes and additions to the company's system of controls:

- Run a criminal background check on all employees who will be hired into a supervisory role.
- Run a criminal background check on any employees who are being promoted into a supervisory role.
- Have the purchasing department maintain a log of all products that have been scrapped. The accounting staff compares this log to the originals of all product destruction forms.
- Have the accounting department maintain an analysis of the scrap proportion for all product destruction authorizations, and report this amount to the production and engineering managers.

The criminal background check recommendations have already been adopted by the human resources department.

Summary

A fraud report is simply an investigative report that focuses on what happened and how to keep it from happening again in the future. It needs to be as detailed as possible, describing each step in the investigation process and the results that were found. The ideal report gives the reader a thorough understanding of what happened, the losses sustained, who perpetrated the fraud and why they did it, and recommendations for mitigating the risk of loss in the future.

A fraud report does not contain any recommendations for disciplinary action against the subject of the investigation, since the fraud examiner is an investigator, not a judge.

Chapter 11
Legal Aspects of Fraud

Introduction

In the last chapter, we discussed the fraud report. Once issued, the information in that report may be used to prosecute the perpetrator on a criminal or civil basis. In this chapter, we describe the differences between civil and criminal prosecution, and how each one is conducted. We also give summary descriptions of the various federal statutes relating to fraud, and the penalties associated with each one.

Types of Prosecution

When a person commits fraud, he or she can be prosecuted on a criminal or civil basis, or both. A criminal prosecution involves situations in which offenses have violated a statute that prohibits an activity. These types of prosecutions can be brought at either the state or federal level. If convicted, a person may spend time in jail and/or be required to pay a fine.

A civil prosecution is based on laws that provide remedies when it is proven that the private rights of an individual have been violated. The outcome of these cases is usually the payment of some amount of financial restitution to the aggrieved party.

It is possible for a person to be pursued under both criminal and civil proceedings. If so, criminal proceedings are usually completed before civil actions are begun.

There are several key differences between these two types of prosecution. The essential differences are:

- *Burden of proof.* A criminal case must be proven "beyond a reasonable doubt," while only a preponderance of the evidence is needed for the jury to reach a verdict in a civil trial. This means it is much easier for an aggrieved party to obtain a favorable outcome in a civil trial.
- *Voting.* A jury in a criminal proceeding must reach a unanimous verdict for the defendant to be found guilty, while this requirement does not apply in a civil trial. Again, this difference makes it easier for the aggrieved party to obtain a favorable outcome in a civil trial.

When a company engages in civil proceedings, the recovery is usually much less than the amount stolen, since the individual has already spent the majority of the funds. The expectation of how much money can be returned can play a major role in an organization's decision to pursue a civil case against a person, since the cost of the lawsuit is not minor.

A variation on what may happen is that the aggrieved company files a claim with its fidelity bonding company. Despite its name, fidelity bonding is actually an insurance policy that reimburses the policy holder for losses caused by the dishonest actions of its employees. The bonding company pays the company the amount of the claim, and then has the option to pursue the employee in court to recover the amount of its payout.

The opportunity for recovery is much higher when the offending party is another business, since it may still have substantial assets. For example, a supplier may have entered into a kickback arrangement with a company employee to sell it over-priced goods. If so, the offended party has a reasonable chance of recovering the lost funds from the supplier. Similarly, when the value of a company's shares decline as the result of a financial statement fraud by management, shareholders may bring a civil action against the company's auditors.

If an organization wants to have an individual prosecuted for a criminal action, they must request it through a law enforcement or other government agency.

When either a civil or criminal case is pursued, it is quite likely that the case will be settled out of court. By doing so, all parties avoid the cost of a trial, while also keeping the situation out of the public eye as much as possible.

The Civil Litigation Process

In a civil litigation case, the process follows six basic steps, which are:

1. *Investigation.* The entity conducts an investigation of the fraud to determine the particulars, including the nature of the fraud, the name of the perpetrator, and the amount stolen.
2. *Complaint.* The organization hires an attorney, who files a complaint that notes the specific violation of the law and the damages being sought. The defendant's attorney may then file a motion that objects to the complaint, based on various defects in the stated case.
3. *Discovery.* The attorneys for both sides collect information concerning all aspects of the case. Each side may file motions, requesting that certain documents be produced by the other side. Once both sides have had a chance to examine these documents, they proceed to taking depositions from anyone associated with the events. A deposition is testimony taken before the start of a trial. Depositions involve questioning by the attorney for the opposing side, with a court reporter noting all questions and answers, which are later converted into a written transcript. Interviewees may be videotaped as well, with both the transcripts and videos being admissible in court.
4. *Motions and negotiation.* The attorneys for both sides may file a variety of motions with the trial judge in relation to any number of issues. The most aggressive motion is for summary judgment, which asks the judge to immediately decide the case because all factual and legal issues can be decided in favor of the party making the motion. At the same time, both sides may be negotiating for settlement, thereby resolving the case.
5. *Trial.* If a case has not yet been resolved, then it goes to trial. If either of the parties wants a jury trial, then it is usually arranged in that manner. Once both sides have presented their cases, the judge instructs the jury on the law to be

applied as they consider their verdict. Once the verdict has been returned, the parties can file motions to have some or all of the verdict set aside, or to have a new trial.

6. *Appeal.* If the motions filed at the end of the trial are rejected, the parties can file an appeal. An appeal states that there was a legal defect in how the original trial was conducted, and requests that a higher court overturn the original verdict or requires that a new trial be held. For example, an appeal could state that inappropriate evidence was included in the original trial, and requests a retrial that excludes the indicated information.

Subpoenas may also be issued in the name of the court, requiring that an individual give testimony in court or appear for a deposition, or to produce certain documents.

The Criminal Litigation Process

A criminal litigation case follows a somewhat different number of steps from those just described for a civil case. The process flow is as follows:

1. *Investigation.* The entity conducts the same investigation just noted for a civil case.

2. *File charges.* The entity contacts the applicable district attorney for the region in which the fraud occurred. The information obtained during the earlier investigation phase may be delivered to the government. The district attorney works with the police to prepare an arrest warrant.

3. *Arrest defendant.* If probable cause exists, the defendant can be arrested. *Probable cause* exists when there is sufficient reason based on known facts to believe that a crime has been committed. A grand jury can determine whether probable cause exists; this approach is commonly used when there is a case of fraud.

4. *Preliminary hearings.* A preliminary hearing is held before a judge shortly after the arrest has occurred, to decide whether there is probable cause for charging the defendant with a crime. The defendant's attorney attempts to show that there is not enough evidence to show probable cause. If probable cause cannot be proven, then the charges are dropped.

5. *Grand jury investigation.* Instead of a preliminary hearing, a grand jury can be used to investigate the matter and decide whether probable cause exists. A grand jury is a group of between 16 and 23 citizens that is tasked with determining the existence of probable cause after reviewing the prosecution's evidence. A grand jury can issue subpoenas to gain access to witnesses and documents.

6. *Arraignment.* During the arraignment, the charges against the defendant are read, and the defendant can plead guilty, not guilty, or does not contest the charges. If the individual pleads not guilty, then a trial will be held. For the other two pleadings, the individual will be sentenced.

7. *Discovery.* There are significant differences between the discovery process for civil and criminal cases. Depositions are rarely allowed in criminal cases.

Also, defendants do not have to disclose any information that could be considered self-incriminating.

8. *Pre-trial motions*. Motions can be filed prior to the trial in the same manner as already described for civil cases.
9. *Trial*. A unanimous jury decision must be produced before a person can be convicted of criminal charges.
10. *Appeal*. Following the issuance of a verdict, the parties can appeal the decision, as described earlier for civil cases.

The Fraud Examiner Role in Lawsuits

Fraud examiners have multiple roles in lawsuits. They may engage in any of the following activities:

- *Expert witness*. An expert witness is used in both civil and criminal fraud trials. An expert witness is a person who is a specialist in a subject, who can present an expert opinion without having been a witness. They give their opinions regarding how frauds were perpetrated, and can compile estimates of how much money was lost to fraud. They may give testimony during both depositions and trials, as well as provide a report that lays out the reasoning behind their decisions.
- *Advisor*. They can advise the attorney for the company in regard to the documents to be requested from the other side, as well as what questions to ask during depositions and the examination of witnesses at trial.
- *Document preparer*. They can advise on the types of documentation to present in court, including those graphics that will most clearly portray the case being made.

The fraud examiner who is willing to be an expert witness must be able to withstand pointed questioning by the attorney for the defense. This attorney intends to question the authority of the fraud examiner, and pick holes in his arguments. Consequently, the examiner needs to carefully formulate his response to each question and only answer the exact question asked, without expanding upon the answer. A lengthy and florid answer will only give the opposing attorney additional verbiage to tear apart. The examiner should also appear as authoritative and sincere as possible, with a complete command of the information used to support his conclusions. Finally, a high-quality expert witness must be able to proficiently translate technical jargon into terms that the jury will readily understand. Not many people can fulfill all of these requirements to become competent expert witnesses.

Federal Statutes Covering Fraudulent Activities

There are a number of federal statutes in the United States that set penalties for different types of fraud. In this section, we provide an overview of these statutes. The discussion is largely a compression of the actual text of the applicable statutes. In the following discussion, the acronym "CFR" is sometimes used; this refers to the Code of Federal Regulations. Also, the term "U.S. Code" refers to the official codification of the federal statutes of the United States. A separate statute is noted in each of the following sub-sections.

17 CFR 240.10b5-1 - Trading "on the basis of" Material Nonpublic Information

Section 240 is targeted at securities fraud. It establishes that a person cannot engage in fraudulent activities in connection with the purchase or sale of securities. This includes making untrue statements of a material fact or omitting to state a material fact in order to make a statement not misleading. The underlying assumption is that the individual is trading securities based on material nonpublic information that is not available to the counterparties in these transactions. Civil liabilities will apply when this type of fraud can be proven.

15 U.S. Code § 78dd–1 - Prohibited Foreign Trade Practices

Originally promulgated as the Foreign Corrupt Practices Act, this section of the U.S. Code prohibits the payment of bribes to foreign officials in order to obtain or retain business. The prohibition only applies to publicly-traded companies and their officers, employees, and agents (such as consultants and distributors). Civil enforcement actions can be brought against violators, which can result in the disgorgement of gains and civil penalties.

18 U.S. Code § 201 - Bribery of Public Officials and Witnesses

Section 201 is targeted at fraud either directed at or caused by public officials or witnesses. This section of the U.S. Code states that anyone who directly or indirectly offers anything of value to a public official with the intent to influence an official act or the official's decision to collude in or allow any fraud, or to influence that person to act in violation of their lawful duty is to be fined not more than three times the monetary equivalent of the thing of value and/or imprisoned for up to 15 years. The same penalty applies to a public official who solicits such items of value in exchange for the activities just enumerated.

The same penalty also applies to an individual who offers anything of value in order to influence the testimony of a person who is a witness in a trial or other type of hearing, as well as to any witness who accepts the item of value.

18 U.S. Code § 500 - Money Orders

This section provides that anyone attempting to use counterfeit or forged money orders, or to alter or steal money orders can be fined and/or imprisoned for up to five years. This crime is investigated by the U.S. Postal Inspection Service, since money orders are issued by the U.S. Postal Service.

18 U.S. Code § 1030 – Fraud and Related Activity in Connection with Computers

This section provides that any intentional or unauthorized access to a computer with the intent of obtaining restricted information pertaining to national security or confidential financial information, or destroying the information on the computer, is subject to a fine and imprisonment of up to either 10 or 20 years, depending on the nature of the offense.

18 U.S. Code § 1037 - Fraud and Related Activity in Connection with Electronic Mail

Section 1037 addresses the pursuit of fraud through the use of e-mails that originate from a protected computer that someone accesses without authorization. If this person sends fraudulent commercial e-mail messages, or intends to deceive recipients as to the origin of these messages, or to falsify the header information in these messages, he or she can be fined and/or imprisoned for up to five years. These amounts can be reduced under certain circumstances. In addition, the perpetrator forfeits any proceeds from these activities, as well as any equipment or software used to commit the offense.

18 U.S. Code § 1341 – Frauds and Swindles

This section states that anyone who acts to defraud others by mailing or receiving items through the postal service can be fined, as well as imprisoned of up to 20 years. If the activity occurs in relation to a declared major disaster or emergency or affects a financial institution, the fine increases to not more than $1,000,000 and/or imprisonment of up to 30 years. This section has proven to be quite useful, since many types of fraud involve the transmission of materials through the Postal Service.

18 U.S. Code § 1342 - Fictitious Name or Address

This section provides that anyone engaged in frauds and swindles, as just described in Section 1341, and who uses a false title, name, or address, or who takes or receives mail matter addressed to that false title, name, or address, can be fined and/or imprisoned for up to five years.

18 U.S. Code § 1344 – Bank Fraud

This section provides that anyone who knowingly executes or attempts to execute a scheme to defraud a financial institution to obtain money or other assets held by the financial institution can be fined up to $1,000,000 and/or imprisoned for up to 30 years.

18 U.S. Code § 1956 - Laundering of Monetary Instruments

This section addresses the laundering of monetary instruments. In this situation, a person knows that the property involved in a financial transaction is from an unlawful activity, and is attempting to conceal the location, source, ownership, or control of the proceeds. The intent of this laundering is to "clean" the monetary instruments, so that they appear to have been legally owned. When laundering can be proven, the perpetrator can be fined up to $500,000 or twice the value of the property involved in the transaction, and is subject to imprisonment for up to 20 years.

The same penalties apply when a person transports, transmits, or transfers a monetary instrument from the United States to a location outside the country, with the intent of promoting an unlawful activity or to conceal the nature, location, source, or ownership of the proceeds.

18 U.S. Code § 1961 – Racketeer Influenced and Corrupt Organizations

This section addresses individuals who engage in a pattern of transgressions as part of a criminal enterprise. A large number of activities can be considered racketeering, including homicide, kidnapping, extortion, witness tampering, robbery, arson, money laundering, securities violations, mail fraud, and counterfeiting. If convicted, violators can be imprisoned for up to 20 years, which can be increased to life in prison if so authorized by the underlying crime. In addition, violators can be fined up to $250,000 or double the amount of the proceeds derived from the underlying activity.

26 U.S. Code § 7201 – Attempt to Evade or Defeat Tax

When anyone willfully attempts to evade the payment of a tax, that person is guilty of a felony, and can be fined up to $100,000 and/or be imprisoned for up to five years, and must pay the costs of prosecution. The fine is increased to $500,000 if the entity is a corporation.

41 U.S. Code § 8701 – Prohibited Conduct (Kickbacks)

This section prohibits anyone from making or receiving payments with the intent of inducing an award from the federal government, or attempting to provide or solicit such payments. This prohibition includes prime contractors and their employees, as well as subcontractors and their employees. Kickback amounts may be withheld from payments made to prime contractors and subcontractors. Penalties can also include twice the amount of each kickback.

Summary

Though we have recommended throughout this book that the perpetrators of fraud always be prosecuted, the lengthy prosecution steps noted in this chapter will make it clear that the process may simply be too expensive for a civil case. A smaller company may not have the financial resources to pursue a civil case, especially when the stolen funds have clearly already been spent. Consequently, it may only be possible to bring up the matter with the local district attorney and hope that the government is willing to pursue criminal charges.

If any type of litigation is pursued, it is quite likely that a fraud examiner will be called upon. This role is a key one in any prosecution effort, in order to clarify the nature of the crime and the amount of assets that were probably lost. A fraud examiner can also provide assistance behind the scenes, constructing questions for witnesses, advising attorneys, and building exhibits for presentation to a jury.

Glossary

A

Accounting anomalies. Unusual processes in the accounting system.

Amortization. The ratable charging of assets to expense over a period of time.

Analytical anomalies. Relationships within or between financial and operational results that do not make sense in relation to the business as a whole.

Arraignment. A proceeding in which the defendant is informed of the charges filed against him, and is asked to file a plea of guilty, not guilty, or some other plea.

B

Balance sheet. A financial statement that presents information about an entity's assets, liabilities, and shareholders' equity.

Bates numbering. A method used to label legal documents with unique numbers.

Benford's law. The observation that smaller digits appear disproportionately more often as leading digits.

Bribery. Giving something of value in order to influence a decision to favor the payer.

Bust-out scam. The practice of building up credit with a company, then placing a large order for a substantial amount of goods, and walking away without paying.

C

Chain of custody. The concept that a record must be maintained that notes the receipt of each document, as well as every transfer of that evidence from person to person.

Computer forensics. The search of electronic records to locate information about frauds.

Contingent liability. A possible obligation that depends on future events that are not under an entity's control.

D

Deposition. Testimony taken before the start of a trial.

Detective control. A control that spots a control breach after it has already happened.

Discovery sampling. A sampling method used to determine whether there is at least one error in a sampling of documents, assuming a certain population error percentage.

Dual custody. When two or more people work together on a task.

E

Employee assistance program. A program that helps employees deal with a number of issues, including substance abuse and other types of addictions, money management problems, health issues, and family-related concerns.

Expert witness. A person who is a specialist in a subject, who can present an expert opinion without having been a witness.

F

Fidelity bonding. An insurance policy that reimburses the policy holder for losses caused by the dishonest actions of its employees.

Financial statements. A collection of reports about an organization's financial results, financial position, and cash flows.

Fixed assets. Assets that are expected to have utility over multiple reporting periods, and whose cost exceeds the minimum capitalization level of a business.

Fraud. A false representation of the facts, resulting in the object of the fraud receiving an injury by acting upon the misrepresented facts.

Fraud report. A report that states the findings of a fraud examiner regarding the outcome of a fraud investigation.

Fraud triangle. The three factors that, when combined, contribute to an environment in which fraud can flourish. The factors are perceived pressure, opportunity, and rationalization.

Free cash flow. The net change in cash generated by the operations of a business during a reporting period, minus cash outlays for working capital, capital expenditures, and dividends during the same period.

G

Grand jury. A group of citizens that is tasked with determining the existence of probable cause after reviewing the prosecution's evidence.

Gross profit. The residual amount after the cost of goods sold is subtracted from sales.

H

Horizontal analysis. The comparison of historical financial information over a series of reporting periods.

I

Income statement. A financial statement that contains the results of an organization's operations for a specific period of time, showing revenues and expenses and the resulting profit or loss.

Intangible assets. A non-physical asset that has a useful life spanning multiple reporting periods.

Invigilation. The use of an excessive number of controls to completely halt all fraud for a short period of time; the results of this period are then compared to the results from a normal period to look for anomalies.

K

Kickback. When a supplier pays a buyer a bribe in exchange for selecting the supplier to supply goods and services to the buyer's company.

L

Lapping. When an employee steals cash by diverting a payment from one customer, and then hides the theft by diverting cash from another customer to offset the receivable from the first customer.

Larceny. The unauthorized taking of property belonging to someone else.

M

Marketable security. An easily traded investment that is readily convertible into cash.

Metadata. Information that describes other data.

Money laundering. The process of altering the sources of cash so that it appears to come from a legitimate source.

Motion. An application to a judge to obtain a ruling in favor of the applicant.

N

Net worth. Assets minus liabilities.

Non-sampling risk. The risk of missing a fraudulent transaction due to an incomplete examination of the available data.

O

Order of liquidity. The presentation of assets in the balance sheet in the order of the amount of time it would usually take to convert them into cash.

Outlier. A value that lies outside the other values in a set of data.

P

Ponzi scheme. A type of fraud under which cash from subsequent investors is used to pay premiums or interest to prior investors.

Preliminary hearing. A hearing to decide whether a person should be tried for the crime charged, based on the existence of a sufficient amount of evidence.

Preventive control. A control that keeps a control breach from occurring.

Probable cause. A finding that there is sufficient reason based on known facts to believe that a crime has been committed.

Profit. The amount by which sales exceed expenses.

R

Rationalization. To invent plausible explanations for actions taken.

Revenue recognition. The process of determining the amount and timing of when revenue is recognized, based on the underlying earnings process.

S

Sales order. An internal document that translates a customer order into a standard format, which is then used to process the order for eventual delivery to the customer.

Sampling risk. The risk that sampling will not detect a case of fraud, because the documentation involving a fraudulent transaction was not selected.

Search warrant. A court order that authorizes access to a location in order to search for evidence of guilt in the prosecution of a criminal action.

Segregation of duties. The division of a task into multiple parts, so that more than one person is required to complete the task.

Shell company. A corporation that has no business operations or assets.

Short selling. The sale of company stock owned by a third party, with the intent of buying back shares on the open market at a later date and returning the shares to the third party.

Skimming. The removal of cash from a system before it can be recorded.

Statement of cash flows. A financial statement that identifies the different types of cash payments made by a business to third parties (cash outflows), as well as payments made to a business by third parties (cash inflows).

Stock option. A financial instrument that gives its holder the right, but not the obligation, to buy shares at a certain price and within a certain date range.

Subpoena. A document requiring the recipient to appear in court or supply certain documents.

Summary judgment. A judgment entered by a court that rules in favor of one party without a full trial.

Surveillance. The act of watching someone in order to detect a crime.

T

Topside entry. A manual adjusting entry made at the corporate level.

V

Vertical analysis. The proportional analysis of a financial statement, where each line item on the statement is listed as a percentage of another item.

Z

Z-score. A statistical measurement of a data point's relationship to the mean of a set of data points.

Index

CPSIA information can be obtained
at www.ICGtesting.com
Printed in the USA
LVHW102358090719
623638LV00003B/64/P

9 781642 210279